Mastering Scala Machine Learning

Advance your skills in efficient data analysis and data processing using the powerful tools of Scala, Spark, and Hadoop

Alex Kozlov

[PACKT] open source ✼
PUBLISHING   community experience distilled

BIRMINGHAM - MUMBAI

Mastering Scala Machine Learning

First published: June 2016

Production reference: 1220616

Published by Packt Publishing Ltd.
Livery Place
35 Livery Street
Birmingham B3 2PB, UK.

ISBN 978-1-78588-088-9

www.packtpub.com

Credits

Author
Alex Kozlov

Reviewer
Rok Kralj

Commissioning Editor
Dipika Gaonkar

Acquisition Editor
Kirk D'costa

Content Development Editor
Samantha Gonsalves

Technical Editor
Suwarna Patil

Copy Editor
Vibha Shukla

Project Coordinator
Sanchita Mandal

Proofreader
Safis Editing

Indexer
Mariammal Chettiyar

Graphics
Disha Haria

Production Coordinator
Arvindkumar Gupta

Cover Work
Arvindkumar Gupta

About the Author

Alex Kozlov is a multidisciplinary big data scientist. He came to Silicon Valley in 1991, got his Ph.D. from Stanford University under the supervision of Prof. Daphne Koller and Prof. John Hennessy in 1998, and has been around a few computer and data management companies since. His latest stint was with Cloudera, the leader in Hadoop, where he was one of the early employees and ended up heading the solution architects group on the West Coast. Before that, he spent time with an online advertising company, Turn, Inc.; and before that, he had the privilege to work with HP Labs researchers at HP Inc., and on data mining software at SGI, Inc. Currently, Alexander is the chief solutions architect at an enterprise security startup, E8 Security, where he came to understand the intricacies of catching bad guys in the Internet universe.

On the non-professional side, Alexander lives in Sunnyvale, CA, together with his beautiful wife, Oxana, and other important family members, including three daughters, Lana, Nika, and Anna, and a cat and dog. His family also included a hamster and a fish at one point.

Alex is an active participant in Silicon Valley technology groups and meetups, and although he is not an official committer of any open source projects, he definitely contributed to many of them in the form of code or discussions. Alexander is an active coder and publishes his open source code at `https://github.com/alexvk`. Other information can be looked up on his LinkedIn page at `https://www.linkedin.com/in/alexvk`.

Acknowlegement

I had a few chances to write a book in the past, but when Packt called me shortly before my 50th birthday, I agreed almost immediately. Scala? Machine learning? Big data? What could be a worse combination of poorly understood and intensely marketed topics? What followed was eight months of sleep deprived existence, putting my ideas on paper—computer keyboard, actually—during which I was able to experimentally find out that my body needs at least three hours of sleep each night and a larger break once in a while. As a whole, the experience was totally worth it. I really appreciate the help of everyone around me, first of all of my family, who had to deal with a lot of sleepless nights and my temporary lack of attention.

I would like to thank my wife for putting up with a lot of extra load and late night writing sessions. I know it's been very hard. I also give deep thanks to my editors, specifically Samantha Gonsalves, who not only nagged me from time to time to keep me on schedule, but also gave very sound advice and put up with my procrastination. Not least, I am very grateful to my colleagues who filled in for me during some very critical stages of E8 Security product releases—we did go through the GA, and at least a couple of releases during this time. A lot of ideas percolated into the E8 product. Particularly, I would like to thank Jeongho Park, Christophe Briguet, Mahendra Kutare, Srinivas Doddi, and Ravi Devireddy. I am grateful to all my Cloudera colleagues for feedback and discussions, specifically Josh Patterson, Josh Wills, Omer Trajman, Eric Sammer, Don Brown, Phillip Zeyliger, Jonathan Hsieh, and many others. Last, but not least, I would like to thank my Ph.D. mentors Walter A. Harrison, Jaswinder Pal Singh, John Hennessy, and Daphne Koller for bringing me into the world of technology and innovation.

www.PacktPub.com

eBooks, discount offers, and more

Did you know that Packt offers eBook versions of every book published, with PDF and ePub files available? You can upgrade to the eBook version at www.PacktPub.com and as a print book customer, you are entitled to a discount on the eBook copy. Get in touch with us at customercare@packtpub.com for more details.

At www.PacktPub.com, you can also read a collection of free technical articles, sign up for a range of free newsletters and receive exclusive discounts and offers on Packt books and eBooks.

https://www2.packtpub.com/books/subscription/packtlib

Do you need instant solutions to your IT questions? PacktLib is Packt's online digital book library. Here, you can search, access, and read Packt's entire library of books.

Why subscribe?

- Fully searchable across every book published by Packt
- Copy and paste, print, and bookmark content
- On demand and accessible via a web browser

Table of Contents

Preface

This book is about machine learning, the functional approach to programming with Scala being the focus, and big data with Spark being the target. When I was offered to write the book about nine months ago, my first reaction was that, while each of the mentioned subjects have been thoroughly investigated and written about, I've definitely taken part in enough discussions to know that combining any pair of them presents challenges, not to mention combining all three of them in one book. The challenge piqued my interest, and the result is this book. Not every chapter is as smooth as I wished it to be, but in the world where technology makes huge strides every day, this is probably expected. I do have a real job and writing is only one way to express my ideas.

Let's start with machine learning. Machine learning went through a head-spinning transformation; it was an offspring of AI and statistics somewhere in the 1990s and later gave birth to data science in or slightly before 2010. There are many definitions of data science, but the most popular one is probably from Josh Wills, with whom I had the privilege to work at Cloudera, which is depicted in *Figure 1*. While the details may be argued about, the truth is that data science is always on the intersection of a few disciplines, and a data scientist is not necessarily is an expert on any one of them. Arguably, the first data scientists worked at Facebook, according to Jeff Hammerbacher, who was also one of the Cloudera founders and an early Facebook employee. Facebook needed interdisciplinary skills to extract value from huge amounts of social data at the time. While I call myself a big data scientist, for the purposes of this book, I'd like to use the term machine learning or ML to keep the focus, as I am mixing too much already here.

One other aspect of ML that came about recently and is actively discussed is that the quantity of data beats the sophistication of the models. One can see this in this book in the example of some Spark MLlib implementations, and word2vec for NLP in particular. Speedier ML models that can respond to new environments faster also often beat the more complex models that take hours to build. Thus, ML and big data make a good match.

Last but not least is the emergence of microservices. I spent a great deal of time on the topic of machine and application communication in this book, and Scala with the Akka actors model comes very naturally here.

Functional programming, at least for a good portion of practical programmers, is more about the style of programming than a programming language itself. While Java 8 started having lambda expressions and streams, which came out of functional programming, one can still write in a functional style without these mechanisms or even write a Java-style code in Scala. The two big ideas that brought Scala to prominence in the big data world are lazy evaluation, which greatly simplifies data processing in a multi-threaded or distributed world, and immutability. Scala has two different libraries for collections: one is mutable and another is immutable. While the distinction is subtle from the application user point of view, immutability greatly increases the options from a compiler perspective, and lazy evaluation cannot be a better match for big data, where REPL postpones most of the number crunching towards later stages of the pipeline, increasing interactivity.

Figure 1: One of the possible definitions of a data scientist

Finally, big data. Big data has definitely occupied the headlines for a couple of years now, and a big reason for this is that the amount of data produced by machines today greatly surpasses anything that a human cannot even produce, but even comprehend, without using the computers. The social network companies, such as Facebook, Google, Twitter, and so on, have demonstrated that enough information can be extracted from these blobs of data to justify the tools specifically targeted towards processing big data, such as Hadoop, MapReduce, and Spark.

We will touch on what Hadoop does later in the book, but originally, it was a Band-Aid on top of commodity hardware to be able to deal with a vast amount of information, which the traditional relational DBs at the time were not equipped to handle (or were able, but at a prohibitive price). While big data is probably too big a subject for me to handle in this book, Spark is the focus and is another implementation of Hadoop MapReduce that removes a few inefficiencies of having to deal with persisting data on disk. Spark is a bit more expensive as it consumes more memory in general and the hardware has to be more reliable, but it is more interactive. Furthermore, Spark works on top of Scala—other languages such as Java and Python too—but Scala is the primary API language, and it found certain synergies in how it expresses data pipelines in Scala.

What this book covers

Chapter 1, Exploratory Data Analysis, covers how every data analyst begins with an exploratory data analysis. There is nothing new here, except that the new tools allow you to look into larger datasets—possibly spread across multiple computers, as easily as if they were just on a local machine. This, of course, does not prevent you from running the pipeline on a single machine, but even then, the laptop I am writing this on has four cores and about 1,377 threads running at the same time. Spark and Scala (parallel collections) allow you to transparently use this entire dowry, sometimes without explicitly specifying the parallelism. Modern servers may have up to 128 hyper-threads available to the OS. This chapter will show you how to start with the new tools, maybe by exploring your old datasets.

Chapter 2, Data Pipelines and Modeling, explains that while data-driven processes existed long before Scala/Spark, the new age demonstrated the emergence of a fully data-driven enterprise where the business is optimized by the feedback from multiple data-generating machines. Big data requires new techniques and architectures to accommodate the new decision making process. Borrowing from a number of academic fields, this chapter proceeds to describe a generic architecture of a data-driven business, where most of the workers' task is monitoring and tuning the data pipelines (or enjoying the enormous revenue per worker that these enterprises can command).

Chapter 3, Working with Spark and MLlib, focuses on the internal architecture of Spark, which we mentioned earlier as a replacement for and/or complement to Hadoop MapReduce. We will specifically stop on a few ML algorithms, which are grouped under the MLlib tag. While this is still a developing topic and many of the algorithms are being moved using a different package now, we will provide a few examples of how to run standard ML algorithms in the `org.apache.spark.mllib` package. We will also explain the modes that Spark can be run under and touch on Spark performance tuning.

Chapter 4, *Supervised and Unsupervised Learning*, explains that while Spark MLlib may be a moving target, general ML principles have been solidly established. Supervised/unsupervised learning is a classical division of ML algorithms that work on row-oriented data—most of the data, really. This chapter is a classic part of any ML book, but we spiced it up a bit to make it more Scala/Spark-oriented.

Chapter 5, *Regression and Classification*, introduces regression and classification, which is another classic subdivision of the ML algorithms, even if it has been shown that classification can be used to regress, and regression to classify, still these are the two classes that use different techniques, precision metrics, and ways to regularize the models. This chapter will take a practical approach while showing you practical examples of regression and classification analysis

Chapter 6, *Working with Unstructured Data,* covers how one of the new features that social data brought with them and brought traditional DBs to their knees is nested and unstructured data. Working with unstructured data requires new techniques and formats, and this chapter is dedicated to the ways to present, store, and evolve these types of data. Scala becomes a big winner here, as it has a natural way to deal with complex data structures in the data pipelines.

Chapter 7, *Working with Graph Algorithms*, explains how graphs present another challenge to the traditional row-oriented DBs. Lately, there has been a resurgence of graph DBs. We will cover two different libraries in this chapter: one is Scala-graph from Assembla, which is a convenient tool to represent and reason with graphs, and the other is Spark's graph class with a few graph algorithms implemented on top of it.

Chapter 8, *Integrating Scala with R and Python*, covers how even though Scala is cool, many people are just too cautious to leave their old libraries behind. In this chapter, I will show how to transparently refer to the legacy code written in R and Python, a request I hear too often. In short, there are too mechanisms: one is using Unix pipelines and another way is to launch R or Python in JVM.

Chapter 9, *NLP in Scala*, focuses on how natural language processing has deal with human-computer interaction and computer's understanding of our often-substandard ways to communicate. I will focus on a few tools that Scala specifically provide for NLP, topic association, and dealing with large amounts of textual information (Spark).

Chapter 10, Advanced Model Monitoring, introduces how developing data pipelines usually means that someone is going to use and debug them. Monitoring is extremely important not only for the end user data pipeline, but also for the developer or designer who is looking for the ways to either optimize the execution or further the design. We cover the standard tools for monitoring systems and distributed clusters of machines as well as how to design a service that has enough hooks to look into its functioning without attaching a debugger. I will also touch on the new emerging field of statistical model monitoring.

What you need for this book

This book is based on open source software. First, it's Java. One can download Java from Oracle's Java Download page. You have to accept the license and choose an appropriate image for your platform. Don't use OpenJDK—it has a few problems with Hadoop/Spark.

Second, Scala. If you are using Mac, I recommend installing Homebrew:

```
$ ruby -e "$(curl -fsSL https://raw.githubusercontent.com/Homebrew/
install/master/install)"
```

Multiple open source packages will also be available to you. To install Scala, run `brew install scala`. Installation on a Linux platform requires downloading an appropriate Debian or RPM package from the `http://www.scala-lang.org/download/` site. We will use the latest version at the time, that is, 2.11.7.

Spark distributions can be downloaded from `http://spark.apache.org/downloads.html`. We use pre-build for Hadoop 2.6 and later image. As it's Java, you need to just unzip the package and start using the scripts from the `bin` subdirectory.

R and Python packages are available at `http://cran.r-project.org/bin` and `http://python.org/ftp/python/$PYTHON_VERSION/Python-$PYTHON_VERSION.tar.xz` sites respectively. The text has specific instruction on how to configure them. Although our use of the packages should be version agnostic, I used R version 3.2.3 and Python version 2.7.11 in this book.

Who this book is for

Professional and emerging data scientists who want to sharpen their skills and see practical examples of working with big data: a data analyst who wants to effectively extract actionable information from large amounts of data and an aspiring statistician who is willing to get beyond the existing boundaries and become a data scientist.

The book style is pretty much hands-on, I don't delve into mathematical proofs or validations, with a few exceptions, and there are more in-depth texts that I recommend throughout the book. However, I will try my best to provide code samples and tricks that you can start using for the standard techniques and libraries as soon as possible.

Conventions

In this book, you will find a number of text styles that distinguish between different kinds of information. Here are some examples of these styles and an explanation of their meaning.

Code words in text, database table names, folder names, filenames, file extensions, pathnames, dummy URLs, user input, and Twitter handles are shown as follows: "We can include other contexts through the use of the include directive."

A block of code is set as follows:

```scala
import scala.util.hashing.MurmurHash3._

val markLow = 0
val markHigh = 4096
val seed = 12345

def consistentFilter(s: String): Boolean = {
  val hash = stringHash(s.split(" ")(0), seed) >>> 16
  hash >= markLow && hash < markHigh
}

val w = new java.io.FileWriter(new java.io.File("out.txt"))
val lines = io.Source.fromFile("chapter01/data/iris/in.txt").getLines
lines.filter(consistentFilter).foreach { s =>
    w.write(s + Properties.lineSeparator)
}
```

Any command-line input or output is written as follows:

```
akozlov@Alexanders-MacBook-Pro]$ scala
Welcome to Scala version 2.11.7 (Java HotSpot(TM) 64-Bit Server VM, Java
1.8.0_40).
Type in expressions to have them evaluated.
Type :help for more information.


scala> import scala.util.Random
import scala.util.Random
```

New terms and **important words** are shown in bold. Words that you see on the screen, for example, in menus or dialog boxes, appear in the text like this: "Run all cells at once by navigating to **Cell | Run All**."

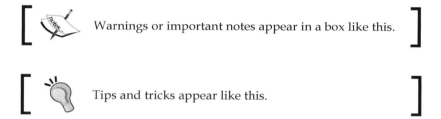

Warnings or important notes appear in a box like this.

Tips and tricks appear like this.

Reader feedback

Feedback from our readers is always welcome. Let us know what you think about this book—what you liked or disliked. Reader feedback is important for us as it helps us develop titles that you will really get the most out of.

To send us general feedback, simply e-mail feedback@packtpub.com, and mention the book's title in the subject of your message.

If there is a topic that you have expertise in and you are interested in either writing or contributing to a book, see our author guide at www.packtpub.com/authors.

Customer support

Now that you are the proud owner of a Packt book, we have a number of things to help you to get the most from your purchase.

Downloading the example code

You can download the example code files for this book from your account at http://www.packtpub.com. If you purchased this book elsewhere, you can visit http://www.packtpub.com/support and register to have the files e-mailed directly to you.

You can download the code files by following these steps:

1. Log in or register to our website using your e-mail address and password.
2. Hover the mouse pointer on the **SUPPORT** tab at the top.
3. Click on **Code Downloads & Errata**.
4. Enter the name of the book in the **Search** box.
5. Select the book for which you're looking to download the code files.
6. Choose from the drop-down menu where you purchased this book from.
7. Click on **Code Download**.

Once the file is downloaded, please make sure that you unzip or extract the folder using the latest version of:

- WinRAR / 7-Zip for Windows
- Zipeg / iZip / UnRarX for Mac
- 7-Zip / PeaZip for Linux

The code bundle for the book is also hosted on GitHub at https://github.com/PacktPublishing/Mastering-Scala-Machine-Learning. We also have other code bundles from our rich catalog of books and videos available at. https://github.com/PacktPublishing/ Check them out!

Downloading the color images of this book

We also provide you with a PDF file that has color images of the screenshots/diagrams used in this book. The color images will help you better understand the changes in the output. You can download this file from https://www.packtpub.com/sites/default/files/downloads/MasteringScalaMachineLearning_ColorImages.pdf.

Errata

Although we have taken every care to ensure the accuracy of our content, mistakes do happen. If you find a mistake in one of our books—maybe a mistake in the text or the code—we would be grateful if you could report this to us. By doing so, you can save other readers from frustration and help us improve subsequent versions of this book. If you find any errata, please report them by visiting http://www.packtpub.com/submit-errata, selecting your book, clicking on the **Errata Submission Form** link, and entering the details of your errata. Once your errata are verified, your submission will be accepted and the errata will be uploaded to our website or added to any list of existing errata under the Errata section of that title.

To view the previously submitted errata, go to https://www.packtpub.com/books/content/support and enter the name of the book in the search field. The required information will appear under the **Errata** section.

Piracy

Piracy of copyrighted material on the Internet is an ongoing problem across all media. At Packt, we take the protection of our copyright and licenses very seriously. If you come across any illegal copies of our works in any form on the Internet, please provide us with the location address or website name immediately so that we can pursue a remedy.

Please contact us at copyright@packtpub.com with a link to the suspected pirated material.

We appreciate your help in protecting our authors and our ability to bring you valuable content.

Questions

If you have a problem with any aspect of this book, you can contact us at questions@packtpub.com, and we will do our best to address the problem.

1
Exploratory Data Analysis

Before I dive into more complex methods to analyze your data later in the book, I would like to stop at basic data exploratory tasks on which almost all data scientists spend at least 80-90% of their productive time. The data preparation, cleansing, transforming, and joining the data alone is estimated to be a $44 billion/year industry alone (*Data Preparation in the Big Data Era* by *Federico Castanedo* and *Best Practices for Data Integration, O'Reilly Media, 2015*). Given this fact, it is surprising that people only recently started spending more time on the science of developing best practices and establishing good habits, documentation, and teaching materials for the whole process of data preparation (*Beautiful Data: The Stories Behind Elegant Data Solutions*, edited by *Toby Segaran* and *Jeff Hammerbacher, O'Reilly Media, 2009* and *Advanced Analytics with Spark: Patterns for Learning from Data at Scale* by *Sandy Ryza et al., O'Reilly Media, 2015*).

Few data scientists would agree on specific tools and techniques—and there are multiple ways to perform the exploratory data analysis, ranging from Unix command line to using very popular open source and commercial ETL and visualization tools. The focus of this chapter is how to use Scala and a laptop-based environment to benefit from techniques that are commonly referred as a functional paradigm of programming. As I will discuss, these techniques can be transferred to exploratory analysis over distributed system of machines using Hadoop/Spark.

What has functional programming to do with it? Spark was developed in Scala for a good reason. Many basic principles that lie at the foundation of functional programming, such as lazy evaluation, immutability, absence of side effects, list comprehensions, and monads go really well with processing data in distributed environments, specifically, when performing the data preparation and transformation tasks on big data. Thanks to abstractions, these techniques work well on a local workstation or a laptop. As mentioned earlier, this does not preclude us from processing very large datasets up to dozens of TBs on modern laptops connected to distributed clusters of storage/processing nodes. We can do it one topic or focus area at the time, but often we even do not have to sample or filter the dataset with proper partitioning. We will use Scala as our primary tool, but will resort to other tools if required.

While Scala is complete in the sense that everything that can be implemented in other languages can be implemented in Scala, Scala is fundamentally a high-level, or even a scripting, language. One does not have to deal with low-level details of data structures and algorithm implementations that in their majority have already been tested by a plethora of applications and time, in, say, Java or C++—even though Scala has its own collections and even some basic algorithm implementations today. Specifically, in this chapter, I'll be focusing on using Scala/Spark only for high-level tasks.

In this chapter, we will cover the following topics:

* Installing Scala
* Learning simple techniques for initial data exploration
* Learning how to downsample the original dataset for faster turnover
* Discussing the implementation of basic data transformation and aggregations in Scala
* Getting familiar with big data processing tools such as Spark and Spark Notebook
* Getting code for some basic visualization of datasets

Getting started with Scala

If you have already installed Scala, you can skip this paragraph. One can get the latest Scala download from `http://www.scala-lang.org/download/`. I used Scala version 2.11.7 on Mac OS X El Capitan 10.11.5. You can use any other version you like, but you might face some compatibility problems with other packages such as Spark, a common problem in open source software as the technology adoption usually lags by a few released versions.

In most cases, you should try to maintain precise match between the recommended versions as difference in versions can lead to obscure errors and a lengthy debugging process.

If you installed Scala correctly, after typing `scala`, you should see something similar to the following:

```
[akozlov@Alexanders-MacBook-Pro ~]$ scala

Welcome to Scala version 2.11.7 (Java HotSpot(TM) 64-Bit Server VM, Java
1.8.0_40).

Type in expressions to have them evaluated.

Type :help for more information.


scala>
```

This is a Scala **read-evaluate-print-loop (REPL)** prompt. Although Scala programs can be compiled, the content of this chapter will be in REPL, as we are focusing on interactivity with, maybe, a few exceptions. The `:help` command provides a some utility commands available in REPL (note the colon at the start):

```
[15:05:20 2.6.0-cdh5.5.0 akozlov@Alexanders-MacBook-Pro chapter01(master)]$ scala
Welcome to Scala version 2.11.7 (Java HotSpot(TM) 64-Bit Server VM, Java 1.8.0_40).
Type in expressions to have them evaluated.
Type :help for more information.

scala> :help
All commands can be abbreviated, e.g., :he instead of :help.
:edit <id>|<line>          edit history
:help [command]            print this summary or command-specific help
:history [num]             show the history (optional num is commands to show)
:h? <string>               search the history
:imports [name name ...]   show import history, identifying sources of names
:implicits [-v]            show the implicits in scope
:javap <path|class>        disassemble a file or class name
:line <id>|<line>          place line(s) at the end of history
:load <path>               interpret lines in a file
:paste [-raw] [path]       enter paste mode or paste a file
:power                     enable power user mode
:quit                      exit the interpreter
:replay [options]          reset the repl and replay all previous commands
:require <path>            add a jar to the classpath
:reset [options]           reset the repl to its initial state, forgetting all session entries
:save <path>               save replayable session to a file
:sh <command line>         run a shell command (result is implicitly => List[String])
:settings <options>        update compiler options, if possible; see reset
:silent                    disable/enable automatic printing of results
:type [-v] <expr>          display the type of an expression without evaluating it
:kind [-v] <expr>          display the kind of expression's type
:warnings                  show the suppressed warnings from the most recent line which had any
```

Distinct values of a categorical field

Now, you have a dataset and a computer. For convenience, I have provided you a small anonymized and obfuscated sample of clickstream data with the book repository that you can get at `https://github.com/alexvk/ml-in-scala.git`. The file in the `chapter01/data/clickstream` directory contains lines with timestamp, session ID, and some additional event information such as URL, category information, and so on at the time of the call. The first thing one would do is apply transformations to find out the distribution of values for different columns in the dataset.

Figure 01-1 shows screenshot shows the output of the dataset in the terminal window of the `gzcat chapter01/data/clickstream/clickstream_sample.tsv.gz |` `less -U` command. The columns are tab (`^I`) separated. One can notice that, as in many real-world big data datasets, many values are missing. The first column of the dataset is recognizable as the timestamp. The file contains complex data such as arrays, structs, and maps, another feature of big data datasets.

Unix provides a few tools to dissect the datasets. Probably, **less, cut, sort**, and **uniq** are the most frequently used tools for text file manipulations. **Awk, sed, perl**, and **tr** can do more complex transformations and substitutions. Fortunately, Scala allows you to transparently use command-line tools from within Scala REPL, as shown in the following screenshot:

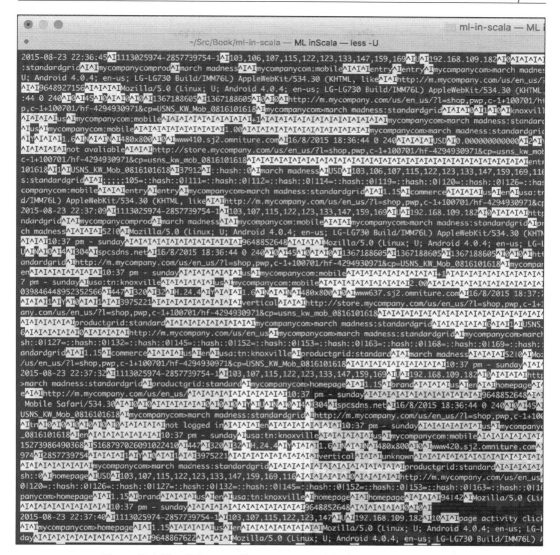

Figure 01-1. The clickstream file as an output of the less -U Unix command

Fortunately, Scala allows you to transparently use command-line tools from within Scala REPL:

```
[akozlov@Alexanders-MacBook-Pro]$ scala

...

scala> import scala.sys.process._
import scala.sys.process._
```

```
scala> val histogram = ( "gzcat chapter01/data/clickstream/clickstream_
sample.tsv.gz" #| "cut -f 10" #| "sort" #| "uniq -c" #| "sort -klnr"
).lineStream

histogram: Stream[String] = Stream(7731 http://www.mycompany.com/us/en_
us/, ?)

scala> histogram take(10) foreach println

7731 http://www.mycompany.com/us/en_us/

3843 http://mycompanyplus.mycompany.com/plus/

2734 http://store.mycompany.com/us/en_us/?l=shop,men_shoes

2400 http://m.mycompany.com/us/en_us/

1750 http://store.mycompany.com/us/en_us/?l=shop,men_mycompanyid

1556 http://www.mycompany.com/us/en_us/c/mycompanyid?sitesrc=id_redir

1530 http://store.mycompany.com/us/en_us/

1393 http://www.mycompany.com/us/en_us/?cp=USNS_KW_0611081618

1379 http://m.mycompany.com/us/en_us/?ref=http%3A%2F%2Fwww.mycompany.
com%2F

1230 http://www.mycompany.com/us/en_us/c/running
```

I used the `scala.sys.process` package to call familiar Unix commands from Scala REPL. From the output, we can immediately see the customers of our Webshop are mostly interested in men's shoes and running, and that most visitors are using the referral code, **KW_0611081618**.

One may wonder when we start using complex Scala types and algorithms. Just wait, a lot of highly optimized tools were created before Scala and are much more efficient for explorative data analysis. In the initial stage, the biggest bottleneck is usually just the disk I/O and slow interactivity. Later, we will discuss more iterative algorithms, which are usually more memory intensive. Also note that the UNIX pipeline operations can be implicitly parallelized on modern multi-core computer architectures, as they are in Spark (we will show it in the later chapters).

It has been shown that using compression, implicit or explicit, on input data files can actually save you the I/O time. This is particularly true for (most) modern semi-structured datasets with repetitive values and sparse content. Decompression can also be implicitly parallelized on modern fast multi-core computer architectures, removing the computational bottleneck, except, maybe in cases where compression is implemented implicitly in hardware (SSD, where we don't need to compress the files explicitly). We also recommend using directories rather than files as a paradigm for the dataset, where the insert operation is reduced to dropping the data file into a directory. This is how the datasets are presented in big data Hadoop tools such as Hive and Impala.

Summarization of a numeric field

Let's look at the numeric data, even though most of the columns in the dataset are either categorical or complex. The traditional way to summarize the numeric data is a five-number-summary, which is a representation of the median or mean, interquartile range, and minimum and maximum. I'll leave the computations of the median and interquartile ranges till the Spark DataFrame is introduced, as it makes these computations extremely easy; but we can compute mean, min, and max in Scala by just applying the corresponding operators:

```
scala> import scala.sys.process._
import scala.sys.process._
scala> val nums = ( "gzcat chapter01/data/clickstream/clickstream_sample.
tsv.gz"  #|  "cut -f 6" ).lineStream
nums: Stream[String] = Stream(0, ?)
scala> val m = nums.map(_.toDouble).min
m: Double = 0.0
scala> val m = nums.map(_.toDouble).sum/nums.size
m: Double = 3.6883642764024662
scala> val m = nums.map(_.toDouble).max
m: Double = 33.0
```

Grepping across multiple fields

Sometimes one needs to get an idea of how a certain value looks across multiple fields—most common are IP/MAC addresses, dates, and formatted messages. For examples, if I want to see all IP addresses mentioned throughout a file or a document, I need to replace the `cut` command in the previous example by `grep -o -E [1-9][0-9]{0,2}(?:\\.[1-9][0-9]{0,2}){3}`, where the `-o` option instructs `grep` to print only the matching parts—a more precise regex for the IP address should be `grep -o -E (?:(?:25[0-5]|2[0-4][0-9]|[01]?[0-9][0-9]?)\.){3}(?:25[0-5]|2[0-4][0-9]|[01]?[0-9][0-9]?)`, but is about 50% slower on my laptop and the original one works in most practical cases. I'll leave it as an excursive to run this command on the sample file provided with the book.

Basic, stratified, and consistent sampling

I've met quite a few data practitioners who scorn sampling. Ideally, if one can process the whole dataset, the model can only improve. In practice, the tradeoff is much more complex. First, one can build more complex models on a sampled set, particularly if the time complexity of the model building is non-linear — and in most situations, if it is at least $N^* log(N)$. A faster model building cycle allows you to iterate over models and converge on the best approach faster. In many situations, *time to action* is beating the potential improvements in the prediction accuracy due to a model built on complete dataset.

Sampling may be combined with appropriate filtering — in many practical situation, focusing on a subproblem at a time leads to better understanding of the whole problem domain. In many cases, this partitioning is at the foundation of the algorithm, like in decision trees, which are considered later. Often the nature of the problem requires you to focus on the subset of original data. For example, a cyber security analysis is often focused around a specific set of IPs rather than the whole network, as it allows to iterate over hypothesis faster. Including the set of all IPs in the network may complicate things initially if not throw the modeling off the right track.

When dealing with rare events, such as clickthroughs in ADTECH, sampling the positive and negative cases with different probabilities, which is also sometimes called oversampling, often leads to better predictions in short amount of time.

Fundamentally, sampling is equivalent to just throwing a coin — or calling a random number generator — for each data row. Thus it is very much like a stream filter operation, where the filtering is on an augmented column of random numbers. Let's consider the following example:

```scala
import scala.util.Random
import util.Properties

val threshold = 0.05

val lines = scala.io.Source.fromFile("chapter01/data/iris/in.txt").
getLines
val newLines = lines.filter(_ =>
    Random.nextDouble() <= threshold
)

val w = new java.io.FileWriter(new java.io.File("out.txt"))
newLines.foreach { s =>
    w.write(s + Properties.lineSeparator)
}
w.close
```

This is all good, but it has the following disadvantages:

- The number of lines in the resulting file is not known beforehand — even though on average it should be 5% of the original file

- The results of the sampling is non-deterministic — it is hard to rerun this process for either testing or verification

To fix the first point, we'll need to pass a more complex object to the function, as we need to maintain the state during the original list traversal, which makes the original algorithm less functional and parallelizable (this will be discussed later):

```scala
import scala.reflect.ClassTag
import scala.util.Random
import util.Properties

def reservoirSample[T: ClassTag](input: Iterator[T],k: Int): Array[T] = {
  val reservoir = new Array[T](k)
  // Put the first k elements in the reservoir.
  var i = 0
  while (i < k && input.hasNext) {
    val item = input.next()
    reservoir(i) = item
    i += 1
  }

  if (i < k) {
    // If input size < k, trim the array size
    reservoir.take(i)
  } else {
    // If input size > k, continue the sampling process.
    while (input.hasNext) {
      val item = input.next
      val replacementIndex = Random.nextInt(i)
      if (replacementIndex < k) {
        reservoir(replacementIndex) = item
      }
      i += 1
    }
    reservoir
  }
}

val numLines=15
```

```
val w = new java.io.FileWriter(new java.io.File("out.txt"))
val lines = io.Source.fromFile("chapter01/data/iris/in.txt").getLines
reservoirSample(lines, numLines).foreach { s =>
    w.write(s + scala.util.Properties.lineSeparator)
}
w.close
```

This will output `numLines` lines. Similarly to reservoir sampling, stratified sampling is guaranteed to provide the same ratios of input/output rows for all strata defined by levels of another attribute. We can achieve this by splitting the original dataset into *N* subsets corresponding to the levels, performing the reservoir sampling, and merging the results afterwards. However, MLlib library, which will be covered in *Chapter 3, Working with Spark and MLlib*, already has stratified sampling implementation:

```
val origLinesRdd = sc.textFile("file://...")
val keyedRdd = origLines.keyBy(r => r.split(",")(0))
val fractions = keyedRdd.countByKey.keys.map(r => (r, 0.1)).toMap
val sampledWithKey = keyedRdd.sampleByKeyExact(fractions)
val sampled = sampledWithKey.map(_._2).collect
```

The other bullet point is more subtle; sometimes we want a consistent subset of values across multiple datasets, either for reproducibility or to join with another sampled dataset. In general, if we sample two datasets, the results will contain random subsets of IDs which might have very little or no intersection. The cryptographic hashing functions come to the help here. The result of applying a hash function such as MD5 or SHA1 is a sequence of bits that is statistically uncorrelated, at least in theory. We will use the `MurmurHash` function, which is part of the `scala.util.hashing` package:

```
import scala.util.hashing.MurmurHash3._

val markLow = 0
val markHigh = 4096
val seed = 12345

def consistentFilter(s: String): Boolean = {
  val hash = stringHash(s.split(" ")(0), seed) >>> 16
  hash >= markLow && hash < markHigh
}

val w = new java.io.FileWriter(new java.io.File("out.txt"))
val lines = io.Source.fromFile("chapter01/data/iris/in.txt").getLines
lines.filter(consistentFilter).foreach { s =>
    w.write(s + Properties.lineSeparator)
}
w.close
```

This function is guaranteed to return exactly the same subset of records based on the value of the first field—it is either all records where the first field equals a certain value or none—and will come up with approximately one-sixteenth of the original sample; the range of hash is 0 to 65,535.

MurmurHash? It is not a cryptographic hash!

Unlike cryptographic hash functions, such as MD5 and SHA1, MurmurHash is not specifically designed to be hard to find an inverse of a hash. It is, however, really fast and efficient. This is what really matters in our use case.

Working with Scala and Spark Notebooks

Often the most frequent values or five-number summary are not sufficient to get the first understanding of the data. The term **descriptive statistics** is very generic and may refer to very complex ways to describe the data. Quantiles, a **Paretto** chart or, when more than one attribute is analyzed, correlations are also examples of descriptive statistics. When sharing all these ways to look at the data aggregates, in many cases, it is also important to share the specific computations to get to them.

Scala or Spark Notebook https://github.com/Bridgewater/scala-notebook, https://github.com/andypetrella/spark-notebook record the whole transformation path and the results can be shared as a JSON-based *.snb file. The Spark Notebook project can be downloaded from http://spark-notebook.io, and I will provide a sample Chapter01.snb file with the book. I will use Spark, which I will cover in more detail in *Chapter 3, Working with Spark and MLlib*.

For this particular example, Spark will run in the local mode. Even in the local mode Spark can utilize parallelism on your workstation, but it is limited to the number of cores and hyperthreads that can run on your laptop or workstation. With a simple configuration change, however, Spark can be pointed to a distributed set of machines and use resources across a distributed set of nodes.

Here is the set of commands to download the Spark Notebook and copy the necessary files from the code repository:

```
[akozlov@Alexanders-MacBook-Pro]$ wget http://s3.eu-central-1.amazonaws.
com/spark-notebook/zip/spark-notebook-0.6.3-scala-2.11.7-spark-1.6.1-
hadoop-2.6.4-with-hive-with-parquet.zip

...

[akozlov@Alexanders-MacBook-Pro]$ unzip -d ~/ spark-notebook-0.6.3-scala-
2.11.7-spark-1.6.1-hadoop-2.6.4-with-hive-with-parquet.zip

...
```

```
[akozlov@Alexanders-MacBook-Pro]$ ln -sf ~/ spark-notebook-0.6.3-scala-
2.11.7-spark-1.6.1-hadoop-2.6.4-with-hive-with-parquet ~/spark-notebook

[akozlov@Alexanders-MacBook-Pro]$ cp chapter01/notebook/Chapter01.snb ~/
spark-notebook/notebooks

[akozlov@Alexanders-MacBook-Pro]$ cp chapter01/ data/kddcup/kddcup.
parquet ~/spark-notebook

[akozlov@Alexanders-MacBook-Pro]$ cd ~/spark-notebook

[akozlov@Alexanders-MacBook-Pro]$ bin/spark-notebook

Play server process ID is 2703

16/04/14 10:43:35 INFO play: Application started (Prod)

16/04/14 10:43:35 INFO play: Listening for HTTP on /0:0:0:0:0:0:0:0:9000

...
```

Now you can open the notebook at `http://localhost:9000` in your browser, as shown in the following screenshot:

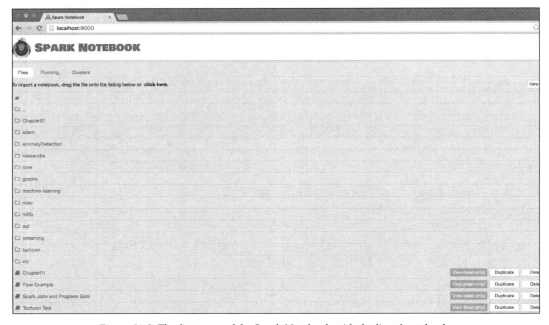

Figure 01-2. The first page of the Spark Notebook with the list of notebooks

Open the `Chapter01` notebook by clicking on it. The statements are organized into cells and can be executed by clicking on the small right arrow at the top, as shown in the following screenshot, or run all cells at once by navigating to **Cell | Run All**:

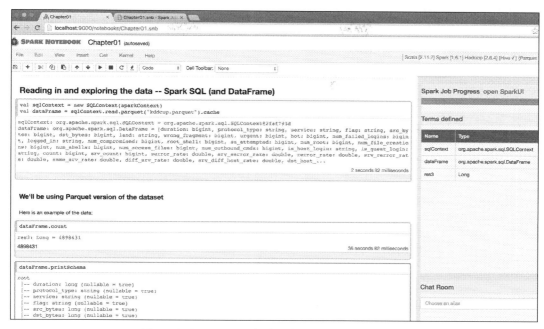

Figure 01-3. Executing the first few cells in the notebook

First, we will look at the discrete variables. For example, to get the other observable attributes. This task would be totally impossible if distribution of the labels, issue the following code:

```
val labelCount = df.groupBy("lbl").count().collect
labelCount.toList.map(row => (row.getString(0), row.getLong(1)))
```

The first time I read the dataset, it took about a minute on MacBook Pro, but Spark caches the data in memory and the subsequent aggregation runs take only about a second. Spark Notebook provides you the distribution of the values, as shown in the following screenshot:

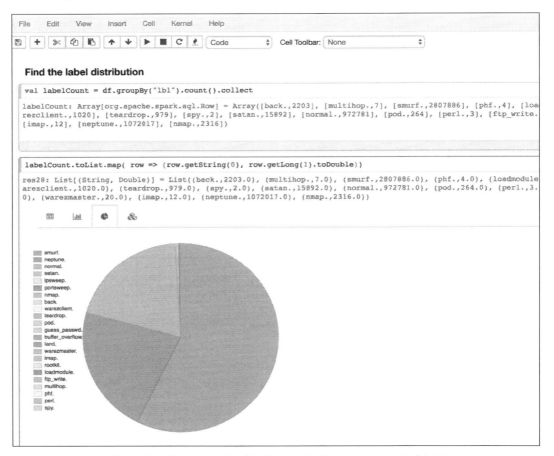

Figure 01-4. Computing the distribution of values for a categorical field

I can also look at crosstab counts for pairs of discrete variables, which gives me an idea of interdependencies between the variables using `http://spark.apache.org/docs/latest/api/scala/index.html#org.apache.spark.sql.DataFrameStatFunctions` — the object does not support computing correlation measures such as chi-square yet:

```
In [63]: dataFrame.stat.crosstab("service", "flag")
         res48: org.apache.spark.sql.DataFrame = [service_flag: string, S0: bigint, RSTO: bigint, RSTR: bigint, RS
         TOS0: bigint, SF: bigint, SH: bigint, REJ: bigint, S1: bigint, OTH: bigint, S2: bigint, S3: bigint]
Out[63]:
```

1 >>   1 second 875 milliseconds

service_flag	S0	RSTO	RSTR	RSTOS0	SF	SH	REJ	S1	OTH	S2	S3
ftp	843	234	6	2	4115	1	0	10	2	1	0
netbios_ssn	842	1	6	0	3	1	202	0	0	0	0
hostnames	837	0	6	0	0	1	206	0	0	0	0
printer	834	202	5	0	2	1	0	1	0	0	0
finger	1634	212	7	2	5031	1	0	3	0	0	1
smtp	1008	349	9	2	95111	1	4	37	2	21	10
harvest	1	0	0	0	0	0	1	0	0	0	0
aol	0	0	0	0	0	0	2	0	0	0	0
name	837	0	8	1	0	1	220	0	0	0	0
whois	843	0	8	1	0	1	220	0	0	0	0
http_8001	1	0	0	0	0	0	1	0	0	0	0
private	820049	1203	4703	91	76524	981	197246	1	33	0	0
sql_net	839	0	6	0	0	1	205	0	1	0	0
shell	834	203	5	0	7	1	0	1	0	0	0
ftp_data	1611	0	9	1	38743	1	238	72	3	6	13
auth	837	4	6	0	2314	1	220	0	0	0	0
ssh	840	16	6	1	9	1	202	0	0	0	0
telnet	1730	315	43	2	2106	1	0	73	3	0	4
gopher	842	3	6	1	14	1	210	0	0	0	0
pop_2	843	1	5	0	2	1	203	0	0	0	0
domain	848	4	6	1	48	1	205	0	0	0	0
pm_dump	0	0	0	0	5	0	0	0	0	0	0
supdup	846	0	7	0	0	1	206	0	0	0	0
netbios_dgm	839	0	7	0	0	1	205	0	0	0	0
discard	841	202	8	2	1	1	4	0	0	0	0

Figure 01-5. Contingency table or crosstab

However, we can see that the most popular service is private and it correlates well with the SF flag. Another way to analyze dependencies is to look at 0 entries. For example, the S2 and S3 flags are clearly related to the SMTP and FTP traffic since all other entries are 0.

Of course, the most interesting correlations are with the target variable, but these are better discovered by supervised learning algorithms that I will cover in *Chapter 3, Working with Spark and MLlib,* and *Chapter 5, Regression and Classification.*

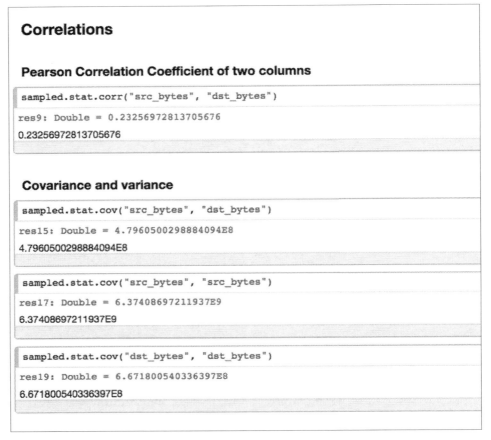

Correlations

Pearson Correlation Coefficient of two columns

```
sampled.stat.corr("src_bytes", "dst_bytes")
res9: Double = 0.23256972813705676
0.23256972813705676
```

Covariance and variance

```
sampled.stat.cov("src_bytes", "dst_bytes")
res15: Double = 4.7960500298884094E8
4.7960500298884094E8
```

```
sampled.stat.cov("src_bytes", "src_bytes")
res17: Double = 6.37408697211937E9
6.37408697211937E9
```

```
sampled.stat.cov("dst_bytes", "dst_bytes")
res19: Double = 6.671800540336397E8
6.671800540336397E8
```

Figure 01-6. Computing simple aggregations using org.apache.spark.sql.DataFrameStatFunctions.

Analogously, we can compute correlations for numerical variables with the dataFrame.stat.corr() and dataFrame.stat.cov() functions (refer to *Figure 01-6*). In this case, the class supports the **Pearson correlation coefficient**. Alternatively, we can use the standard SQL syntax on the parquet file directly:

```
sqlContext.sql("SELECT lbl, protocol_type, min(duration),
   avg(duration), stddev(duration), max(duration) FROM
   parquet.`kddcup.parquet` group by lbl, protocol_type")
```

Finally, I promised you to compute percentiles. Computing percentiles usually involves sorting the whole dataset, which is expensive; however, if the tile is one of the first or the last ones, usually it is possible to optimize the computation:

```
val pct = sqlContext.sql("SELECT duration FROM
    parquet.`kddcup.parquet` where protocol_type =
    'udp'").rdd.map(_.getLong(0)).cache
pct.top((0.05*pct.count).toInt).last
```

Computing the exact percentiles for a more generic case is more computationally expensive and is provided as a part of the Spark Notebook example code.

Basic correlations

You probably noticed that detecting correlations from contingency tables is hard. Detecting patterns takes practice, but many people are much better at recognizing the patterns visually. Detecting actionable patterns is one of the primary goals of machine learning. While advanced supervised machine learning techniques that will be covered in *Chapter 4*, *Supervised and Unsupervised Learning* and *Chapter 5*, *Regression and Classification* exist, initial analysis of interdependencies between variables can help with the right transformation of variables or selection of the best inference technique.

Multiple well-established visualization tools exist and there are multiple sites, such as http://www.kdnuggets.com, which specialize on ranking and providing recommendations on data analysis, data explorations, and visualization software. I am not going to question the validity and accuracy of such rankings in this book, and very few sites actually mention Scala as a specific way to visualize the data, even if this is possible with, say, a D3.js package. A good visualization is a great way to deliver your findings to a larger audience. One look is worth a thousand words.

For the purposes of this chapter, I will use **Grapher** that is present on every Mac OS notebook. To open **Grapher**, go to Utilities (*shift + command + U* in Finder) and click on the **Grapher** icon (or search by name by pressing *command + space*). Grapher presents many options, including the following **Log-Log** and **Polar** coordinates:

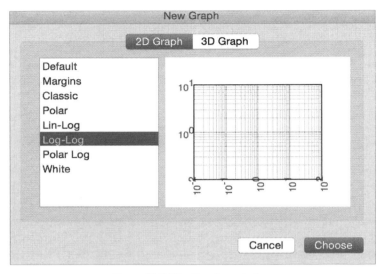

Figure 01-7. The Grapher window

Fundamentally, the amount of information that can be delivered through visualization is limited by the number of pixels on the screen, which, for most modern computers, is in millions and color variations, which arguably can also be in millions (*Judd, Deane B.; Wyszecki, Günter (1975). Color in Business, Science and Industry. Wiley Series in Pure and Applied Optics (3rd ed.). New York*). If I am working on a multidimensional TB dataset, the dataset first needs to be summarized, processed, and reduced to a size that can be viewed on a computer screen.

For the purpose of illustration, I will use the Iris UCI dataset that can be found at `https://archive.ics.uci.edu/ml/datasets/Iris`. To bring the dataset into the tool, type the following code (on Mac OS):

```
[akozlov@Alexanders-MacBook-Pro]$ pbcopy < chapter01/data/iris/in.txt
```

Open the new **Point Set** in the **Grapher** (*command + alt + P*), press **Edit Points...**
and paste the data by pressing *command + V*. The tools has line-fitting capabilities
with basic linear, polynomial, and exponential families and provides the popular
chi-squared metric to estimate the goodness of the fit with respect to the number
of free parameters:

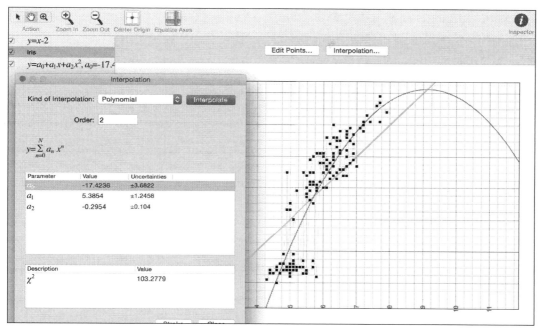

Figure 01-8. Fitting the Iris dataset using Grapher on Mac OS X

We will cover how to estimate the goodness of model fit in the following chapters.

Summary

I've tried to establish a common ground to perform a more complex data science later in the book. Don't expect these to be a complete set of exploratory techniques, as the exploratory techniques can extend to running very complex modes. However, we covered simple aggregations, sampling, file operations such as read and write, working with tools such as notebooks and Spark DataFrames, which brings familiar SQL constructs into the arsenal of an analyst working with Spark/Scala.

The next chapter will take a completely different turn by looking at the data pipelines as a part of a data-driven enterprise and cover the data discovery process from the business perspective: what are the ultimate goals we are trying to accomplish by doing the data analysis. I will cover a few traditional topics of ML, such as supervised and unsupervised learning, after this before delving into more complex representations of the data, where Scala really shows it's advantage over SQL.

Data Pipelines and Modeling

We have looked at basic hands-on tools for exploring the data in the previous chapter, thus we now can delve into more complex topics of statistical model building and optimal control or science-driven tools and problems. I will go ahead and say that we will only touch on some topics in optimal control since this book really is just about ML in Scala and not the theory of data-driven business management, which might be an exciting topic for a book on its own.

In this chapter, I will stay away from specific implementations in Scala and discuss the problem of building a data-driven enterprise at a high level. Later chapters will address how to solve these smaller pieces of the puzzle. A special emphasis will be given to handing uncertainty. Uncertainty usually comes in several favors: first, there can be noise in the information we are provided with. Secondly, the information can be incomplete. The system may have some degree of freedom in filling the missing pieces, which results in uncertainty. Finally, there may be variations in the interpretation of the models and the resulting metrics. The final point is subtle, as most classic textbooks assume that we can measure things directly. Not only the measurements may be noisy, but the definition of the measure may change in time — try measuring satisfaction or happiness. Certainly, we can avoid the ambiguity by saying that we can optimize only measurable metrics, as people usually do, but it will significantly limit the application domain in practice. Nothing prevents the scientific machinery from handling the uncertainty in the interpretation into account as well.

The predictive models are often built just for data understanding. From the linguistic derivation, model is a simplified representation of the actual complex buildings or processes for exactly the purpose of making a point and convincing people, one or another way. The ultimate goal for predictive modeling, the modeling I am concerned about in this book and this chapter specifically, is to optimize the business processes by taking the most important factors into account in order to make the world a better place. This was certainly a sentence with a lot of uncertainty entrenched, but at least it looks like a much better goal than optimizing a click-through rate.

Let's look at a traditional business decision-making process: a traditional business might involve a set of C-level executives making decisions based on information that is usually obtained from a set of dashboards with graphical representation of the data in one or several DBs. The promise of an automated data-driven business is to be able to automatically make most of the decisions provided the uncertainties eliminating human bias. This is not to say that we no longer need C-level executives, but the C-level executives will be busy helping the machines to make the decisions instead of the other way around.

In this chapter, we will cover the following topics:

- Going through the basics of influence diagrams as a tool for decision making
- Looking at variations of the pure decision making optimization in the context of adaptive **Markov Decision** making process and **Kelly Criterion**
- Getting familiar with at least three different practical strategies for exploration-exploitation trade-off
- Describing the architecture of a data-driven enterprise
- Discussing major architectural components of a decision-making pipeline
- Getting familiar with standard tools for building data pipelines

Influence diagrams

While the decision making process can have multiple facets, a book about decision making under uncertainty would be incomplete without mentioning influence diagrams (*Influence Diagrams for Team Decision Analysis*, Decision Analysis 2 (4): 207–228), which help the analysis and understanding of the decision-making process. The decision may be as mundane as selection of the next news article to show to a user in a personalized environment or a complex one as detecting malware on an enterprise network or selecting the next research project.

Depending on the weather she can try and go on a boat trip. We can represent the decision-making process as a diagram. Let's decide whether to take a river boat tour during her stay in Portland, Oregon:

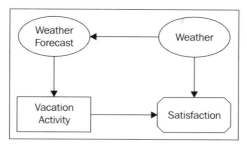

Figure 02-1. A simple vacation influence diagram to represent a simple decision-making process. The diagram contains decision nodes such as Vacation Activity, observable and unobservable information nodes such as Weather Forecast and Weather, and finally the value node such as Satisfaction

The preceding diagram represents this situation. The decision whether to participate in the activity is clearly driven by the potential to get certain satisfaction, which is a function of the decision itself and the weather at the time of the activity. While the actual weather conditions are unknown at the time of the trip planning, we believe there is a certain correlation between the weather forecast and the actual weather experienced during the trip, which is represented by the edge between the **Weather** and **Weather Forecast** nodes. The **Vacation Activity** node is the decision node, it has only one parent as the decision is made solely based on **Weather Forecast**. The final node in the DAG is **Satisfaction**, which is a function of the actual whether and the decision we made during the trip planning — obviously, *yes + good weather* and *no + bad weather* are likely to have the highest scores. The *yes + bad weather* and *no + good weather* would be a bad outcome — the latter case is probably just a missed opportunity, but not necessarily a bad decision, provided an inaccurate weather forecast.

The absence of an edge carries an independence assumption. For example, we believe that **Satisfaction** should not depend on **Weather Forecast**, as the latter becomes irrelevant once we are on the boat. Once the vacation plan is finalized, the actual weather during the boating activity can no longer affect the decision, which was made solely based on the weather forecast; at least in our simplified model, where we exclude the option of buying a trip insurance.

The graph shows different stages of decision making and the flow of information (we will provide an actual graph implementation in Scala in *Chapter 7, Working with Graph Algorithms*). There is only one piece of information required to make the decision in our simplified diagram: the weather forecast. Once the decision is made, we can no longer change it, even if we have information about the actual weather at the time of the trip. The weather and the decision data can be used to model her satisfaction with the decision she has made.

Let's map this approach to an advertising problem as an illustration: the ultimate goal is to get user satisfaction with the targeted ads, which results in additional revenue for an advertiser. The satisfaction is the function of user-specific environmental state, which is unknown at the time of decision making. Using machine learning algorithms, however, we can forecast this state based on the user's recent Web visit history and other information that we can gather, such as geolocation, browser-agent string, time of day, category of the ad, and so on (refer to *Figure 02-2*).

While we are unlikely to measure the level of dopamine in the user's brain, which will certainly fall under the realm of measurable metrics and probably reduce the uncertainty, we can measure the user satisfaction indirectly by the user's actions, either the fact that they responded to the ad or even the measure of time the user spent between the clicks to browse relevant information, which can be used to estimate the effectiveness of our modeling and algorithms. Here is an influence diagram, similar to the one for "vacation", adjusted for the advertising decision-making process:

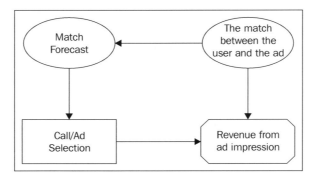

Figure 02-2. The vacation influence diagram adjusted to the online advertising decision-making case. The decisions for online advertising can be made thousand times per second

The actual process might be more complex, representing a chain of decisions, each one depending on a few previous time slices. For example, the so-called **Markov Chain Decision Process**. In this case, the diagram might be repeated over multiple time slices.

Yet another example might be Enterprise Network Internet malware analytics system. In this case, we try to detect network connections indicative of either **command and control (C2)**, lateral movement, or data exfiltration based on the analysis of network packets flowing through the enterprise switches. The goal is to minimize the potential impact of an outbreak with minimum impact on the functioning systems.

One of the decisions we might take is to reimage a subset of nodes or to at least isolate them. The data we collect may contain uncertainty—many benign software packages may send traffic in suspicious ways, and the models need to differentiate between them based on the risk and potential impact. One of the decisions in this specific case may be to collect additional information.

I will leave it to the reader to map this and other potential business cases to the corresponding diagram as an exercise. Let's consider a more complex optimization problem now.

Sequential trials and dealing with risk

What if my preferences for making an extra few dollars outweigh the risk of losing the same amount? I will stop on why one's preferences might be asymmetric in a little while in this section, and there is scientific evidence that this asymmetry is ingrained in our minds for evolutionary reasons, but you are right, I have to optimize the expected value of the asymmetric function of the parameterized utility now, as follows:

$$\frac{\partial E\left(F\left(u\left(z\right)\right)\right)}{\partial z} \cdot \left(2.1\right)$$

Why would an asymmetric function surface in the analysis? One example is repeated bets or re-investments, also known as the Kelly Criterion problem. Although originally, the Kelly Criterion was developed for a specific case of binary outcome as in a gambling machine and the optimization of the fraction of money to bet in each round (*A New Interpretation of Information Rate*, Bell System Technical Journal 35 (4): 917–926, 1956), a more generic formulation as an re-investment problem involves a probabilistic distribution of possible returns.

The return over multiple bets is a product of individual return rates on each of the bets—the return rate is the ratio between the bankroll after the bet to the original bankroll before each individual bet, as follows:

$$R = r_1 r_2 \ldots r_N$$

This does not help us much to optimize the total return as we don't know how to optimize the product of *i.i.d.* random variables. However, we can convert the product to a sum using log transformation and apply the **central limit theorem (CLT)** to approximate the sum of *i.i.d.* variables (provided that the distribution of r_i is subect to CLT conditions, for example, has a finite mean and variance), as follows:

$$E(R) =$$
$$E\left(\exp\left(\log(r_1) + \log(r_2) + \ldots + \log(r_N)\right)\right) \cdot =$$
$$\exp\left(N \times E\left(\log(r)\right) + O\left(\sqrt{N}\right)\right) =$$
$$\exp\left(E\left(\log(r)\right)\right)^N \left(1 + O\left(\frac{1}{\sqrt{N}}\right)\right)$$

Thus, the cumulative result of making N bets would look like the result of making N bets with expected return of $\exp\left(E\left(\log(r_i)\right)\right)$, and not $E(r_i)$!

As I mentioned before, the problem is most often applied for the case of binary bidding, although it can be easily generalized, in which case there is an additional parameter: x, the amount of money to bid in each round. Let's say I make a profit of W with probability p or completely lose my bet otherwise with the probability *(1-p)*. Optimizing the expected return with respect to the following additional parameter:

$$E\left(\log(r(x))\right) = p\log(1 + xW) + (1 - p)\log(1 - x) \cdot (2.2)$$

$$\frac{\partial E(\log(r(x)))}{\partial x} = \frac{pW}{1 + xW} - \frac{(1 - p)}{1 - x} = 0 \cdot (2.3)$$

$$x = p - \left[\frac{1 - p}{W}\right] \cdot (2.4)$$

The last equation is the Kelly Criterion ratio and gives you the optimal amount to bet.

The reason that one might bet less than the total amount is that even if the average return is positive, there is still a possibility to lose the whole bankroll, particularly, in highly skewed situations. For example, even if the probability of making *10 x* on your bet is *0.105* (*W = 10*, the expected return is *5%*), the combinatorial analysis show that even after *60* bets, there is roughly a *50%* chance that the overall return will be negative, and there is an *11%* chance, in particular, of losing *(57 - 10 x 3) = 27* times your bet or more:

```
akozlov@Alexanders-MacBook-Pro$ scala
Welcome to Scala version 2.11.7 (Java HotSpot(TM) 64-Bit Server VM, Java
1.8.0_40).
Type in expressions to have them evaluated.
Type :help for more information.27

scala> def logFactorial(n: Int) = { (1 to n).map(Math.log(_)).sum }
logFactorial: (n: Int)Double

scala> def cmnp(m: Int, n: Int, p: Double) = {
     |     Math.exp(logFactorial(n) -
     |     logFactorial(m) +
     |     m*Math.log(p) -
     |     logFactorial(n-m) +
     |     (n-m)*Math.log(1-p))
     | }
cmnp: (m: Int, n: Int, p: Double)Double

scala> val p = 0.105
p: Double = 0.105

scala> val n = 60
n: Int = 60

scala> var cumulative = 0.0
cumulative: Double = 0.0

scala> for(i <- 0 to 14) {
     |     val prob = cmnp(i,n,p)
     |     cumulative += prob
```

```
    |    println(f"We expect $i wins with $prob%.6f probability
$cumulative%.3f cumulative (n = $n, p = $p).")
    | }
```

We expect 0 wins with 0.001286 probability 0.001 cumulative (n = 60, p = 0.105).

We expect 1 wins with 0.009055 probability 0.010 cumulative (n = 60, p = 0.105).

We expect 2 wins with 0.031339 probability 0.042 cumulative (n = 60, p = 0.105).

We expect 3 wins with 0.071082 probability 0.113 cumulative (n = 60, p = 0.105).

We expect 4 wins with 0.118834 probability 0.232 cumulative (n = 60, p = 0.105).

We expect 5 wins with 0.156144 probability 0.388 cumulative (n = 60, p = 0.105).

We expect 6 wins with 0.167921 probability 0.556 cumulative (n = 60, p = 0.105).

We expect 7 wins with 0.151973 probability 0.708 cumulative (n = 60, p = 0.105).

We expect 8 wins with 0.118119 probability 0.826 cumulative (n = 60, p = 0.105).

We expect 9 wins with 0.080065 probability 0.906 cumulative (n = 60, p = 0.105).

We expect 10 wins with 0.047905 probability 0.954 cumulative (n = 60, p = 0.105).

We expect 11 wins with 0.025546 probability 0.979 cumulative (n = 60, p = 0.105).

We expect 12 wins with 0.012238 probability 0.992 cumulative (n = 60, p = 0.105).

We expect 13 wins with 0.005301 probability 0.997 cumulative (n = 60, p = 0.105).

We expect 14 wins with 0.002088 probability 0.999 cumulative (n = 60, p = 0.105).

Note that to recover the *27 x* amount, one would need to play only $\log(27)/\log(1.05)=68$ additional rounds on average with these favourable odds, but one must have something to bet to start with. The Kelly Criterion provides that the optimal is to bet only *1.55%* of our bankroll. Note that if I bet the whole bankroll, I would lose all my money with 89.5% certainty in the first round (the probability of a win is only *0.105*). If I bet only a fraction of the bankroll, the chances of staying in the game are infinitely better, but the overall returns are smaller. The plot of expected log of return is shown in *Figure 02-3* as a function of the portions of the bankroll to bet, *x*, and possible distribution of outcomes in 60 bets that I just computed. In 24% of the games we'll do worse than the lower curve, in 39% worse than the next curve, in about half—44%—a gambler we'll do the same or better than the black curve in the middle, and in 30% of cases better than the top one. The optimal Kelly Criterion value for *x* is *0.0155*, which will eventually optimize the overall return over infinitely many rounds:

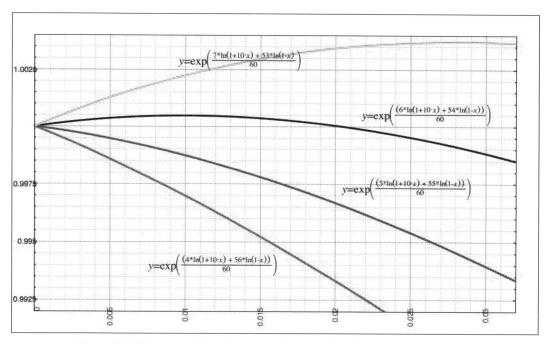

Figure 02-3. The expected log of return as a function of the bet amount and possible outcomes in 60 rounds (see equation (2.2))

The Kelly Criterion has been criticized for being both too aggressive (gamblers tend to overestimate their winning potential/ratio and underestimate the probability of a ruin), as well as for being too conservative (the value at risk should be the total available capital, not just the bankroll), but it demonstrates one of the examples where we need to compensate our intuitive understanding of the "benefit" with some additional transformations.

From the financial point of view, the Kelly Criterion is a much better description of risk than the standard definition as volatility or variance of the returns. For a generic parametrized payoff distribution, *y(z)*, with a probability distribution function, *f(z)*, the equation (2.3) can be reformulated as follows. after the substitution *r(x) = 1 + x y(z)*, where *x* is still the amount to bet:

$$\frac{\partial E\left(\log\left(1+xy\left(z\right)\right)\right)}{\partial x} = E\left(\frac{y\left(z\right)}{1+xy\left(z\right)}\right) = 0$$

$$\int_{z=-\infty}^{\infty} \frac{y\left(z\right)f\left(z\right)}{1+xy\left(z\right)}dz = 0 \cdot \left(2.5\right)$$

It can also be written in the following manner in the discrete case:

$$= \sum_i \frac{y\left(z_i\right)p\left(z_i\right)}{1+xy\left(z_i\right)} = 0 \ \left(2.6\right)$$

Here, the denominator emphasizes the contributions from the regions with negative payoffs. Specifically, the possibility of losing all your bankroll is exactly where the denominator $\left(1+xy\left(z\right)\right)$ is zero.

As I mentioned before, interestingly, risk aversion is engrained in our intuitions and there seems to be a natural risk-aversion system of preferences encoded in both humans and primates (*A Monkey Economy as Irrational as Ours* by Laurie Santos, TED talk, 2010). Now enough about monkeys and risk, let's get into another rather controversial subject—the exploration-exploitation trade-off, where one might not even know the payoff trade-offs initially.

Exploration and exploitation

The exploration-exploitation trade-off is another problem that has its apparent origin within gambling, even though the real applications range from allocation of funding to research projects to self-driving cars. The traditional formulation is a multi-armed bandit problem, which refers to an imaginary slot machine with one or more arms. Sequential plays of each arm generate $i.i.d.$ returns with unknown probabilities for each arm; the successive plays are independent in the simplified models. The rewards are assumed to be independent across the arms. The goal is to maximize the reward—for example, the amount of money won, and to minimize the learning loss, or the amount spend on the arms with less than optimal winning rate, provided an agreed upon arm selection policy. The obvious trade-off is between the **exploration** in search of an arm that produces the best return and **exploitation** of the best-known arm with optimal return:

$$r_{opt} = \max_{i=1\ldots K} E(r_i)$$

The **pseudo-regret** is then the difference:

$$R_N = N r_{opt} - \sum_{i=1}^{N} E\left(r_{s_i}\right)$$

Here, s_i is the ith arm selection out of N trials. The multi-armed bandit problem was extensively studied in the 1930s and again during the early 2000s, with the application in finance and ADTECH. While in general, due to stochastic nature of the problem, it is not possible to provide a bound on the expected regret better than the square root of N, the pseudo-regret can be controlled so that we are able to bound it by a log of N (*Regret Analysis of Stochastic and Nonstochastic Multi-armed Bandit Problems* by Sebastien Bubeck and Nicolo Cesa-Bianchi, http://arxiv.org/pdf/1204.5721.pdf).

One of the most common strategies used in practice is epsilon strategies, where the optimal arm is chosen with the probability of $(1-\varepsilon)$ and one of the other arms with the remaining probability. The drawback of this approach is that we might spend a lot of exploration resources on the arms that are never going to provide any rewards. The UCB strategy improves the epsilon strategy by choosing an arm with the largest estimate of the return, plus some multiple or fraction of the standard deviation of the return estimates. The approach needs the recomputation of the best arm to pull at each round and suffers from approximations made to estimate the mean and standard deviation. Besides, UCB requires the recomputation of the estimates for each successive pull, which might be a scalability problem.

Finally, the Thompson sampling strategy uses a fixed random sample from Beta-Bernoulli posterior estimates and assigns the next arm to the one that gives the minimal expected regret, for which real data can be used to avoid parameter recomputation. Although the specific numbers may depend on the assumptions, one available comparison for these model performances is provided in the following diagram:

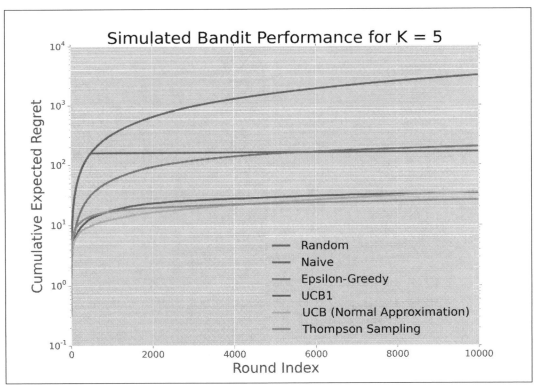

Figure 02-3. The simulation results for different exploration exploitation strategies for K = 5, one-armed bandits, and different strategies.

Figure 02-3 shows simulation results for different strategies (taken from the Rich Relevance website at http://engineering.richrelevance.com/recommendations-thompson-sampling). The **Random** strategy just allocates the arms at random and corresponds to pure exploration. The **Naive** strategy is random up to a certain threshold and than switches to pure Exxploitation mode. **Upper Confidence Bound (UCB)** with 95% confidence level. UCB1 is a modification of UCB to take into account the log-normality of the distributions. Finally the Thompson sampling strategy makes a random sample from actual posterior distribution to optimize the regret.

Exploration/exploitation models are known to be very sensitive to the initial conditions and outliers, particularly on the low-response side. One can spend enormous amount of trials on the arms that are essentially dead.

Other improvements on the strategies are possible by estimating better priors based on additional information, such as location, or limiting the set of arms to explore — K — due to such additional information, but these aspects are more domain-specific (such as personalization or online advertising).

Unknown unknowns

Unknown unknowns have been largely made famous due to a phrase from a response the United States Secretary of Defense, Donald Rumsfeld, gave to a question at a United States **Department of Defense (DoD)** news briefing on February 12, 2002 about the lack of evidence linking the government of Iraq with the supply of weapons of mass destruction to terrorist groups, and books by Nassim Taleb (*The Black Swan: The Impact of the Highly Improbable* by Nassim Taleb, Random House, 2007).

Turkey paradox

Arguably, the unknown unknown is better explained by the turkey paradox. Suppose you have a family of turkeys playing in the backyard and enjoying protection and free food. Across the fence, there is another family of turkeys. This all works day after day, and month after month, until Thanksgiving comes — Thanksgiving Day is a national holiday celebrated in Canada and the United States, where it's customary to roast the turkeys in an oven. The turkeys are very likely to be harvested and consumed at this point, although from the turkey's point of view, there is no discernable signal that anything will happen on the second Monday of October in Canada and the fourth Thursday of November in the United States. No amount of modeling on the within-the-year data can fix this prediction problem from the turkey's point of view besides the additional year-over-year information.

The unknown unknown is something that is not in the model and cannot be anticipated to be in the model. In reality, the only unknown unknowns that are of interest are the ones that affect the model so significantly that the results that were previously virtually impossible, or possible with infinitesimal probability, now become the reality. Given that most of the practical distributions are from exponential family with really thin tails, the deviation from normal does not have to be more than a few sigmas to have devastating results on the standard model assumptions. While one has still to come up with an actionable strategy of how to include the unknown factors in the model—a few ways have been proposed, including fractals, but few if any are actionable—the practitioners have to be aware of the risks, and here the definition of the risk is exactly the possibility of delivering the models useless. Of course, the difference between the known unknown and unknown unknown is exactly that we understand the risks and what needs to be explored.

As we looked at the basic scope of problems that the decision-making systems are facing, let's look at the data pipelines, the software systems that provide information for making the decisions, and more practical aspects of designing the data pipeline for a data-driven system.

Basic components of a data-driven system

In short, a data-driven architecture contains the following components—at least all the systems I've seen have them—or can be reduced to these components:

- **Data ingest**: We need to collect the data from systems and devices. Most of the systems have logs, or at least an option to write files into a local filesystem. Some can have capabilities to report information to network-based interfaces such as syslog, but the absence of persistence layer usually means potential data loss, if not absence of audit information.

- **Data transformation layer**: It was also historically called **extract, transform, and load** (**ETL**). Today the data transformation layer can also be used to have real-time processing, where the aggregates are computed on the most recent data. The data transformation layer is also traditionally used to reformat and index the data to be efficiently accessed by a UI component of algorithms down the pipeline.

- **Data analytics and machine learning engine**: The reason this is not part of the standard data transformation layer is usually that this layer requires quite different skills. The mindset of people who build reasonable statistical models is usually different from people who make terabytes of data move fast, even though occasionally I can find people with both skills. Usually, these unicorns are called data scientists, but the skills in any specific field are usually inferior to ones who specialize in a particular field. We need more of either, though. Another reason is that machine learning, and to a certain extent, data analysis, requires multiple aggregations and passes over the same data, which as opposed to a more stream-like ETL transformations, requires a different engine.

- **UI component**: Yes, UI stands for user interface, which most often is a set of components that allow you to communicate with the system via a browser (it used to be a native GUI, but these days the web-based JavaScript or Scala-based frameworks are much more powerful and portable). From the data pipeline and modeling perspective, this component offers an API to access internal representation of data and models.

- **Actions engine**: This is usually a configurable rules engine to optimize the provided metrics based on insights. The actions may be either real-time, like in online advertising, in which case the engine should be able to supply real-time scoring information, or a recommendation for a user action, which can take the form of an e-mail alert.

- **Correlation engine**: This is an emerging component that may analyze the output of data analysis and machine learning engine to infer additional insights into data or model behavior. The actions might also be triggered by an output from this layer.

- **Monitoring**: This is a complex system will be incomplete without logging, monitoring, and some way to change system parameters. The purpose of monitoring is to have a nested decision-making system regarding the optimal health of the system and either to mitigate the problem(s) automatically or to alert the system administrators about the problem(s).

Let's discuss each of the components in detail in the following sections.

Data ingest

With the proliferation of smart devices, information gathering has become less of a problem and more of a necessity for any business that does more than a type-written text. For the purpose of this chapter, I will assume that the device or devices are connected to the Internet or have some way of passing this information via home dialing or direct network connection.

The major purpose of this component is to collect all relevant information that can be relevant for further data-driven decision making. The following table provides details on the most common implementations of the data ingest:

Framework	When used	Comments
Syslog	Syslog is one of the most common standards to pass messages between the machines on Unix. Syslog usually listens on port 514 and the transport protocol can be configured either with UDP (unreliable) or with TCP. The latest enhanced implementation on CentOS and Red Hat Linux is rsyslog, which includes many advanced options such as regex-based filtering that is useful for system-performance tuning and debugging. Apart from slightly inefficient raw message representation—plain text, which might be inefficient for long messages with repeated strings—the syslog system can support tens of thousands of messages per second.	Syslog is one of the oldest protocols developed in the 1980s by Eric Allman as part of Sendmail. While it does not guarantee delivery or durability, particularly for distributed systems, it is one of the most widespread protocols for message passing. Some of the later frameworks, such as Flume and Kafka, have syslog interfaces as well.
Rsync	Rsync is a younger framework developed in the 1990s. If the data is put in the flat files on a local filesystem, rsync might be an option. While rsync is more traditionally used to synchronize two directories, it also can be run periodically to transfer log data in batches. Rsync uses a recursive algorithm invented by an Australian computer programmer, Andrew Tridgell, for efficiently detecting the differences and transmitting a structure (such as a file) across a communication link when the receiving computer already has a similar, but not identical, version of the same structure. While it incurs extra communication, it is better from the point of durability, as the original copy can always be retrieved. It is particularly appropriate if the log data is known to arrive in batches in the first place (such as uploads or downloads).	Rsync has been known to be hampered by network bottlenecks, as it ultimately passes more information over the network when comparing the directory structures. However, the transferred files may be compressed when passed over the network. The network bandwidth can be limited per command-line flags.

Framework	When used	Comments
Flume	Flume is one of the youngest frameworks developed by Cloudera in 2009-2011 and open sourced. Flume—we refer to the more popular flume-ng implementation as Flume as opposed to an older regular Flume—consists of sources, pipes, and sinks that may be configured on multiple nodes for high availability and redundancy purposes. Flume was designed to err on the reliability side at the expense of possible duplication of data. Flume passes the messages in the **Avro** format, which is also open sourced and the transfer protocol, as well as messages can be encoded and compressed.	While Flume originally was developed just to ship records from a file or a set of files, it can also be configured to listen to a port, or even grab the records from a database. Flume has multiple adapters including the preceding syslog.
Kafka	Kafka is the latest addition to the log-processing framework developed by LinkedIn and is open sourced. Kafka, compared to the previous frameworks, is more like a distributed reliable message queue. Kafka keeps a partitioned, potentially between multiple distributed machines; buffer and one can subscribe to or unsubscribe from getting messages for a particular topic. Kafka was built with strong reliability guarantees in mind, which is achieved through replication and consensus protocol.	Kafka might not be appropriate for small systems (< five nodes) as the benefits of the fully distributed system might be evident only at larger scales. Kafka is commercially supported by Confluent.

The transfer of information usually occurs in batches, or micro batches if the requirements are close to real time. Usually the information first ends up in a file, traditionally called log, in a device's local filesystem, and then is transferred to a central location. Recently developed Kafka and Flume are often used to manage these transfers, together with a more traditional syslog, rsync, or netcat. Finally, the data can be placed into a local or distributed storage such as HDFS, Cassandra, or Amazon S3.

Data transformation layer

After the data ends up in HDFS or other storage, the data needs to be made available for processing. Traditionally, the data is processed on a schedule and ends up partitioned by time-based buckets. The processing can happen daily or hourly, or even on a sub-minute basis with the new Scala streaming framework, depending on the latency requirements. The processing may involve some preliminary feature construction or vectorization, even though it is traditionally considered a machine-learning task. The following table summarizes some available frameworks:

Framework	When used	Comments
Oozie	This is one of the oldest open source frameworks developed by Yahoo. This has good integration with big data Hadoop tools. It has limited UI that lists the job history.	The whole workflow is put into one big XML file, which might be considered a disadvantage from the modularity point of view.
Azkaban	This is an alternative open source workflow-scheduling framework developed by LinkedIn. Compared to Oozie, this arguably has a better UI. The disadvantage is that all high-level tasks are executed locally, which might present a scalability problem.	The idea behind Azkaban is to create a fully modularized drop-in architecture where the new jobs/tasks can be added with as few modifications as possible.
StreamSets	StreamSets is the latest addition build by the former Informix and Cloudera developers. It has a very developed UI and supports a much richer set of input sources and output destinations.	This is a fully UI-driven tool with an emphasis on data curation, for example, constantly monitoring the data stream for problems and abnormalities.

Separate attention should be given to stream-processing frameworks, where the latency requirements are reduced to one or a few records at a time. First, stream processing usually requires much more resources dedicated to processing, as it is more expensive to process individual records at a time as opposed to batches of records, even if it is tens or hundreds of records. So, the architect needs to justify the additional costs based on the value of more recent result, which is not always warranted. Second, stream processing requires a few adjustments to the architecture as handling the more recent data becomes a priority; for example, a delta architecture where the more recent data is handled by a separate substream or a set of nodes became very popular recently with systems such as **Druid** (http://druid.io).

Data analytics and machine learning

For the purpose of this chapter, **Machine Learning (ML)** is any algorithm that can compute aggregates or summaries that are actionable. We will cover more complex algorithms from *Chapter 3, Working with Spark and MLlib* to *Chapter 6, Working with Unstructured Data*, but in some cases, a simple sliding-window average and deviation from the average may be sufficient signal for taking an action. In the past few years, it just works in A/B testing somehow became a convincing argument for model building and deployment. I am not speculating that solid scientific principles might or might not apply, but many fundamental assumptions such as *i.i.d.*, balanced designs, and the thinness of the tail just fail to hold for many big data situation. Simpler models tend to be faster and to have better performance and stability.

For example, in online advertising, one might just track average performance of a set of ads over a certain similar properties over times to make a decision whether to have this ad displayed. The information about anomalies, or deviation from the previous behavior, may be a signal a new unknown unknown, which signals that the old data no longer applies, in which case, the system has no choice but to start the new exploration cycle.

I will talk about more complex non-structured, graph, and pattern mining later in *Chapter 6, Working with Unstructured Data*, *Chapter 8, Integrating Scala with R and Python* and *Chapter 9, NLP in Scala*.

UI component

Well, UI is for wimps! Just joking...maybe it's too harsh, but in reality, UI usually presents a syntactic sugar that is necessary to convince the population beyond the data scientists. A good analyst should probably be able to figure out t-test probabilities by just looking at a table with numbers.

However, one should probably apply the same methodologies we used at the beginning of the chapter, assessing the usefulness of different components and the amount of cycles put into them. The presence of a good UI is often justified, but depends on the target audience.

First, there are a number of existing UIs and reporting frameworks. Unfortunately, most of them are not aligned with the functional programming methodologies. Also, the presence of complex/semi-structured data, which I will describe in *Chapter 6, Working with Unstructured Data* in more detail, presents a new twist that many frameworks are not ready to deal with without implementing some kind of DSL. Here are a few frameworks for building the UI in a Scala project that I find particularly worthwhile:

Framework	When used	Comments
Scala Swing	If you used Swing components in Java and are proficient with them, Scala Swing is a good choice for you. Swing component is arguably the least portable component of Java, so your mileage can vary on different platforms.	The `Scala.swing` package uses the standard Java Swing library under the hood, but it has some nice additions. Most notably, as it's made for Scala, it can be used in a much more concise way than the standard Swing.
Lift	Lift is a secure, developer-centric, scalable, and interactive framework written in Scala. Lift is open sourced under Apache 2.0 license.	The open source Lift framework was launched in 2007 by David Polak, who was dissatisfied with certain aspects of the Ruby on Rails framework. Any existing Java library and web container can be used in running Lift applications. Lift web applications are thus packaged as WAR files and deployed on any servlet 2.4 engine (for example, Tomcat 5.5.xx, Jetty 6.0, and so on). Lift programmers may use the standard Scala/Java development toolchain, including IDEs such as Eclipse, NetBeans, and IDEA. Dynamic web content is authored via templates using standard HTML5 or XHTML editors. Lift applications also benefit from native support for advanced web development techniques, such as Comet and Ajax.

Framework	When used	Comments
Play	Play is arguably better aligned with Scala as a functional language than any other platform—it is officially supported by Typesafe, the commercial company behind Scala. The Play framework 2.0 builds on Scala, Akka, and sbt to deliver superior asynchronous request handling, fast and reliable. Typesafe templates, and a powerful build system with flexible deployment options. Play is open sourced under Apache 2.0 license.	The open source Play framework was created in 2007 by Guillaume Bort, who sought to bring a fresh web development experience inspired by modern web frameworks like Ruby on Rails to the long-suffering Java web development community. Play follows a familiar stateless model-view-controller architectural pattern, with a philosophy of convention-over-configuration and an emphasis on developer productivity. Unlike traditional Java web frameworks with their tedious compile-package-deploy-restart cycles, updates to Play applications are instantly visible with a simple browser refresh.
Dropwizard	The dropwizard (`www.dropwizard.io`) project is an attempt to build a generic RESTful framework in both Java and Scala, even though one might end up using more Java than Scala. What is nice about this framework is that it is flexible enough to be used with arbitrary complex data (including semi-structured).This is licensed under Apache License 2.0.	RESTful API assumes state, while functional languages shy away from using state. Unless you are flexible enough to deviate from a pure functional approach, this framework is probably not good enough for you.
Slick	While Slick is not a UI component, it is Typesafe's modern database query and access library for Scala, which can serve as a UI backend. It allows you to work with the stored data almost as if you were using Scala collections, while at the same time, giving you full control over when a database access occurs and what data is transferred. You can also use SQL directly. Use it if all of your data is purely relational. This is open sourced under BSD-Style license.	Slick was started in 2012 by Stefan Zeiger and maintained mainly by Typesafe. It is useful for mostly relational data.

Framework	When used	Comments
NodeJS	Node.js is a JavaScript runtime, built on Chrome's V8 JavaScript engine. Node.js uses an event-driven, non-blocking I/O model that makes it lightweight and efficient. Node.js' package ecosystem, npm, is the largest ecosystem of open source libraries in the world. It is open sourced under MIT License.	Node.js was first introduced in 2009 by Ryan Dahl and other developers working at Joyent. Originally Node.js supported only Linux, but now it runs on OS X and Windows.
AngularJS	AngularJS (`https://angularjs.org`) is a frontend development framework, built to simplify development of one-page web applications. This is open sourced under MIT License.	AngularJS was originally developed in 2009 by Misko Hevery at Brat Tech LLC. AngularJS is mainly maintained by Google and by a community of individual developers and corporations, and thus is specifically for Android platform (support for IE8 is dropped in versions 1.3 and later).

Actions engine

While this is the heart of the data-oriented system pipeline, it is also arguably the easiest one. Once the system of metrics and values is known, the system decides, based on the known equations, whether to take a certain set of actions or not, based on the information provided. While the triggers based on a threshold is the most common implementation, the significance of probabilistic approaches that present the user with a set of possibilities and associated probabilities is emerging — or just presenting the user with the top N relevant choices like a search engine does.

The management of the rules might become pretty involved. It used to be that managing the rules with a rule engine, such as **Drools** (`http://www.drools.org`), was sufficient. However, managing complex rules becomes an issue that often requires development of a DSL (*Domain-Specific Languages* by Martin Fowler, Addison-Wesley, 2010). Scala is particularly fitting language for the development of such an actions engine.

Correlation engine

The more complex the decision-making system is, the more it requires a secondary decision-making system to optimize its management. DevOps is turning into DataOps (*Getting Data Right* by Michael Stonebraker et al., Tamr, 2015). Data collected about the performance of a data-driven system are used to detect anomalies and semi-automated maintenance.

Models are often subject to time drift, where the performance might deteriorate either due to the changes in the data collection layers or the behavioral changes in the population (I will cover model drift in *Chapter 10, Advanced Model Monitoring*). Another aspect of model management is to track model performance, and in some cases, use "collective" intelligence of the models by various consensus schemes.

Monitoring

Monitoring a system involves collecting information about system performance either for audit, diagnostic, or performance-tuning purposes. While it is related to the issues raised in the previous sections, monitoring solution often incorporates diagnostic and historical storage solutions and persistence of critical data, such as a black box on an airplane. In the Java and, thus, Scala world, a popular tool of choice is Java performance beans, which can be monitored in the Java Console. While Java natively supports MBean for exposing JVM information over JMX, **Kamon** (http://kamon.io) is an open source library that uses this mechanism to specifically expose Scala and Akka metrics.

Some other popular monitoring open source solutions are **Ganglia** (http://ganglia.sourceforge.net/) and **Graphite** (http://graphite.wikidot.com).

I will stop here, as I will address system and model monitoring in more detail in *Chapter 10, Advanced Model Monitoring*.

Optimization and interactivity

While the data collected can be just used for understanding the business, the final goal of any data-driven business is to optimize the business behavior by automatically making data-based and model-based decisions. We want to reduce human intervention to minimum. The following simplified diagram can be depicted as a cycle:

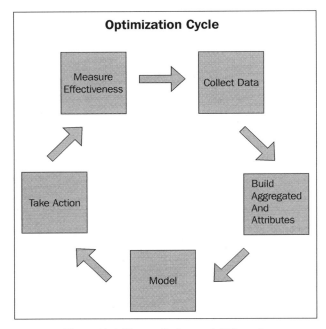

Figure 02-4. The predictive model life cycle

The cycle is repeated over and over for new information coming into the system. The parameters of the system may be tuned to improve the overall system performance.

Feedback loops

While humans are still likely to be kept in the loop for most of the systems, last few years saw an emergence of systems that can manage the complete feedback loop on their own—ranging from advertisement systems to self-driving cars.

The classical formulation of this problem is the optimal control theory, which is also an optimization problem to minimize cost functional, given a set of differential equations describing the system. An optimal control is a set of control policies to minimize the cost functional given constraints. For example, the problem might be to find a way to drive the car to minimize its fuel consumption, given that it must complete a given course in a time not exceeding some amount. Another control problem is to maximize profit for showing ads on a website, provided the inventory and time constraints. Most software packages for optimal control are written in other languages such as C or MATLAB (PROPT, SNOPT, RIOTS, DIDO, DIRECT, and GPOPS), but can be interfaced with Scala.

However, in many cases, the parameters for the optimization or the state transition, or differential equations, are not known with certainty. **Markov Decision Processes (MDPs)** provide a mathematical framework to model decision making in situations where outcomes are partly random and partly under the control of the decision maker. In MDPs, we deal with a discrete set of possible states and a set of actions. The "rewards" and state transitions depend both on the state and actions. MDPs are useful for studying a wide range of optimization problems solved via dynamic programming and reinforcement learning.

Summary

In this chapter, I described a high-level architecture and approach to design a data-driven enterprise. I also introduced you to influence diagrams, a tool for understanding how the decisions are made in traditional and data-driven enterprises. I stopped on a few key models, such as Kelly Criterion and multi-armed bandit, essential to demonstrate the issues from the mathematical point of view. I built on top of this to introduce some Markov decision process approaches where we deal with decision policies based on the results of the previous decisions and observations. I delved into more practical aspects of building a data pipeline for decision-making, describing major components and frameworks that can be used to built them. I also discussed the issues of communicating the data and modeling results between different stages and nodes, presenting the results to the user, feedback loop, and monitoring.

In the next chapter, I will describe MLlib, a library for machine learning over distributed set of nodes written in Scala.

Working with Spark and MLlib

Now that we are powered with the knowledge of where and how statistics and machine learning fits in the global data-driven enterprise architecture, let's stop at the specific implementations in Spark and MLlib, a machine learning library on top of Spark. Spark is a relatively new member of the big data ecosystem that is optimized for memory usage as opposed to disk. The data can be still spilled to disk as necessary, but Spark does the spill only if instructed to do so explicitly, or if the active dataset does not fit into the memory. Spark stores lineage information to recompute the active dataset if a node goes down or the information is erased from memory for some other reason. This is in contrast to the traditional MapReduce approach, where the data is persisted to the disk after each map or reduce task.

Spark is particularly suited for iterative or statistical machine learning algorithms over a distributed set of nodes and can scale out of core. The only limitation is the total memory and disk space available across all Spark nodes and the network speed. I will cover the basics of Spark architecture and implementation in this chapter.

One can direct Spark to execute data pipelines either on a single node or across a set of nodes with a simple change in the configuration parameters. Of course, this flexibility comes at a cost of slightly heavier framework and longer setup times, but the framework is very parallelizable and as most of modern laptops are already multithreaded and sufficiently powerful, this usually does not present a big issue.

In this chapter, we will cover the following topics:

- Installing and configuring Spark if you haven't done so yet
- Learning the basics of Spark architecture and why it is inherently tied to the Scala language
- Learning why Spark is the next technology after sequential implementations and Hadoop MapReduce
- Learning about Spark components

- Looking at the simple implementation of word count in Scala and Spark
- Looking at the streaming word count implementation
- Seeing how to create Spark DataFrames from either a distributed file or a distributed database
- Learning about Spark performance tuning

Setting up Spark

If you haven't done so yet, you can download the pre-build Spark package from `http://spark.apache.org/downloads.html`. The latest release at the time of writing is **1.6.1**:

Figure 03-1. The download site at http://spark.apache.org with recommended selections for this chapter

Alternatively, you can build the Spark by downloading the full source distribution from https://github.com/apache/spark:

```
$ git clone https://github.com/apache/spark.git
Cloning into 'spark'...
remote: Counting objects: 301864, done.
...
$ cd spark
$sh ./ dev/change-scala-version.sh 2.11
...
$./make-distribution.sh --name alex-build-2.6-yarn --skip-java-test --tgz
-Pyarn -Phive -Phive-thriftserver -Pscala-2.11 -Phadoop-2.6
...
```

The command will download the necessary dependencies and create the spark-2.0.0-SNAPSHOT-bin-alex-spark-build-2.6-yarn.tgz file in the Spark directory; the version is 2.0.0, as it is the next release version at the time of writing. In general, you do not want to build from trunk unless you are interested in the latest features. If you want a released version, you can checkout the corresponding tag. Full list of available versions is available via the git branch -r command. The spark*.tgz file is all you need to run Spark on any machine that has Java JRE.

The distribution comes with the docs/building-spark.md document that describes other options for building Spark and their descriptions, including incremental Scala compiler, zinc. Full Scala 2.11 support is in the works for the next Spark 2.0.0 release.

Understanding Spark architecture

A parallel execution involves splitting the workload into subtasks that are executed in different threads or on different nodes. Let's see how Spark does this and how it manages execution and communication between the subtasks.

Task scheduling

Spark workload splitting is determined by the number of partitions for **Resilient Distributed Dataset (RDD)**, the basic abstraction in Spark, and the pipeline structure. An RDD represents an immutable, partitioned collection of elements that can be operated on in parallel. While the specifics might depend on the mode in which Spark runs, the following diagram captures the Spark task/resource scheduling:

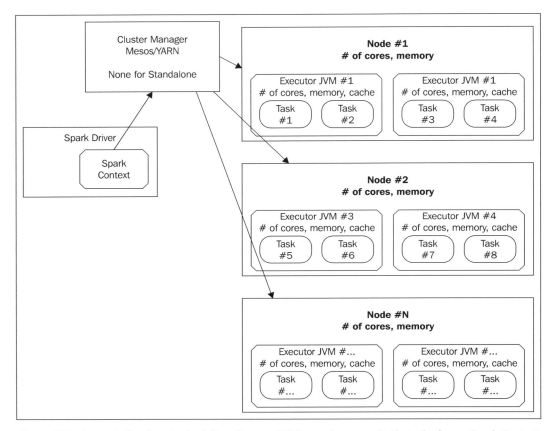

Figure 03-2. A generic Spark task scheduling diagram. While not shown explicitly in the figure, Spark Context opens an HTTP UI, usually on port 4040 (the concurrent contexts will open 4041, 4042, and so on), which is present during a task execution. Spark Master UI is usually 8080 (although it is changed to 18080 in CDH) and Worker UI is usually 7078. Each node can run multiple executors, and each executor can run multiple tasks.

You will find that Spark, as well as Hadoop, has a lot of parameters. Some of them are specified as environment variables (refer to the $SPARK_HOME/conf/spark-env.sh file), and yet some can be given as a command-line parameter. Moreover, some files with pre-defined names can contain parameters that will change the Spark behavior, such as core-site.xml. This might be confusing, and I will cover as much as possible in this and the following chapters. If you are working with **Hadoop Distributed File System (HDFS)**, then the core-site.xml and hdfs-site.xml files will contain the pointer and specifications for the HDFS master. The requirement for picking this file is that it has to be on CLASSPATH Java process, which, again, may be set by either specifying HADOOP_CONF_DIR or SPARK_CLASSPATH environment variables. As is usual with open source, you need to grep the code sometimes to understand how various parameters work, so having a copy of the source tree on your laptop is a good idea.

Each node in the cluster can run one or more executors, and each executor can schedule a sequence of tasks to perform the Spark operations. Spark driver is responsible for scheduling the execution and works with the cluster scheduler, such as Mesos or YARN to schedule the available resources. Spark driver usually runs on the client machine, but in the latest release, it can also run in the cluster under the cluster manager. YARN and Mesos have the ability to dynamically manage the number of executors that run concurrently on each node, provided the resource constraints.

In the Standalone mode, **Spark Master** does the work of the cluster scheduler—it might be less efficient in allocating resources, but it's better than nothing in the absence of preconfigured Mesos or YARN. Spark standard distribution contains shell scripts to start Spark in Standalone mode in the sbin directory. Spark Master and driver communicate directly with one or several Spark workers that run on individual nodes. Once the master is running, you can start Spark shell with the following command:

```
$ bin/spark-shell --master spark://<master-address>:7077
```

Note that you can always run Spark in local mode, which means that all tasks will be executed in a single JVM, by specifying --master local[2], where 2 is the number of threads that have to be at least 2. In fact, we will be using the local mode very often in this book for running small examples.

Spark shell is an application from the Spark point of view. Once you start a Spark application, you will see it under **Running Applications** in the Spark Master UI (or in the corresponding cluster manager), which can redirect you to the Spark application HTTP UI at port 4040, where one can see the subtask execution timeline and other important properties such as environment setting, classpath, parameters passed to the JVM, and information on resource usage (refer to *Figure 3-3*):

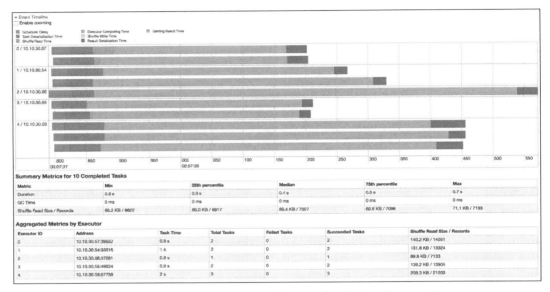

Figure 03-3. Spark Driver UI in Standalone mode with time decomposition

As we saw, with Spark, one can easily switch between local and cluster mode by providing the `--master` command-line option, setting a `MASTER` environment variable, or modifying `spark-defaults.conf`, which should be on the classpath during the execution, or even set explicitly using the `setters` method on the `SparkConf` object directly in Scala, which will be covered later:

Cluster Manager	MASTER env variable	Comments
Local (single node, multiple threads)	`local[n]`	*n* is the number of threads to use, should be greater than or equal to 2. If you want Spark to communicate with other Hadoop tools such as Hive, you still need to point it to the cluster by either setting the `HADOOP_CONF_DIR` environment variable or copying the Hadoop `*-site.xml` configuration files into the `conf` subdirectory.

Cluster Manager	MASTER env variable	Comments
Standalone (Daemons running on the nodes)	`spark:// master- address>:7077`	This has a set of start/stop scripts in the `$SPARK_ HOME/sbin` directory. This also supports the HA mode. More details can be found at `https:// spark.apache.org/docs/latest/spark- standalone.html`.
Mesos	`mesos:// host:5050` or `mesos://zk:// host:2181` (multimaster)	Here, you need to set `MESOS_NATIVE_JAVA_ LIBRARY=<path to libmesos.so>` and `SPARK_EXECUTOR_URI=<URL of spark- 1.5.0.tar.gz>`. The default is fine-grained mode, where each Spark task runs as a separate Mesos task. Alternatively, the user can specify the coarse-grained mode, where the Mesos tasks persists for the duration of the application. The advantage is lower total start-up costs. This can use dynamic allocation (refer to the following URL) in coarse-grained mode. More details can be found at `https://spark.apache.org/docs/ latest/running-on-mesos.html`.
YARN	`yarn`	Spark driver can run either in the cluster or on the client node, which is managed by the `--deploy- mode` parameter (cluster or client, shell can only run in the client mode). Set `HADOOP_CONF_DIR` or `YARN_CONF_DIR` to point to the YARN config files. Use the `--num-executors` flag or `spark. executor.instances` property to set a fixed number of executors (default). Set `spark.dynamicAllocation.enabled` to `true` to dynamically create/kill executors depending on the application demand. More details are available at `https://spark. apache.org/docs/latest/running-on- yarn.html`.

The most common ports are 8080, the master UI, and 4040, the application UI. Other Spark ports are summarized in the following table:

Standalone ports				
From	**To**	**Default Port**	**Purpose**	**Configuration Setting**
Browser	Standalone Master	8080	Web UI	`spark.master.ui.port / SPARK_MASTER_WEBUI_PORT`

Standalone ports				
From	**To**	**Default Port**	**Purpose**	**Configuration Setting**
Browser	Standalone worker	8081	Web UI	`spark.worker.ui.port` / `SPARK_WORKER_WEBUI_PORT`
Driver / Standalone worker	Standalone Master	7077	Submit job to cluster / Join cluster	`SPARK_MASTER_PORT`
Standalone master	Standalone worker	(random)	Schedule executors	`SPARK_WORKER_PORT`
Executor / Standalone master	Driver	(random)	Connect to application / Notify executor state changes	`spark.driver.port`
Other ports				
From	**To**	**Default Port**	**Purpose**	**Configuration Setting**
Browser	Application	4040	Web UI	`spark.ui.port`
Browser	History server	18080	Web UI	`spark.history.ui.port`
Driver	Executor	(random)	Schedule tasks	`spark.executor.port`
Executor	Driver	(random)	File server for files and jars	`spark.fileserver.port`
Executor	Driver	(random)	HTTP broadcast	`spark.broadcast.port`

Also, some of the documentation is available with the source distribution in the `docs` subdirectory, but may be out of date.

Spark components

Since the emergence of Spark, multiple applications that benefit from Spark's ability to cache RDDs have been written: Shark, Spork (Pig on Spark), graph libraries (GraphX, GraphFrames), streaming, MLlib, and so on; some of these will be covered here and in later chapters.

In this section, I will cover major architecture components to collect, store, and analyze the data in Spark. While I will cover a more complete data life cycle architecture in *Chapter 2, Data Pipelines and Modeling*, here are Spark-specific components:

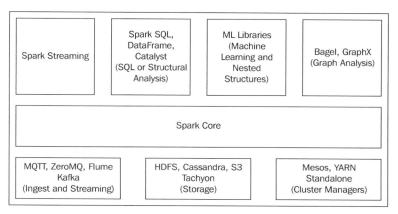

Figure 03-4. Spark architecture and components.

MQTT, ZeroMQ, Flume, and Kafka

All of these are different ways to reliably move data from one place to another without loss and duplication. They usually implement a publish-subscribe model, where multiple writers and readers can write and read from the same queues with different guarantees. Flume stands out as a first distributed log and event management implementation, but it is slowly replaced by Kafka, a fully functional publish-subscribe distributed message queue optionally persistent across a distributed set of nodes developed at LinkedIn. We covered Flume and Kafka briefly in the previous chapter. Flume configuration is file-based and is traditionally used to deliver messages from a Flume source to one or several Flume sinks. One of the popular sources is `netcat` — listening on raw data over a port. For example, the following configuration describes an agent receiving data and then writing them to HDFS every 30 seconds (default):

```
# Name the components on this agent
a1.sources = r1
a1.sinks = k1
```

```
a1.channels = c1

# Describe/configure the source
a1.sources.r1.type = netcat
a1.sources.r1.bind = localhost
a1.sources.r1.port = 4987

# Describe the sink (the instructions to configure and start HDFS are
provided in the Appendix)
a1.sinks.k1.type=hdfs
a1.sinks.k1.hdfs.path=hdfs://localhost:8020/flume/netcat/data
a1.sinks.k1.hdfs.filePrefix=chapter03.example
a1.sinks.k1.channel=c1
a1.sinks.k1.hdfs.writeFormat = Text

# Use a channel which buffers events in memory
a1.channels.c1.type = memory
a1.channels.c1.capacity = 1000
a1.channels.c1.transactionCapacity = 100

# Bind the source and sink to the channel
a1.sources.r1.channels = c1
a1.sinks.k1.channel = c1
```

This file is included as part of the code provided with this book in the chapter03/ conf directory. Let's download and start Flume agent (check the MD5 sum with one provided at http://flume.apache.org/download.html):

```
$ wget http://mirrors.ocf.berkeley.edu/apache/flume/1.6.0/apache-flume-
1.6.0-bin.tar.gz

$ md5sum apache-flume-1.6.0-bin.tar.gz

MD5 (apache-flume-1.6.0-bin.tar.gz) = defd21ad8d2b6f28cc0a16b96f652099

$ tar xf apache-flume-1.6.0-bin.tar.gz

$ cd apache-flume-1.6.0-bin

$ ./bin/flume-ng agent -Dlog.dir=. -Dflume.log.level=DEBUG,console -n a1
-f ../chapter03/conf/flume.conf

Info: Including Hadoop libraries found via (/Users/akozlov/hadoop-2.6.4/
bin/hadoop) for HDFS access

Info: Excluding /Users/akozlov/hadoop-2.6.4/share/hadoop/common/lib/
slf4j-api-1.7.5.jar from classpath

Info: Excluding /Users/akozlov/hadoop-2.6.4/share/hadoop/common/lib/
slf4j-log4j12-1.7.5.jar from classpath

...
```

Now, in a separate window, you can type a `netcat` command to send text to the Flume agent:

```
$ nc localhost 4987
Hello
OK
World
OK

...
```

The Flume agent will first create a *.tmp file and then rename it to a file without extension (the file extension can be used to filter out files being written to):

```
$ bin/hdfs dfs -text /flume/netcat/data/chapter03.example.1463052301372
16/05/12 04:27:25 WARN util.NativeCodeLoader: Unable to load native-
hadoop library for your platform... using builtin-java classes where
applicable
1463052302380   Hello
1463052304307   World
```

Here, each row is a Unix time in milliseconds and data received. In this case, we put the data into HDFS, from where they can be analyzed by a Spark/Scala program, we can exclude the files being written to by the *.tmp filename pattern. However, if you are really interested in up-to-the-last-minute values, Spark, as well as some other platforms, supports streaming, which I will cover in a few sections.

HDFS, Cassandra, S3, and Tachyon

HDFS, Cassandra, S3, and Tachyon are the different ways to get the data into persistent storage and compute nodes as necessary with different guarantees. HDFS is a distributed storage implemented as a part of Hadoop, which serves as the backend for many products in the Hadoop ecosystem. HDFS divides each file into blocks, which are 128 MB in size by default, and stores each block on at least three nodes. Although HDFS is reliable and supports HA, a general complain about HDFS storage is that it is slow, particularly for machine learning purposes. Cassandra is a general-purpose key/value storage that also stores multiple copies of a row and can be configured to support different levels of consistency to optimize read or write speeds. The advantage that Cassandra over HDFS model is that it does not have a central master node; the reads and writes are completed based on the consensus algorithm. This, however, may sometimes reflect on the Cassandra stability. S3 is the Amazon storage: The data is stored off-cluster, which affects the I/O speed. Finally, the recently developed Tachyon claims to utilize node's memory to optimize access to working sets across the nodes.

Additionally, new backends are being constantly developed, for example, Kudu from Cloudera (`http://getkudu.io/kudu.pdf`) and **Ignite File System** (**IGFS**) from GridGain (`http://apacheignite.gridgain.org/v1.0/docs/igfs`). Both are open source and Apache-licensed.

Mesos, YARN, and Standalone

As we mentioned before, Spark can run under different cluster resource schedulers. These are various implementations to schedule Spark's containers and tasks on the cluster. The schedulers can be viewed as cluster kernels, performing functions similar to the operating system kernel: resource allocation, scheduling, I/O optimization, application services, and UI.

Mesos is one of the original cluster managers and is built using the same principles as the Linux kernel, only at a different level of abstraction. A Mesos slave runs on every machine and provides API's for resource management and scheduling across entire datacenter and cloud environments. Mesos is written in C++.

YARN is a more recent cluster manager developed by Yahoo. Each node in YARN runs a **Node Manager**, which communicates with the **Resource Manager** which may run on a separate node. The resource manager schedules the task to satisfy memory and CPU constraints. The Spark driver itself can run either in the cluster, which is called the cluster mode for YARN. Otherwise, in the client mode, only Spark executors run in the cluster and the driver that schedules Spark pipelines runs on the same machine that runs Spark shell or submit program. The Spark executors will talk to the local host over a random open port in this case. YARN is written in Java with the consequences of unpredictable GC pauses, which might make latency's long tail fatter.

Finally, if none of these resource schedulers are available, the standalone deployment mode starts a `org.apache.spark.deploy.worker.Worker` process on each node that communicates with the Spark Master process run as `org.apache.spark.deploy.master.Master`. The worker process is completely managed by the master and can run multiple executors and tasks (refer to *Figure 3-2*).

In practical implementations, it is advised to track the program parallelism and required resources through driver's UI and adjust the parallelism and available memory, increasing the parallelism if necessary. In the following section, we will start looking at how Scala and Scala in Spark address different problems.

Applications

Let's consider a few practical examples and libraries in Spark/Scala starting with a very traditional problem of word counting.

Word count

Most modern machine learning algorithms require multiple passes over data. If the data fits in the memory of a single machine, the data is readily available and this does not present a performance bottleneck. However, if the data becomes too large to fit into RAM, one has a choice of either dumping pieces of the data on disk (or database), which is about 100 times slower, but has a much larger capacity, or splitting the dataset between multiple machines across the network and transferring the results. While there are still ongoing debates, for most practical systems, analysis shows that storing the data over a set of network connected nodes has a slight advantage over repeatedly storing and reading it from hard disks on a single node, particularly if we can split the workload effectively between multiple CPUs.

> An average disk has bandwidth of about 100 MB/sec and transfers with a few mms latency, depending on the rotation speed and caching. This is about 100 times slower than reading the data from memory, depending on the data size and caching implementation again. Modern data bus can transfer data at over 10 GB/sec. While the network speed still lags behind the direct memory access, particularly with standard TCP/IP kernel networking layer overhead, specialized hardware can reach tens of GB/sec and if run in parallel, it can be potentially as fast as reading from the memory. In practice, the network-transfer speeds are somewhere between 1 to 10 GB/sec, but still faster than the disk in most practical systems. Thus, we can potentially fit the data into combined memory of all the cluster nodes and perform iterative machine learning algorithms across a system of them.

One problem with memory, however, is that it is does not persist across node failures and reboots. A popular big data framework, Hadoop, made possible with the help of the original Dean/Ghemawat paper (Jeff Dean and Sanjay Ghemawat, *MapReduce: Simplified Data Processing on Large Clusters*, OSDI, 2004.), is using exactly the disk layer persistence to guarantee fault tolerance and store intermediate results. A Hadoop MapReduce program would first run a map function on each row of a dataset, emitting one or more key/value pairs. These key/value pairs then would be sorted, grouped, and aggregated by key so that the records with the same key would end up being processed together on the same reducer, which might be running on same or another node. The reducer applies a reduce function that traverses all the values that were emitted for the same key and aggregates them accordingly. The persistence of intermediate results would guarantee that if a reducer fails for one or another reason, the partial computations can be discarded and the reduce computation can be restarted from the checkpoint-saved results. Many simple ETL-like applications traverse the dataset only once with very little information preserved as state from one record to another.

For example, one of the traditional applications of MapReduce is word count. The program needs to count the number of occurrences of each word in a document consisting of lines of text. In Scala, the word count is readily expressed as an application of the foldLeft method on a sorted list of words:

```
val lines = scala.io.Source.fromFile("...").getLines.toSeq
val counts = lines.flatMap(line => line.split("\\W+")).sorted.
  foldLeft(List[(String,Int)]()){ (r,c) =>
    r match {
      case (key, count) :: tail =>
        if (key == c) (c, count+1) :: tail
        else (c, 1) :: r
      case Nil =>
        List((c, 1))
    }
  }
```

If I run this program, the output will be a list of (word, count) tuples. The program splits the lines into words, sorts the words, and then matches each word with the latest entry in the list of (word, count) tuples. The same computation in MapReduce would be expressed as follows:

```
val linesRdd = sc.textFile("hdfs://...")
val counts = linesRdd.flatMap(line => line.split("\\W+"))
    .map(_.toLowerCase)
    .map(word => (word, 1)).
    .reduceByKey(_+_)
counts.collect
```

First, we need to process each line of the text by splitting the line into words and generation (word, 1) pairs. This task is easily parallelized. Then, to parallelize the global count, we need to split the counting part by assigning a task to do the count for a subset of words. In Hadoop, we compute the hash of the word and divide the work based on the value of the hash.

Once the map task finds all the entries for a given hash, it can send the key/value pairs to the reducer, the sending part is usually called shuffle in MapReduce vernacular. A reducer waits until it receives all the key/value pairs from all the mappers, combines the values—a partial combine can also happen on the mapper, if possible—and computes the overall aggregate, which in this case is just sum. A single reducer will see all the values for a given word.

Let's look at the log output of the word count operation in Spark (Spark is very verbose by default, you can manage the verbosity level by modifying the conf/log4j.properties file by replacing INFO with ERROR or FATAL):

```
$ wget http://mirrors.sonic.net/apache/spark/spark-1.6.1/spark-1.6.1-bin-
hadoop2.6.tgz
$ tar xvf spark-1.6.1-bin-hadoop2.6.tgz
$ cd spark-1.6.1-bin-hadoop2.6
$ mkdir leotolstoy
$ (cd leotolstoy; wget http://www.gutenberg.org/files/1399/1399-0.txt)
$ bin/spark-shell
Welcome to


      ____              __
     / __/__  ___ _____/ /__
    _\ \/ _ \/ _ `/ __/  '_/
   /___/ .__/\_,_/_/ /_/\_\   version 1.6.1
      /_/


Using Scala version 2.11.7 (Java HotSpot(TM) 64-Bit Server VM, Java
1.8.0_40)
Type in expressions to have them evaluated.
Type :help for more information.
Spark context available as sc.
SQL context available as sqlContext.
scala> val linesRdd = sc.textFile("leotolstoy", minPartitions=10)
linesRdd: org.apache.spark.rdd.RDD[String] = leotolstoy
MapPartitionsRDD[3] at textFile at <console>:27
```

At this stage, the only thing that happened is metadata manipulations, Spark has not touched the data itself. Spark estimates that the size of the dataset and the number of partitions. By default, this is the number of HDFS blocks, but we can specify the minimum number of partitions explicitly with the minPartitions parameter:

```
scala> val countsRdd = linesRdd.flatMap(line => line.split("\\W+")).
     | map(_.toLowerCase).
     | map(word => (word, 1)).
     | reduceByKey(_+_)
countsRdd: org.apache.spark.rdd.RDD[(String, Int)] = ShuffledRDD[5] at
reduceByKey at <console>:31
```

We just defined another RDD derived from the original `linesRdd`:

```scala
scala> countsRdd.collect.filter(_._2 > 99)

res3: Array[(String, Int)] = Array((been,1061), (them,841), (found,141),
(my,794), (often,105), (table,185), (this,1410), (here,364),
(asked,320), (standing,132), ("",13514), (we,592), (myself,140),
(is,1454), (carriage,181), (got,277), (won,153), (girl,117), (she,4403),
(moment,201), (down,467), (me,1134), (even,355), (come,667),
(new,319), (now,872), (upon,207), (sister,115), (veslovsky,110),
(letter,125), (women,134), (between,138), (will,461), (almost,124),
(thinking,159), (have,1277), (answer,146), (better,231), (men,199),
(after,501), (only,654), (suddenly,173), (since,124), (own,359),
(best,101), (their,703), (get,304), (end,110), (most,249), (but,3167),
(was,5309), (do,846), (keep,107), (having,153), (betsy,111), (had,3857),
(before,508), (saw,421), (once,334), (side,163), (ough...
```

Word count over 2 GB of text data—40,291 lines and 353,087 words—took under a second to read, split, and group by words.

With extended logging, you could see the following:

- Spark opens a few ports to communicate with the executors and users
- Spark UI runs on port 4040 on `http://localhost:4040`
- You can read the file either from local or distributed storage (HDFS, Cassandra, and S3)
- Spark will connect to Hive if Spark is built with Hive support
- Spark uses lazy evaluation and executes the pipeline only when necessary or when output is required
- Spark uses internal scheduler to split the job into tasks, optimize the execution, and execute the tasks
- The results are stored into RDDs, which can either be saved or brought into RAM of the node executing the shell with collect method

The art of parallel performance tuning is to split the workload between different nodes or threads so that the overhead is relatively small and the workload is balanced.

Streaming word count

Spark supports listening on incoming streams, partitioning it, and computing aggregates close to real-time. Currently supported sources are Kafka, Flume, HDFS/S3, Kinesis, Twitter, as well as the traditional MQs such as ZeroMQ and MQTT. In Spark, streaming is implemented as micro-batches. Internally, Spark divides input data into micro-batches, usually from subseconds to minutes in size and performs RDD aggregation operations on these micro-batches.

For example, let's extend the Flume example that we covered earlier. We'll need to modify the Flume configuration file to create a Spark polling sink. Instead of HDFS, replace the sink section:

```
# The sink is Spark
a1.sinks.k1.type=org.apache.spark.streaming.flume.sink.SparkSink
a1.sinks.k1.hostname=localhost
a1.sinks.k1.port=4989
```

Now, instead of writing to HDFS, Flume will wait for Spark to poll for data:

```
object FlumeWordCount {
  def main(args: Array[String]) {
    // Create the context with a 2 second batch size
    val sparkConf = new SparkConf().setMaster("local[2]")
      .setAppName("FlumeWordCount")
    val ssc = new StreamingContext(sparkConf, Seconds(2))
    ssc.checkpoint("/tmp/flume_check")
    val hostPort=args(0).split(":")
    System.out.println("Opening a sink at host: [" + hostPort(0) +
      "] port: [" + hostPort(1).toInt + "]")
    val lines = FlumeUtils.createPollingStream(ssc, hostPort(0),
      hostPort(1).toInt, StorageLevel.MEMORY_ONLY)
    val words = lines
      .map(e => new String(e.event.getBody.array)).
        map(_.toLowerCase).flatMap(_.split("\\W+"))
      .map(word => (word, 1L))
      .reduceByKeyAndWindow(_+_, _-_, Seconds(6),
        Seconds(2)).print
    ssc.start()
    ssc.awaitTermination()
  }
}
```

To run the program, start the Flume agent in one window:

```
$ ./bin/flume-ng agent -Dflume.log.level=DEBUG,console -n a1 -f ../
chapter03/conf/flume-spark.conf
...
```

Then run the `FlumeWordCount` object in another:

```
$ cd ../chapter03
$ sbt "run-main org.akozlov.chapter03.FlumeWordCount localhost:4989
...
```

Now, any text typed to the `netcat` connection will be split into words and counted every two seconds for a six second sliding window:

```
$ echo "Happy families are all alike; every unhappy family is unhappy in
its own way" | nc localhost 4987
...
-------------------------------------------
Time: 1464161488000 ms
-------------------------------------------
(are,1)
(is,1)
(its,1)
(family,1)
(families,1)
(alike,1)
(own,1)
(happy,1)
(unhappy,2)
(every,1)
...


-------------------------------------------
Time: 1464161490000 ms
-------------------------------------------
(are,1)
(is,1)
(its,1)
(family,1)
(families,1)
(alike,1)
(own,1)
(happy,1)
(unhappy,2)
(every,1)
...
```

Spark/Scala allows to seamlessly switch between the streaming sources. For example, the same program for Kafka publish/subscribe topic model looks similar to the following:

```scala
object KafkaWordCount {
  def main(args: Array[String]) {
    // Create the context with a 2 second batch size
    val sparkConf = new SparkConf().setMaster("local[2]")
      .setAppName("KafkaWordCount")
    val ssc = new StreamingContext(sparkConf, Seconds(2))
    ssc.checkpoint("/tmp/kafka_check")
    System.out.println("Opening a Kafka consumer at zk:
      [" + args(0) + "] for group group-1 and topic example")
    val lines = KafkaUtils.createStream(ssc, args(0), "group-1",
      Map("example" -> 1), StorageLevel.MEMORY_ONLY)
    val words = lines
      .flatMap(_._2.toLowerCase.split("\\W+"))
      .map(word => (word, 1L))
      .reduceByKeyAndWindow(_+_, _-_, Seconds(6),
        Seconds(2)).print
    ssc.start()
    ssc.awaitTermination()
  }
}
```

To start the Kafka broker, first download the latest binary distribution and start ZooKeeper. ZooKeeper is a distributed-services coordinator and is required by Kafka even in a single-node deployment:

```
$ wget http://apache.cs.utah.edu/kafka/0.9.0.1/kafka_2.11-0.9.0.1.tgz
...
$ tar xf kafka_2.11-0.9.0.1.tgz
$ bin/zookeeper-server-start.sh config/zookeeper.properties
...
```

In another window, start the Kafka server:

```
$ bin/kafka-server-start.sh config/server.properties
...
```

Run the KafkaWordCount object:

```
$ sbt "run-main org.akozlov.chapter03.KafkaWordCount localhost:2181"
...
```

Now, publishing the stream of words into the Kafka topic will produce the window counts:

```
$ echo "Happy families are all alike; every unhappy family is unhappy
in its own way" | ./bin/kafka-console-producer.sh --broker-list
localhost:9092 --topic example

...

$ sbt "run-main org.akozlov.chapter03.FlumeWordCount localhost:4989

...

-------------------------------------------
Time: 1464162712000 ms
-------------------------------------------
(are,1)

(is,1)

(its,1)

(family,1)

(families,1)

(alike,1)

(own,1)

(happy,1)

(unhappy,2)

(every,1)
```

As you see, the programs output every two seconds. Spark streaming is sometimes called **micro-batch processing**. Streaming has many other applications (and frameworks), but this is too big of a topic to be entirely considered here and needs to be covered separately. I'll cover some ML on streams of data in *Chapter 5, Regression and Classification*. Now, let's get back to more traditional SQL-like interfaces.

Spark SQL and DataFrame

DataFrame was a relatively recent addition to Spark, introduced in version 1.3, allowing one to use the standard SQL language for data analysis. We already used some SQL commands in *Chapter 1, Exploratory Data Analysis* for the exploratory data analysis. SQL is really great for simple exploratory analysis and data aggregations.

According to the latest poll results, about 70% of Spark users use DataFrame. Although DataFrame recently became the most popular framework for working with tabular data, it is a relatively heavyweight object. The pipelines that use DataFrames may execute much slower than the ones that are based on Scala's vector or LabeledPoint, which will be discussed in the next chapter. The evidence from different developers is that the response times can be driven to tens or hundreds of milliseconds depending on the query, from submillisecond on simpler objects.

Spark implements its own shell for SQL, which can be invoked in addition to the standard Scala REPL shell: `./bin/spark-sql` can be used to access the existing Hive/Impala or relational DB tables:

```
$ ./bin/spark-sql

...

spark-sql> select min(duration), max(duration), avg(duration) from
kddcup;

...

0   58329   48.34243046395876
Time taken: 11.073 seconds, Fetched 1 row(s)
```

In standard Spark's REPL, the same query can be performed by running the following command:

```
$ ./bin/spark-shell

...

scala> val df = sqlContext.sql("select min(duration), max(duration),
avg(duration) from kddcup"
16/05/12 13:35:34 INFO parse.ParseDriver: Parsing command: select
min(duration), max(duration), avg(duration) from alex.kddcup_parquet
16/05/12 13:35:34 INFO parse.ParseDriver: Parse Completed
df: org.apache.spark.sql.DataFrame = [_c0: bigint, _c1: bigint, _c2:
double]
scala> df.collect.foreach(println)

...

16/05/12 13:36:32 INFO scheduler.DAGScheduler: Job 2 finished: collect at
<console>:22, took 4.593210 s
[0,58329,48.34243046395876]
```

ML libraries

Spark, particularly with memory-based storage systems, claims to substantially improve the speed of data access within and between nodes. ML seems to be a natural fit, as many algorithms require multiple passes over the data, or repartitioning. MLlib is the open source library of choice, although private companies are catching, up with their own proprietary implementations.

As I will chow in *Chapter 5, Regression and Classification*, most of the standard machine learning algorithms can be expressed as an optimization problem. For example, classical linear regression minimizes the sum of squares of y distance between the regression line and the actual value of y:

$$\frac{\partial}{\partial X} \sum_{i=1}^{N} \left(y_i - \hat{y}_i \right)^2$$

Here, $\hat{y}_i$ are the predicted values according to the linear expression:

$$\hat{y} = A^T X + B$$

A is commonly called the slope, and B the intercept. In a more generalized formulation, a linear optimization problem is to minimize an additive function:

$$C(w) = \frac{1}{N} \sum_{i=1}^{N} L\left(w \middle| x_i, y_i \right) + \lambda \, R(w)$$

Here, $L\left(w \middle| x_i, y_i \right)$ is a loss function and $R(w)$ is a regularization function. The regularization function is an increasing function of model complexity, for example, the number of parameters (or a natural logarithm thereof). Most common loss functions are given in the following table:

	Loss function L	Gradient
Linear	$\frac{1}{2}\left(y_i - A^T X \right)^2$	$(A^T X - y_i)X$
Logistic	$\ln\left(1 + \exp\left(-yw^T x \right) \right)$	$-y\left[1 - \dfrac{1}{1 + \exp\left(-yw^T x \right)} \right]x$

	Loss function L	Gradient
Hinge	$\max\left(0, 1 - yw^T x\right)$	$-yx \ if \ yw^T x < 1, 0 \ otherwise$

The purpose of the regularizer is to penalize more complex models to avoid overfitting and improve generalization error: more MLlib currently supports the following regularizers:

	Regularizer R	Gradient
L2	$\frac{1}{2}\|w\|_2^2$	w
L1	$\|w\|_1$	$sign(w)$
Elastic net	$\alpha\|w\|_1 + (1 - \alpha)\frac{1}{2}\|w\|_2^2$	$\alpha \ sign(w) + (1 - \alpha) \ w$

Here, *sign(w)* is the vector of the signs of all entries of *w*.

Currently, MLlib includes implementation of the following algorithms:

- Basic statistics:
    - Summary statistics
    - Correlations
    - Stratified sampling
    - Hypothesis testing
    - Streaming significance testing
    - Random data generation

- Classification and regression:
    - Linear models (SVMs, logistic regression, and linear regression)
    - Naive Bayes
    - Decision trees
    - Ensembles of trees (Random Forests and Gradient-Boosted Trees)
    - Isotonic regression

- Collaborative filtering:
    - ◦ **Alternating least squares (ALS)**

- Clustering:
    - ◦ k-means
    - ◦ Gaussian mixture
    - ◦ **Power Iteration Clustering (PIC)**
    - ◦ **Latent Dirichlet allocation (LDA)**
    - ◦ Bisecting k-means
    - ◦ Streaming k-means

- Dimensionality reduction:
    - ◦ **Singular Value Decomposition (SVD)**
    - ◦ **Principal Component Analysis (PCA)**

- Feature extraction and transformation
- Frequent pattern mining:
    - ◦ FP-growth
    - ◦ Association rules
    - ◦ PrefixSpan

- Optimization:
    - ◦ **Stochastic Gradient Descent (SGD)**
    - ◦ **Limited-Memory BFGS (L-BFGS)**

I will go over some of the algorithms in *Chapter 5, Regression and Classification*. More complex non-structured machine learning methods will be considered in *Chapter 6, Working with Unstructured Data*.

SparkR

R is an implementation of popular S programming language created by John Chambers while working at Bell Labs. R is currently supported by the **R Foundation for Statistical Computing**. R's popularity has increased in recent years according to polls. SparkR provides a lightweight frontend to use Apache Spark from R. Starting with Spark 1.6.0, SparkR provides a distributed DataFrame implementation that supports operations such as selection, filtering, aggregation, and so on, which is similar to R DataFrames, dplyr, but on very large datasets. SparkR also supports distributed machine learning using MLlib.

SparkR required R version 3 or higher, and can be invoked via the `./bin/sparkR` shell. I will cover SparkR in *Chapter 8, Integrating Scala with R and Python*.

Graph algorithms – GraphX and GraphFrames

Graph algorithms are one of the hardest to correctly distribute between nodes, unless the graph itself is naturally partitioned, that is, it can be represented by a set of disconnected subgraphs. Since the social networking analysis on a multi-million node scale became popular due to companies such as Facebook, Google, and LinkedIn, researches have been coming up with new approaches to formalize the graph representations, algorithms, and types of questions asked.

GraphX is a modern framework for graph computations described in a 2013 paper (*GraphX: A Resilient Distributed Graph System on Spark* by Reynold Xin, Joseph Gonzalez, Michael Franklin, and Ion Stoica, GRADES (SIGMOD workshop), 2013). It has graph-parallel frameworks such as Pregel, and PowerGraph as predecessors. The graph is represented by two RDDs: one for vertices and another one for edges. Once the RDDs are joined, GraphX supports either Pregel-like API or MapReduce-like API, where the map function is applied to the node's neighbors and reduce is the aggregation step on top of the map results.

At the time of writing, GraphX includes the implementation for the following graph algorithms:

- PageRank
- Connected components
- Triangle counting
- Label propagation
- SVD++ (collaborative filtering)
- Strongly connected components

As GraphX is an open source library, changes to the list are expected. GraphFrames is a new implementation from Databricks that fully supports the following three languages: Scala, Java, and Python, and is build on top of DataFrames. I'll discuss specific implementations in *Chapter 7, Working with Graph Algorithms*.

Spark performance tuning

While efficient execution of the data pipeline is prerogative of the task scheduler, which is part of the Spark driver, sometimes Spark needs hints. Spark scheduling is primarily driven by the two parameters: CPU and memory. Other resources, such as disk and network I/O, of course, play an important part in Spark performance as well, but neither Spark, Mesos or YARN can currently do anything to actively manage them.

The first parameter to watch is the number of RDD partitions, which can be specified explicitly when reading the RDD from a file. Spark usually errs on the side of too many partitions as it provides more parallelism, and it does work in many cases as the task setup/teardown times are relatively small. However, one might experiment with decreasing the number of partitions, especially if one does aggregations.

The default number of partitions per RDD and the level of parallelism is determined by the `spark.default.parallelism` parameter, defined in the `$SPARK_HOME/conf/spark-defaults.conf` configuration file. The number of partitions for a specific RDD can also be explicitly changed by the `coalesce()` or `repartition()` methods.

The total number of cores and available memory is often the reason for deadlocks as the tasks cannot proceed further. One can specify the number of cores for each executor with the `--executor-cores` flag when invoking spark-submit, spark-shell, or PySpark from the command line. Alternatively, one can set the corresponding parameters in the `spark-defaults.conf` file discussed earlier. If the number of cores is set too high, the scheduler will not be able to allocate resources on the nodes and will deadlock.

In a similar way, `--executor-memory` (or the `spark.executor.memory` property) specifies the requested heap size for all the tasks (the default is 1g). If the executor memory is specified too high, again, the scheduler may be deadlocked or will be able to schedule only a limited number of executors on a node.

The implicit assumption in Standalone mode when counting the number of cores and memory is that Spark is the only running application—which may or may not be true. When running under Mesos or YARN, it is important to configure the cluster scheduler that it has the resources available to schedule the executors requested by the Spark Driver. The relevant YARN properties are: `yarn.nodemanager.resource.cpu-vcores` and `yarn.nodemanager.resource.memory-mb`. YARN may round the requested memory up a little. YARN's `yarn.scheduler.minimum-allocation-mb` and `yarn.scheduler.increment-allocation-mb` properties control the minimum and increment request values respectively.

JVMs can also use some memory off heap, for example, for interned strings and direct byte buffers. The value of the `spark.yarn.executor.memoryOverhead` property is added to the executor memory to determine the full memory request to YARN for each executor. It defaults to max (*384, .07 * spark.executor.memory*).

Since Spark can internally transfer the data between executors and client node, efficient serialization is very important. I will consider different serialization frameworks in *Chapter 6, Working with Unstructured Data*, but Spark uses Kryo serialization by default, which requires the classes to be registered explicitly in a static method. If you see a serialization error in your code, it is likely because the corresponding class has not been registered or Kryo does not support it, as it happens with too nested and complex data types. In general, it is recommended to avoid complex objects to be passed between the executors unless the object serialization can be done very efficiently.

Driver has similar parameters: `spark.driver.cores`, `spark.driver.memory`, and `spark.driver.maxResultSize`. The latter one sets the limit for the results collected from all the executors with the `collect` method. It is important to protect the driver process from out-of-memory exceptions. The other way to avoid out-of-memory exceptions and consequent problems are to either modify the pipeline to return aggregated or filtered results or use the `take` method instead.

Running Hadoop HDFS

A distributed processing framework wouldn't be complete without distributed storage. One of them is HDFS. Even if Spark is run on local mode, it can still use a distributed file system at the backend. Like Spark breaks computations into subtasks, HDFS breaks a file into blocks and stores them across a set of machines. For HA, HDFS stores multiple copies of each block, the number of copies is called replication level, three by default (refer to *Figure 3-5*).

NameNode is managing the HDFS storage by remembering the block locations and other metadata such as owner, file permissions, and block size, which are file-specific. **Secondary Namenode** is a slight misnomer: its function is to merge the metadata modifications, edits, into fsimage, or a file that serves as a metadata database. The merge is required, as it is more practical to write modifications of fsimage to a separate file instead of applying each modification to the disk image of the fsimage directly (in addition to applying the corresponding changes in memory). Secondary **Namenode** cannot serve as a second copy of the **Namenode**. A **Balancer** is run to move the blocks to maintain approximately equal disk usage across the servers—the initial block assignment to the nodes is supposed to be random, if enough space is available and the client is not run within the cluster. Finally, the **Client** communicates with the **Namenode** to get the metadata and block locations, but after that, either reads or writes the data directly to the node, where a copy of the block resides. The client is the only component that can be run outside the HDFS cluster, but it needs network connectivity with all the nodes in the cluster.

If any of the node dies or disconnects from the network, the **Namenode** notices the change, as it constantly maintains the contact with the nodes via heartbeats. If the node does not reconnect to the **Namenode** within 10 minutes (by default), the **Namenode** will start replicating the blocks in order to achieve the required replication level for the blocks that were lost on the node. A separate block scanner thread in the **Namenode** will scan the blocks for possible bit rot—each block maintains a checksum—and will delete corrupted and orphaned blocks:

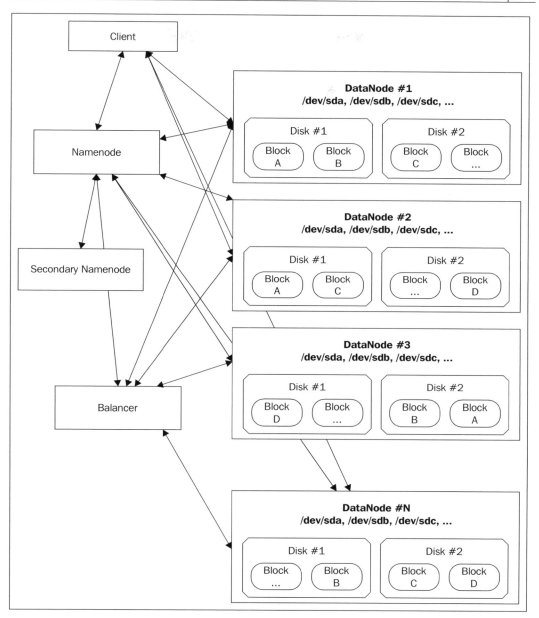

Figure 03-5. This is the HDFS architecture. Each block is stored in three separate locations (the replication level).

1. To start HDFS on your machine (with replication level 1), download a Hadoop distribution, for example, from `http://hadoop.apache.org`:

```
$ wget ftp://apache.cs.utah.edu/apache.org/hadoop/common/h/hadoop-
2.6.4.tar.gz

--2016-05-12 00:10:55--  ftp://apache.cs.utah.edu/apache.org/
hadoop/common/hadoop-2.6.4/hadoop-2.6.4.tar.gz

            => 'hadoop-2.6.4.tar.gz.1'

Resolving apache.cs.utah.edu... 155.98.64.87

Connecting to apache.cs.utah.edu|155.98.64.87|:21... connected.

Logging in as anonymous ... Logged in!

==> SYST ... done.    ==> PWD ... done.

==> TYPE I ... done.  ==> CWD (1) /apache.org/hadoop/common/
hadoop-2.6.4 ... done.

==> SIZE hadoop-2.6.4.tar.gz ... 196015975

==> PASV ... done.    ==> RETR hadoop-2.6.4.tar.gz ... done.

...

$ wget ftp://apache.cs.utah.edu/apache.org/hadoop/common/
hadoop-2.6.4/hadoop-2.6.4.tar.gz.mds

--2016-05-12 00:13:58--  ftp://apache.cs.utah.edu/apache.org/
hadoop/common/hadoop-2.6.4/hadoop-2.6.4.tar.gz.mds

            => 'hadoop-2.6.4.tar.gz.mds'

Resolving apache.cs.utah.edu... 155.98.64.87

Connecting to apache.cs.utah.edu|155.98.64.87|:21... connected.

Logging in as anonymous ... Logged in!

==> SYST ... done.    ==> PWD ... done.

==> TYPE I ... done.  ==> CWD (1) /apache.org/hadoop/common/
hadoop-2.6.4 ... done.

==> SIZE hadoop-2.6.4.tar.gz.mds ... 958

==> PASV ... done.    ==> RETR hadoop-2.6.4.tar.gz.mds ... done.

...

$ shasum -a 512 hadoop-2.6.4.tar.gz

493cc1a3e8ed0f7edee506d99bfabbe2aa71a4776e4bff5b852c6279b4c828a
0505d4ee5b63a0de0dcfecf70b4bb0ef801c767a068eaeac938b8c58d8f21beec
hadoop-2.6.4.tar.gz

$ cat !$.mds

hadoop-2.6.4.tar.gz:    MD5 = 37 01 9F 13 D7 DC D8 19  72 7B E1 58
44 0B 94 42
```

```
hadoop-2.6.4.tar.gz:    SHA1 = 1E02 FAAC 94F3 35DF A826   73AC BA3E
7498 751A 3174

hadoop-2.6.4.tar.gz: RMD160 = 2AA5 63AF 7E40 5DCD 9D6C  D00E EBB0
750B D401 2B1F

hadoop-2.6.4.tar.gz: SHA224 = F4FDFF12 5C8E754B DAF5BCFC 6735FCD2
C6064D58

                              36CB9D80 2C12FC4D
hadoop-2.6.4.tar.gz: SHA256 = C58F08D2 E0B13035 F86F8B0B 8B65765A
B9F47913

                              81F74D02 C48F8D9C EF5E7D8E
hadoop-2.6.4.tar.gz: SHA384 = 87539A46 B696C98E 5C7E352E 997B0AF8
0602D239

                              5591BF07 F3926E78 2D2EF790 BCBB6B3C
EAF5B3CF

                              ADA7B6D1 35D4B952
hadoop-2.6.4.tar.gz: SHA512 = 493CC1A3 E8ED0F7E DEE506D9 9BFABBE2
AA71A477

                              6E4BFF5B 852C6279 B4C828A0 505D4EE5
B63A0DE0

                              DCFECF70 B4BB0EF8 01C767A0 68EAEAC9
38B8C58D

                              8F21BEEC


$ tar xf hadoop-2.6.4.tar.gz
$ cd hadoop-2.6.4
```

2. To get the minimal HDFS configuration, modify the `core-site.xml` and `hdfs-site.xml` files, as follows:

```
$ cat << EOF > etc/hadoop/core-site.xml
<configuration>
    <property>
        <name>fs.defaultFS</name>
        <value>hdfs://localhost:8020</value>
    </property>
</configuration>
EOF
$ cat << EOF > etc/hadoop/hdfs-site.xml
```

```
<configuration>
    <property>
        <name>dfs.replication</name>
        <value>1</value>
    </property>
</configuration>
EOF
```

This will put the Hadoop HDFS metadata and data directories under the `/tmp/hadoop-$USER` directories. To make this more permanent, we can add the `dfs.namenode.name.dir`, `dfs.namenode.edits.dir`, and `dfs.datanode.data.dir` parameters, but we will leave these out for now. For a more customized distribution, one can download a Cloudera version from `http://archive.cloudera.com/cdh`.

3. First, we need to write an empty metadata:

```
$ bin/hdfs namenode -format
16/05/12 00:55:40 INFO namenode.NameNode: STARTUP_MSG:
/************************************************************
STARTUP_MSG: Starting NameNode
STARTUP_MSG:    host = alexanders-macbook-pro.local/192.168.1.68
STARTUP_MSG:    args = [-format]
STARTUP_MSG:    version = 2.6.4
STARTUP_MSG:    classpath =
...
```

4. Then start the `namenode`, `secondarynamenode`, and `datanode` Java processes (I usually open three different command-line windows to see the logs, but in a production environment, these are usually daemonized):

```
$ bin/hdfs namenode &
...
$ bin/hdfs secondarynamenode &
...
$ bin/hdfs datanode &
...
```

5. We are now ready to create the first HDFS file:

```
$ date | bin/hdfs dfs -put - date.txt
...
$ bin/hdfs dfs -ls
Found 1 items
-rw-r--r-- 1 akozlov supergroup 29 2016-05-12 01:02 date.txt
$ bin/hdfs dfs -text date.txt
Thu May 12 01:02:36 PDT 2016
```

6. Of course, in this particular case, the actual file is stored only on one node, which is the same node we run `datanode` on (localhost). In my case, it is the following:

```
$ cat /tmp/hadoop-akozlov/dfs/data/current/BP-1133284427-
192.168.1.68-1463039756191/current/finalized/subdir0/subdir0/
blk_1073741827
Thu May 12 01:02:36 PDT 2016
```

7. The Namenode UI can be found at `http://localhost:50070` and displays a host of information, including the HDFS usage and the list of DataNodes, the slaves of the HDFS Master node as follows:

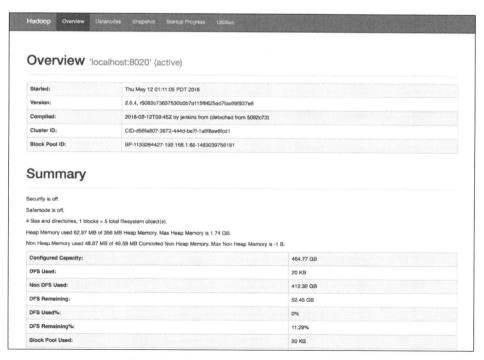

Figure 03-6. A snapshot of HDFS NameNode UI.

The preceding figure shows HDFS Namenode HTTP UI in a single node deployment (usually, `http://<namenode-address>:50070`). The **Utilities | Browse the file system** tab allows you to browse and download the files from HDFS. Nodes can be added by starting DataNodes on a different node and pointing to the Namenode with the `fs.defaultFS=<namenode-address>:8020` parameter. The Secondary Namenode HTTP UI is usually at `http:<secondarynamenode-address>:50090`.

Scala/Spark by default will use the local file system. However, if the `core-site/xml` file is on the classpath or placed in the `$SPARK_HOME/conf` directory, Spark will use HDFS as the default.

Summary

In this chapter, I covered the Spark/Hadoop and their relationship with Scala and functional programming at a very high level. I considered a classic word count example and it's implementation in Scala and Spark. I also provided high-level components of Spark ecosystem with specific examples of word count and streaming. I now have all the components to start looking at the specific implementation of classic machine learning algorithms in Scala/Spark. In the next chapter, I will start by covering supervised and unsupervised learning—a traditional division of learning algorithms for structured data.

4

Supervised and Unsupervised Learning

I covered the basics of the MLlib library in the previous chapter, but MLlib, at least at the time of writing this book, is more like a fast-moving target that is gaining the lead rather than a well-structured implementation that everyone uses in production or even has a consistent and tested documentation. In this situation, as people say, rather than giving you the fish, I will try to focus on well-established concepts behind the libraries and teach the process of fishing in this book in order to avoid the need to drastically modify the chapters with each new MLlib release. For better or worse, this increasingly seems to be a skill that a data scientist needs to possess.

Statistics and machine learning inherently deal with uncertainty, due to one or another reason we covered in *Chapter 2, Data Pipelines and Modeling*. While some datasets might be completely random, the goal here is to find trends, structure, and patterns beyond what a random number generator will provide you. The fundamental value of ML is that we can generalize these patterns and improve on at least some metrics. Let's see what basic tools are available within Scala/Spark.

In this chapter, I am covering supervised and unsupervised leaning, the two historically different approaches. Supervised learning is traditionally used when we have a specific goal to predict a label, or a specific attribute of a dataset. Unsupervised learning can be used to understand internal structure and dependencies between any attributes of a dataset, and is often used to group the records or attributes in meaningful clusters. In practice, both methods can be used to complement and aid each other.

In this chapter, we will cover the following topics:

- Learning standard models for supervised learning – decision trees and logistic regression
- Discussing the staple of unsupervised learning – k-means clustering and its derivatives
- Understanding metrics and methods to evaluate the effectiveness of the above algorithms
- Having a glimpse of extending the above methods on special cases of streaming data, sparse data, and non-structured data

Records and supervised learning

For the purpose of this chapter, a record is an observation or measurement of one or several attributes. We assume that the observations might contain noise ε_{ij} (or be inaccurate for one or other reason):

$$x_i = \widehat{x}_i + \varepsilon_{ij}$$

While we believe that there is some pattern or correlation between the attributes, the one that we are after and want to uncover, the noise is uncorrelated across either the attributes or the records. In statistical terms, we say that the values for each record are drawn from the same distribution and are independent (or *i.i.d.* in statistical terms). The order of records does not matter. One of the attributes, usually the first, might be designated to be the label.

Supervised learning is when the goal is to predict the label yi:

$$y_i = f\left(x_1, \ldots, x_N\right)$$

Here, N is the number of remaining attributes. In other words, the goal is to generalize the patterns so that we can predict the label by just knowing the other attributes, whether because we cannot physically get the measurement or just want to explore the structure of the dataset without having the immediate goal to predict the label.

The unsupervised learning is when we don't use the label — we just try to explore the structure and correlations to understand the dataset to, potentially, predict the label better. The number of problems in this latter category has increased recently with the emergence of learning for unstructured data and streams, each of which, I'll be covering later in the book in separate chapters.

Iris dataset

I will demonstrate the concept of records and labels based on one of the most famous datasets in machine learning, the Iris dataset (`https://archive.ics.uci.edu/ml/datasets/Iris`). The Iris dataset contains 50 records for each of the three types of Iris flower, 150 lines of total five fields. Each line is a measurement of the following:

- Sepal length in cm
- Sepal width in cm
- Petal length in cm
- Petal width in cm

With the final field being the type of the flower (*setosa*, *versicolor*, or *virginica*). The classic problem is to predict the label, which, in this case, is a categorical attribute with three possible values as a function of the first four attributes:

$$label = f\left(x_1, x_2, x_3, x_4\right)$$

One option would be to draw a plane in the four-dimensional space that separates all four labels. Unfortunately, as one can find out, while one of the classes is clearly separable, the remaining two are not, as shown in the following multidimensional scatterplot (we have used Data Desk software to create it):

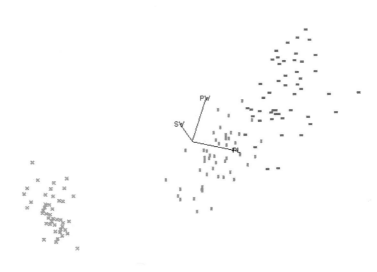

Figure 04-1. The Iris dataset as a three-dimensional plot. The Iris setosa records, shown by crosses, can be separated from the other two types based on petal length and width.

The colors and shapes are assigned according to the following table:

Label	Color	Shape
Iris setosa	Blue	x
Iris versicolor	Green	Vertical bar
Iris virginica	Purple	Horizontal bar

The *Iris setosa* is separable because it happens to have a very short petal length and width compared to the two other types.

Let's see how we can use MLlib to find that separating multidimensional plane.

Labeled point

The labeled datasets used to have a very special place in ML—we will discuss unsupervised learning later in the chapter, where we do not need a label, so MLlib has a special data type to represent a record with a `org.apache.spark.mllib.regression.LabeledPoint` label (refer to `https://spark.apache.org/docs/latest/mllib-data-types.html#labeled-point`). To read the Iris dataset from a text file, we need to transform the original UCI repository file into the so-called LIBSVM text format. While there are plenty of converters from CSV to LIBSVM format, I'd like to use a simple AWK script to do the job:

```
awk -F, '/setosa/ {print "0 1:"$1" 2:"$2" 3:"$3" 4:"$4;}; /versicolor/
{print "1 1:"$1" 2:"$2" 3:"$3" 4:"$4;}; /virginica/ {print "1 1:"$1"
2:"$2" 3:"$3" 4:"$4;};' iris.csv > iris-libsvm.txt
```

Why do we need LIBSVM format?

LIBSVM is the format that many libraries use. First, LIBSVM takes only continuous attributes. While a lot of datasets in the real world contain discrete or categorical attributes, internally they are always converted to a numerical representation for efficiency reasons, even if the L1 or L2 metrics on the resulting numerical attribute does not make much sense in the unordered discrete values. Second, the LIBSVM format allows for efficient sparse data representation. While the Iris dataset is not sparse, almost all of the modern big data sources are sparse, and the format allows for efficient storage by only storing the provided values. Many modern big data key-value and traditional RDBMS databases actually do the same for efficiency reasons.

The code might be more complex for missing values, but we know that the Iris dataset is not sparse—otherwise we'd complement our code with a bunch of if statements. We mapped the last two labels to 1 for our purpose now.

SVMWithSGD

Now, let's run the **Linear Support Vector Machine (SVM)** SVMWithSGD code from MLlib:

```
$ bin/spark-shell

Welcome to


      ____              __
     / __/__  ___ _____/ /__
    _\ \/ _ \/ _ `/ __/  '_/
   /___/ .__/\_,_/_/ /_/\_\   version 1.6.1
      /_/


Using Scala version 2.10.5 (Java HotSpot(TM) 64-Bit Server VM, Java
1.8.0_40)
Type in expressions to have them evaluated.
Type :help for more information.
Spark context available as sc.
SQL context available as sqlContext.


scala> import org.apache.spark.mllib.classification.{SVMModel,
SVMWithSGD}
import org.apache.spark.mllib.classification.{SVMModel, SVMWithSGD}

scala> import org.apache.spark.mllib.evaluation.
BinaryClassificationMetrics
import org.apache.spark.mllib.evaluation.BinaryClassificationMetrics

scala> import org.apache.spark.mllib.util.MLUtils
import org.apache.spark.mllib.util.MLUtils

scala> val data = MLUtils.loadLibSVMFile(sc, "iris-libsvm.txt")
data: org.apache.spark.rdd.RDD[org.apache.spark.mllib.regression.
LabeledPoint] = MapPartitionsRDD[6] at map at MLUtils.scala:112

scala> val splits = data.randomSplit(Array(0.6, 0.4), seed = 123L)
splits: Array[org.apache.spark.rdd.RDD[org.apache.spark.mllib.
regression.LabeledPoint]] = Array(MapPartitionsRDD[7] at randomSplit at
<console>:26, MapPartitionsRDD[8] at randomSplit at <console>:26)

scala> val training = splits(0).cache()
training: org.apache.spark.rdd.RDD[org.apache.spark.mllib.regression.
LabeledPoint] = MapPartitionsRDD[7] at randomSplit at <console>:26

scala> val test = splits(1)
```

```
test: org.apache.spark.rdd.RDD[org.apache.spark.mllib.regression.
LabeledPoint] = MapPartitionsRDD[8] at randomSplit at <console>:26

scala> val numIterations = 100

numIterations: Int = 100

scala> val model = SVMWithSGD.train(training, numIterations)

model: org.apache.spark.mllib.classification.SVMModel = org.apache.
spark.mllib.classification.SVMModel: intercept = 0.0, numFeatures = 4,
numClasses = 2, threshold = 0.0

scala> model.clearThreshold()

res0: model.type = org.apache.spark.mllib.classification.SVMModel:
intercept = 0.0, numFeatures = 4, numClasses = 2, threshold = None

scala> val scoreAndLabels = test.map { point =>
     |     val score = model.predict(point.features)
     |     (score, point.label)
     | }

scoreAndLabels: org.apache.spark.rdd.RDD[(Double, Double)] =
MapPartitionsRDD[212] at map at <console>:36

scala> val metrics = new BinaryClassificationMetrics(scoreAndLabels)

metrics: org.apache.spark.mllib.evaluation.BinaryClassificationMetrics =
org.apache.spark.mllib.evaluation.BinaryClassificationMetrics@692e4a35

scala> val auROC = metrics.areaUnderROC()

auROC: Double = 1.0


scala> println("Area under ROC = " + auROC)

Area under ROC = 1.0

scala> model.save(sc, "model")

SLF4J: Failed to load class "org.slf4j.impl.StaticLoggerBinder".

SLF4J: Defaulting to no-operation (NOP) logger implementation

SLF4J: See http://www.slf4j.org/codes.html#StaticLoggerBinder for further
details.
```

So, you just run one of the most complex algorithms in the machine learning toolbox: SVM. The result is a separating plane that distinguishes *Iris setosa* flowers from the other two types. The model in this case is exactly the intercept and the coefficients of the plane that best separates the labels:

```
scala> model.intercept
res5: Double = 0.0


scala> model.weights
```

```
res6: org.apache.spark.mllib.linalg.Vector = [-0.2469448809675877,-
1.0692729424287566,1.7500423423258127,0.8105712661836376]
```

If one looks under the hood, the model is stored in a `parquet` file, which can be dumped using `parquet-tool`:

```
$ parquet-tools dump model/data/part-r-00000-7a86b825-569d-4c80-8796-
8ee6972fd3b1.gz.parquet
...
DOUBLE weights.values.array
--------------------------------------------------------------------------
-------------------------------------------------------------------------
*** row group 1 of 1, values 1 to 4 ***
value 1: R:0 D:3 V:-0.2469448809675877
value 2: R:1 D:3 V:-1.0692729424287566
value 3: R:1 D:3 V:1.7500423423258127
value 4: R:1 D:3 V:0.8105712661836376


DOUBLE intercept
--------------------------------------------------------------------------
-------------------------------------------------------------------------
*** row group 1 of 1, values 1 to 1 ***
value 1: R:0 D:1 V:0.0
...
```

The **Receiver Operating Characteristic (ROC)** is a common measure of the classifier to be able to correctly rank the records according to their numeric label. We will consider precision metrics in more detail in *Chapter 9, NLP in Scala*.

What is ROC?

ROC has emerged in signal processing with the first application to measure the accuracy of analog radars. The common measure of accuracy is area under ROC, which, shortly, is the probability of two randomly chosen points to be ranked correctly according to their labels (the *0* label should always have a lower rank than the *1* label). AUROC has a number of attractive characteristics:

- The value, at least theoretically, does not depend on the oversampling rate, that is, the rate at which we see *0* labels as opposed to *1* labels.

- The value does not depend on the sample size, excluding the expected variance due to the limited sample size.

- Adding a constant to the final score does not change the ROC, thus the intercept can always be set to *0*. Computing the ROC requires a sort with respect to the generated score.

Of course, separating the remaining two labels is a harder problem since the plane that separated *Iris versicolor* from *Iris virginica* does not exist: the AUROC score will be less than *1.0*. However, the SVM method will find the plane that best differentiates between the latter two classes.

Logistic regression

Logistic regression is one of the oldest classification methods. The outcome of the logistic regression is also a set of weights, which define the hyperplane, but the loss function is logistic loss instead of *L2*:

$$\ln\left(1 + \exp\left(-yw^T x\right)\right)$$

Logit function is a frequent choice when the label is binary (as $y = +/- 1$ in the above equation):

```
$ bin/spark-shell
Welcome to


      ____              __
     / __/__  ___ _____/ /__
    _\ \/ _ \/ _ `/ __/  '_/
   /___/ .__/\_,_/_/ /_/\_\   version 1.6.1
      /_/


Using Scala version 2.10.5 (Java HotSpot(TM) 64-Bit Server VM, Java
1.8.0_40)
Type in expressions to have them evaluated.
Type :help for more information.
Spark context available as sc.
SQL context available as sqlContext.


scala> import org.apache.spark.SparkContext
import org.apache.spark.SparkContext
scala> import org.apache.spark.mllib.classification.
{LogisticRegressionWithLBFGS, LogisticRegressionModel}
import org.apache.spark.mllib.classification.
{LogisticRegressionWithLBFGS, LogisticRegressionModel}
scala> import org.apache.spark.mllib.evaluation.MulticlassMetrics
import org.apache.spark.mllib.evaluation.MulticlassMetrics
scala> import org.apache.spark.mllib.regression.LabeledPoint
import org.apache.spark.mllib.regression.LabeledPoint
scala> import org.apache.spark.mllib.linalg.Vectors
import org.apache.spark.mllib.linalg.Vectors
scala> import org.apache.spark.mllib.util.MLUtils
import org.apache.spark.mllib.util.MLUtils
scala> val data = MLUtils.loadLibSVMFile(sc, "iris-libsvm-3.txt")
data: org.apache.spark.rdd.RDD[org.apache.spark.mllib.regression.
LabeledPoint] = MapPartitionsRDD[6] at map at MLUtils.scala:112
scala> val splits = data.randomSplit(Array(0.6, 0.4))
```

```
splits: Array[org.apache.spark.rdd.RDD[org.apache.spark.mllib.
regression.LabeledPoint]] = Array(MapPartitionsRDD[7] at randomSplit at
<console>:29, MapPartitionsRDD[8] at randomSplit at <console>:29)

scala> val training = splits(0).cache()

training: org.apache.spark.rdd.RDD[org.apache.spark.mllib.regression.
LabeledPoint] = MapPartitionsRDD[7] at randomSplit at <console>:29

scala> val test = splits(1)

test: org.apache.spark.rdd.RDD[org.apache.spark.mllib.regression.
LabeledPoint] = MapPartitionsRDD[8] at randomSplit at <console>:29

scala> val model = new LogisticRegressionWithLBFGS().setNumClasses(3).
run(training)

model: org.apache.spark.mllib.classification.LogisticRegressionModel =
org.apache.spark.mllib.classification.LogisticRegressionModel: intercept
= 0.0, numFeatures = 8, numClasses = 3, threshold = 0.5

scala> val predictionAndLabels = test.map { case LabeledPoint(label,
features) =>
     |    val prediction = model.predict(features)
     |    (prediction, label)
     | }

predictionAndLabels: org.apache.spark.rdd.RDD[(Double, Double)] =
MapPartitionsRDD[67] at map at <console>:37

scala> val metrics = new MulticlassMetrics(predictionAndLabels)

metrics: org.apache.spark.mllib.evaluation.MulticlassMetrics = org.
apache.spark.mllib.evaluation.MulticlassMetrics@6d5254f3

scala> val precision = metrics.precision

precision: Double = 0.9516129032258065

scala> println("Precision = " + precision)

Precision = 0.9516129032258065

scala> model.intercept

res5: Double = 0.0

scala> model.weights

res7: org.apache.spark.mllib.linalg.Vector = [10.644978886788556,-
26.850171485157578,3.852594349297618,8.74629386938248,4.288703063075211,-
31.029289381858273,9.790312529377474,22.058196856491996]
```

The labels in this case can be any integer in the range *[0, k)*, where *k* is the total number of classes (the correct class will be determined by building multiple binary logistic regression models against the pivot class, which in this case, is the class with the *0* label) (*The Elements of Statistical Learning* by *Trevor Hastie, Robert Tibshirani, Jerome Friedman, Springer Series in Statistics*).

The accuracy metric is precision, or the percentage of records predicted correctly (which is 95% in our case).

Decision tree

The preceding two methods describe linear models. Unfortunately, the linear approach does not always work for complex interactions between attributes. Assume that the label looks like an exclusive *OR: 0 if X ≠ Y and 1 if X = Y:*

X	Y	Label
1	0	0
0	1	0
1	1	1
0	0	1

There is no hyperplane that can differentiate between the two labels in the *XY* space. Recursive split solution, where the split on each level is made on only one variable or a linear combination thereof might work a bit better in these case. Decision trees are also known to work well with sparse and interaction-rich datasets:

```
$ bin/spark-shell
Welcome to
      ____              __
     / __/__  ___ _____/ /__
    _\ \/ _ \/ _ `/ __/  '_/
   /___/ .__/\_,_/_/ /_/\_\   version 1.6.1
      /_/

Using Scala version 2.10.5 (Java HotSpot(TM) 64-Bit Server VM, Java
1.8.0_40)
Type in expressions to have them evaluated.
Type :help for more information.
Spark context available as sc.
SQL context available as sqlContext.

scala> import org.apache.spark.mllib.tree.DecisionTree
import org.apache.spark.mllib.tree.DecisionTree
scala> import org.apache.spark.mllib.tree.model.DecisionTreeModel
```

```
import org.apache.spark.mllib.tree.model.DecisionTreeModel
scala> import org.apache.spark.mllib.util.MLUtils
import org.apache.spark.mllib.util.MLUtils
scala> import org.apache.spark.mllib.tree.configuration.Strategy
import org.apache.spark.mllib.tree.configuration.Strategy
scala> import org.apache.spark.mllib.tree.configuration.Algo.
Classification
import org.apache.spark.mllib.tree.configuration.Algo.Classification
scala> import org.apache.spark.mllib.tree.impurity.{Entropy, Gini}
import org.apache.spark.mllib.tree.impurity.{Entropy, Gini}
scala> val data = MLUtils.loadLibSVMFile(sc, "iris-libsvm-3.txt")
data: org.apache.spark.rdd.RDD[org.apache.spark.mllib.regression.
LabeledPoint] = MapPartitionsRDD[6] at map at MLUtils.scala:112


scala> val splits = data.randomSplit(Array(0.7, 0.3), 11L)
splits: Array[org.apache.spark.rdd.RDD[org.apache.spark.mllib.
regression.LabeledPoint]] = Array(MapPartitionsRDD[7] at randomSplit at
<console>:30, MapPartitionsRDD[8] at randomSplit at <console>:30)
scala> val (trainingData, testData) = (splits(0), splits(1))
trainingData: org.apache.spark.rdd.RDD[org.apache.spark.mllib.regression.
LabeledPoint] = MapPartitionsRDD[7] at randomSplit at <console>:30
testData: org.apache.spark.rdd.RDD[org.apache.spark.mllib.regression.
LabeledPoint] = MapPartitionsRDD[8] at randomSplit at <console>:30
scala> val strategy = new Strategy(Classification, Gini, 10, 3, 10)
strategy: org.apache.spark.mllib.tree.configuration.Strategy = org.
apache.spark.mllib.tree.configuration.Strategy@4110e631
scala> val dt = new DecisionTree(strategy)
dt: org.apache.spark.mllib.tree.DecisionTree = org.apache.spark.mllib.
tree.DecisionTree@33d89052
scala> val model = dt.run(trainingData)
model: org.apache.spark.mllib.tree.model.DecisionTreeModel =
DecisionTreeModel classifier of depth 6 with 21 nodes
scala> val labelAndPreds = testData.map { point =>
     |    val prediction = model.predict(point.features)
     |    (point.label, prediction)
     | }
labelAndPreds: org.apache.spark.rdd.RDD[(Double, Double)] =
MapPartitionsRDD[32] at map at <console>:36
```

```scala
scala> val testErr = labelAndPreds.filter(r => r._1 != r._2).count.
toDouble / testData.count()

testErr: Double = 0.02631578947368421

scala> println("Test Error = " + testErr)

Test Error = 0.02631578947368421


scala> println("Learned classification tree model:\n" + model.
toDebugString)
Learned classification tree model:
DecisionTreeModel classifier of depth 6 with 21 nodes
  If (feature 3 <= 0.4)
   Predict: 0.0
  Else (feature 3 > 0.4)
   If (feature 3 <= 1.7)
    If (feature 2 <= 4.9)
     If (feature 0 <= 5.3)
      If (feature 1 <= 2.8)
       If (feature 2 <= 3.9)
        Predict: 1.0
       Else (feature 2 > 3.9)
        Predict: 2.0
      Else (feature 1 > 2.8)
       Predict: 0.0
     Else (feature 0 > 5.3)
      Predict: 1.0
    Else (feature 2 > 4.9)
     If (feature 0 <= 6.0)
      If (feature 1 <= 2.4)
       Predict: 2.0
      Else (feature 1 > 2.4)
       Predict: 1.0
     Else (feature 0 > 6.0)
      Predict: 2.0
   Else (feature 3 > 1.7)
    If (feature 2 <= 4.9)
     If (feature 1 <= 3.0)
```

```
       Predict: 2.0
    Else (feature 1 > 3.0)
       Predict: 1.0
    Else (feature 2 > 4.9)
       Predict: 2.0
scala> model.save(sc, "dt-model")
SLF4J: Failed to load class "org.slf4j.impl.StaticLoggerBinder".
SLF4J: Defaulting to no-operation (NOP) logger implementation
SLF4J: See http://www.slf4j.org/codes.html#StaticLoggerBinder for further
details.
```

As you can see, the error (misprediction) rate on hold-out 30% sample is only 2.6%. The 30% sample of 150 is only 45 records, which means we missed only 1 record from the whole test set. Certainly, the result might and will change with a different seed, and we need a more rigorous cross-validation technique to prove the accuracy of the model, but this is enough for a rough estimate of model performance.

Decision tree generalizes on regression case, that is, when the label is continuous in nature. In this case, the splitting criterion is minimization of weighted variance, as opposed to entropy gain or gini in the case of classification. I will talk more about the differences in *Chapter 5, Regression and Classification*.

There are a number of parameters, which can be tuned to improve the performance:

Parameter	Description	Recommended value
maxDepth	This is the maximum depth of the tree. Deep trees are costly and usually are more likely to overfit. Shallow trees are more efficient and better for bagging/boosting algorithms such as AdaBoost.	This depends on the size of the original dataset. It is worth experimenting and plotting the accuracy of the resulting tree versus the parameter to find out the optimum.
minInstancesPerNode	This also limits the size of the tree: once the number of instances falls under this threshold, no further splitting occurs.	The value is usually 10-100, depending on the complexity of the original dataset and the number of potential labels.
maxBins	This is used only for continuous attributes: the number of bins to split the original range.	Large number of bins increase computation and communication cost. One can also consider the option of pre-discretizing the attribute based on domain knowledge.

Parameter	Description	Recommended value
`minInfoGain`	This is the amount of information gain (entropy), impurity (gini), or variance (regression) gain to split a node.	The default is *0*, but you can increase the default to limit the tree size and reduce the risk of overfitting.
`maxMemoryInMB`	This is the amount of memory to be used for collecting sufficient statistics.	The default value is conservatively chosen to be 256 MB to allow the decision algorithm to work in most scenarios. Increasing `maxMemoryInMB` can lead to faster training (if the memory is available) by allowing fewer passes over the data. However, there may be decreasing returns as `maxMemoryInMB` grows, as the amount of communication on each iteration can be proportional to `maxMemoryInMB`.
`subsamplingRate`	This is the fraction of the training data used for learning the decision tree.	This parameter is most relevant for training ensembles of trees (using `RandomForest` and `GradientBoostedTrees`), where it can be useful to subsample the original data. For training a single decision tree, this parameter is less useful since the number of training instances is generally not the main constraint.
`useNodeIdCache`	If this is set to true, the algorithm will avoid passing the current model (tree or trees) to executors on each iteration.	This can be useful with deep trees (speeding up computation on workers) and for large random forests (reducing communication on each iteration).

Parameter	Description	Recommended value
`checkpointDir:`	This is the directory for checkpointing the node ID cache RDDs.	This is an optimization to save intermediate results to avoid recomputation in case of node failure. Set it in large clusters or with unreliable nodes.
`checkpointInterval`	This is the frequency for checkpointing the node ID cache RDDs.	Setting this too low will cause extra overhead from writing to HDFS and setting this too high can cause problems if executors fail and the RDD needs to be recomputed.

Bagging and boosting – ensemble learning methods

As a portfolio of stocks has better characteristics compared to individual equities, models can be combined to produce better classifiers. Usually, these methods work really well with decision trees as the training technique can be modified to produce models with large variations. One way is to train the model on random subsets of the original data or random subsets of attributes, which is called random forest. Another way is to generate a sequence of models, where misclassified instances are reweighted to get a larger weight in each subsequent iteration. It has been shown that this method has a relation to gradient descent methods in the model parameter space. While these are valid and interesting techniques, they usually require much more space in terms of model storage and are less interpretable compared to bare decision tree models. For Spark, the ensemble models are currently under development—the umbrella issue is SPARK-3703 (`https://issues.apache.org/jira/browse/SPARK-3703`).

Unsupervised learning

If we get rid of the label in the Iris dataset, it would be nice if some algorithm could recover the original grouping, maybe without the exact label names— *setosa*, *versicolor*, and *virginica*. Unsupervised learning has multiple applications in compression and encoding, CRM, recommendation engines, and security to uncover internal structure without actually having the exact labels. The labels sometimes can be given base on the singularity in attribute value distributions. For example, *Iris setosa* can be described as a *Flower with Small Leaves*.

While a supervised learning problem can always be cast as unsupervised by disregarding the label, the reverse is also true. A clustering algorithm can be cast as a density-estimation problem by assigning label *1* to all vectors and generating random vectors with label *0* (*The Elements of Statistical Learning* by *Trevor Hastie, Robert Tibshirani, Jerome Friedman, Springer Series in Statistics*). The difference between the two is formal and it's even fuzzier with non-structured and nested data. Often, running unsupervised algorithms in labeled datasets leads to a better understanding of the dependencies and thus a better selection and performance of the supervised algorithm.

One of the most popular algorithms for clustering and unsupervised learning in k-means (and its variants, k-median and k-center, will be described later):

```
$ bin/spark-shell
Welcome to


      ____              __
     / __/__  ___ _____/ /__
    _\ \/ _ \/ _ `/ __/  '_/
   /___/ .__/\_,_/_/ /_/\_\   version 1.6.1
      /_/

Using Scala version 2.10.5 (Java HotSpot(TM) 64-Bit Server VM, Java
1.8.0_40)
Type in expressions to have them evaluated.
Type :help for more information.
Spark context available as sc.
SQL context available as sqlContext.


scala> import org.apache.spark.mllib.clustering.{KMeans, KMeansModel}
import org.apache.spark.mllib.clustering.{KMeans, KMeansModel}
scala> import org.apache.spark.mllib.linalg.Vectors
import org.apache.spark.mllib.linalg.Vectors
scala> val iris = sc.textFile("iris.txt")
iris: org.apache.spark.rdd.RDD[String] = MapPartitionsRDD[4] at textFile
at <console>:23


scala> val vectors = data.map(s => Vectors.dense(s.split('\t').map(_.
toDouble))).cache()
```

```
vectors: org.apache.spark.rdd.RDD[org.apache.spark.mllib.linalg.Vector] =
MapPartitionsRDD[5] at map at <console>:25
```

```
scala> val numClusters = 3

numClusters: Int = 3

scala> val numIterations = 20

numIterations: Int = 20

scala> val clusters = KMeans.train(vectors, numClusters, numIterations)

clusters: org.apache.spark.mllib.clustering.KMeansModel = org.apache.
spark.mllib.clustering.KMeansModel@5dc9cb99

scala> val centers = clusters.clusterCenters

centers: Array[org.apache.spark.mllib.linalg.Vector] =
Array([5.005999999999999,3.4180000000000006,1.4640000000000002,
0.2439999999999999], [6.853846153846535,3.076923076923076,
5.715384615384614,2.0538461538461537], [5.883606557377049,
2.740983606557377,4.388524590163936,1.4344262295081966])

scala> val SSE = clusters.computeCost(vectors)

WSSSE: Double = 78.94506582597859

scala> vectors.collect.map(x => clusters.predict(x))

res18: Array[Int] = Array(0, 0, 0, 0, 0, 0, 0, 0, 0, 0, 0, 0, 0, 0, 0, 0,
0, 0, 0, 0, 0, 0, 0, 0, 0, 0, 0, 0, 0, 0, 0, 0, 0, 0, 0, 0, 0, 0, 0, 0,
0, 0, 0, 0, 0, 0, 0, 0, 0, 0, 1, 2, 1, 2, 2, 2, 2, 2, 2, 2, 2, 2, 2, 2,
2, 2, 2, 2, 2, 2, 2, 2, 2, 2, 2, 2, 2, 1, 2, 2, 2, 2, 2, 2, 2, 2, 2, 2,
2, 2, 2, 2, 2, 2, 2, 2, 2, 2, 2, 2, 1, 2, 1, 1, 1, 1, 2, 1, 1, 1, 1, 1,
1, 2, 2, 1, 1, 1, 1, 2, 1, 2, 1, 2, 1, 1, 2, 2, 1, 1, 1, 1, 1, 2, 1, 1,
1, 1, 2, 1, 1, 1, 2, 1, 1, 1, 2, 1, 1, 2)

scala> println("Sum of Squared Errors = " + SSE)

Sum of Squared Errors = 78.94506582597859

scala> clusters.save(sc, "model")

SLF4J: Failed to load class "org.slf4j.impl.StaticLoggerBinder".

SLF4J: Defaulting to no-operation (NOP) logger implementation

SLF4J: See http://www.slf4j.org/codes.html#StaticLoggerBinder for further
details.
```

One can see that the first center, the one with index 0, has petal length and width of 1.464 and 0.244, which is much shorter than the other two — 5.715 and 2.054, 4.389 and 1.434). The prediction completely matches the first cluster, corresponding to *Iris setosa*, but has a few mispredictions for the other two.

The measure of cluster quality might depend on the (desired) labels if we want to achieve a desired classification result, but since the algorithm has no information about the labeling, a more common measure is the sum of distances from centroids to the points in each of the clusters. Here is a graph of WSSSE, depending on the number of clusters:

```scala
scala> 1.to(10).foreach(i => println("i: " + i + " SSE: " + KMeans.
train(vectors, i, numIterations).computeCost(vectors)))

i: 1 WSSSE: 680.8244

i: 2 WSSSE: 152.3687064773393

i: 3 WSSSE: 78.94506582597859

i: 4 WSSSE: 57.47327326549501

i: 5 WSSSE: 46.53558205128235

i: 6 WSSSE: 38.9647878510374

i: 7 WSSSE: 34.311167589868646

i: 8 WSSSE: 32.607859500805034

i: 9 WSSSE: 28.231729411088438

i: 10 WSSSE: 29.435054384424078
```

As expected, the average distance is decreasing as more clusters are configured. A common method to determine the optimal number of clusters—in our example, we know that there are three types of flowers—is to add a penalty function. A common penalty is the log of the number of clusters as we expect a convex function. What would be the coefficient in front of log? If each vector is associated with its own cluster, the sum of all distances will be zero, so if we would like a metric that achieves approximately the same value at both ends of the set of possible values, 1 to 150, the coefficient should be 680.8244/log(150):

```scala
scala> for (i <- 1.to(10)) println(i + " -> " + ((KMeans.train(vectors,
i, numIterations).computeCost(vectors)) + 680 * scala.math.log(i) /
scala.math.log(150)))

1 -> 680.8244

2 -> 246.436635016484

3 -> 228.03498068120865

4 -> 245.48126639400738

5 -> 264.9805962616268

6 -> 285.48857890531764

7 -> 301.56808340425164

8 -> 315.321639004243

9 -> 326.47262191671723

10 -> 344.87130979355675
```

Here is how the sum of the squared distances with penalty looks as a graph:

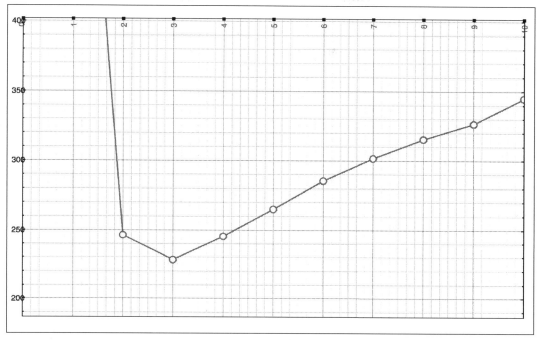

Figure 04-2. The measure of the clustering quality as a function of the number of clusters

Besides k-means clustering, MLlib also has implementations of the following:

- Gaussian mixture
- **Power Iteration Clustering (PIC)**
- **Latent Dirichlet Allocation (LDA)**
- Streaming k-means

The Gaussian mixture is another classical mechanism, particularly known for spectral analysis. Gaussian mixture decomposition is appropriate, where the attributes are continuous and we know that they are likely to come from a set of Gaussian distributions. For example, while the potential groups of points corresponding to clusters may have the average for all attributes, say **Var1** and **Var2**, the points might be centered around two intersecting hyperplanes, as shown in the following diagram:

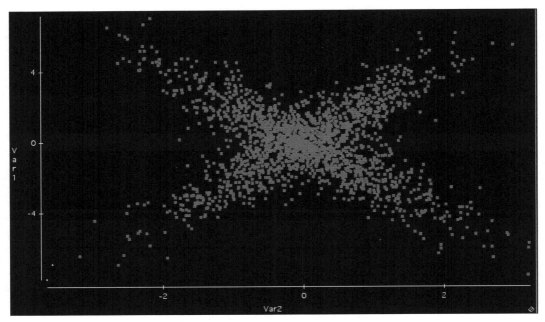

Figure 04-3. A mixture of two Gaussians that cannot be properly described by k-means clustering

This renders the k-means algorithm ineffective as it will not be able to distinguish between the two (of course a simple non-linear transformation such as a distance to one of the hyperplanes will solve the problem, but this is where domain knowledge and expertise as a data scientist are handy).

PIC is using clustering vertices of a graph provided pairwise similarity measures given as edge properties. It computes a pseudo-eigenvector of the normalized affinity matrix of the graph via power iteration and uses it to cluster vertices. MLlib includes an implementation of PIC using GraphX as its backend. It takes an RDD of (srcId, dstId, similarity) tuples and outputs a model with the clustering assignments. The similarities must be non-negative. PIC assumes that the similarity measure is symmetric. A pair (srcId, dstId) regardless of the ordering should appear at most once in the input data. If a pair is missing from the input, their similarity is treated as zero.

LDA can be used for clustering documents based on keyword frequencies. Rather than estimating a clustering using a traditional distance, LDA uses a function based on a statistical model of how text documents are generated.

Finally, streaming k-means is a modification of the k-means algorithm, where the clusters can be adjusted with new batches of data. For each batch of data, we assign all points to their nearest cluster, compute new cluster centers based on the assignment, and then update each cluster parameters using the equations:

$$c_{t+1} = \frac{a \, n_t c_t + n_t' c_t'}{a n_t + n_t'}$$

$$n_{t+1} = a \, n_t + n_t'$$

Here, c_t and c_t' are the centers of from the old model and the ones computed for the new batch and n_t and n_t' are the number of vectors from the old model and for the new batch. By changing the a parameter, we can control how much information from the old runs can influence the clustering—*0* means the new cluster centers are totally based on the points in the new batch, while *1* means that we accommodate for all points that we have seen so far.

k-means clustering has many modifications. For example, k-medians computes the cluster centers as medians of the attribute values, not mean, which works much better for some distributions and with *L1* target distance metric (absolute value of the difference) as opposed to *L2* (the sum of squares). K-medians centers are not necessarily present as a specific point in the dataset. K-medoids is another algorithm from the same family, where the resulting cluster center has to be an actual instance in the input set and we actually do not need to have the global sort, only the pairwise distances between the points. Many variations of the techniques exist on how to choose the original seed cluster centers and converge on the optimal number of clusters (besides the simple log trick I have shown).

Another big class of clustering algorithms is hierarchical clustering. Hierarchical clustering is either done from the top—akin to the decision tree algorithms—or from the bottom; we first find the closest neighbors, pair them, and continue the pairing process up the hierarchy until all records are merged. The advantage of hierarchical clustering is that it can be made deterministic and relatively fast, even though the cost of one iteration in k-means is probably going to be better. However, as mentioned, the unsupervised problem can actually be converted to a density-estimation supervised problem, with all the supervised learning techniques available. So have fun understanding the data!

Problem dimensionality

The larger the attribute space or the number of dimensions, the harder it is to usually predict the label for a given combination of attribute values. This is mostly due to the fact that the total number of possible distinct combinations of attributes increases exponentially with the dimensionality of the attribute space—at least in the case of discrete variables (in case of continuous variables, the situation is more complex and depends on the metrics used), and it is becoming harder to generalize.

The effective dimensionality of the problem might be different from the dimensionality of the input space. For example, if the label depends only on the linear combination of the (continuous) input attributes, the problem is called linearly separable and its internal dimensionality is one—we still have to find the coefficients for this linear combination like in logistic regression though.

This idea is also sometimes referred to as a **Vapnik–Chervonenkis (VC)** dimension of a problem, model, or algorithm—the expressive power of the model depending on how complex the dependencies that it can solve, or shatter, might be. More complex problems require algorithms with higher VC dimensions and larger training sets. However, using an algorithm with higher VC dimension on a simple problem can lead to overfitting and worse generalization to new data.

If the units of input attributes are comparable, say all of them are meters or units of time, PCA, or more generally, kernel methods, can be used to reduce the dimensionality of the input space:

```
$ bin/spark-shell
Welcome to


      ____              __
     / __/__  ___ _____/ /__
    _\ \/ _ \/ _ `/ __/  '_/
   /___/ .__/\_,_/_/ /_/\_\   version 1.6.1
```

/_/

Using Scala version 2.10.5 (Java HotSpot(TM) 64-Bit Server VM, Java 1.8.0_40)

Type in expressions to have them evaluated.

Type :help for more information.

Spark context available as sc.

SQL context available as sqlContext.

```scala
scala> import org.apache.spark.mllib.regression.LabeledPoint
import org.apache.spark.mllib.regression.LabeledPoint
scala> import org.apache.spark.mllib.feature.PCA
import org.apache.spark.mllib.feature.PCA
scala> import org.apache.spark.mllib.util.MLUtils
import org.apache.spark.mllib.util.MLUtils
scala> val pca = new PCA(2).fit(data.map(_.features))
pca: org.apache.spark.mllib.feature.PCAModel = org.apache.spark.mllib.feature.PCAModel@4eee0b1a


scala> val reduced = data.map(p => p.copy(features = pca.transform(p.features)))
reduced: org.apache.spark.rdd.RDD[org.apache.spark.mllib.regression.LabeledPoint] = MapPartitionsRDD[311] at map at <console>:39
scala> reduced.collect().take(10)
res4: Array[org.apache.spark.mllib.regression.LabeledPoint] =
Array((0.0,[-2.827135972679021,-5.641331045573367]), (0.0,[-2.7959524821488393,-5.145166883252959]), (0.0,[-2.621523558165053,-5.173781212203953]), (0.0,[-2.764905900474235,-5.0035994150569865]), (0.0,[-2.7827501159516546,-5.6486482943774305]), (0.0,[-3.231445736773371,-6.062506444034109]), (0.0,[-2.6904524156023393,-5.232619219784292]), (0.0,[-2.8848611044591506,-5.485129079769268]), (0.0,[-2.6233845324473357,-4.743925704477387]), (0.0,[-2.8374984110638493,-5.208032027056245]))


scala> import scala.language.postfixOps
import scala.language.postfixOps


scala> pca pc
res24: org.apache.spark.mllib.linalg.DenseMatrix =
```

```
-0.36158967738145065    -0.6565398832858496

0.08226888989221656     -0.7297123713264776

-0.856572105290527      0.17576740342866465

-0.35884392624821626    0.07470647013502865
```

```scala
scala> import org.apache.spark.mllib.classification.{SVMModel,
SVMWithSGD}
import org.apache.spark.mllib.classification.{SVMModel, SVMWithSGD}
scala> import org.apache.spark.mllib.evaluation.
BinaryClassificationMetrics
import org.apache.spark.mllib.evaluation.BinaryClassificationMetrics
scala> val splits = reduced.randomSplit(Array(0.6, 0.4), seed = 1L)
splits: Array[org.apache.spark.rdd.RDD[org.apache.spark.mllib.regression.
LabeledPoint]] = Array(MapPartitionsRDD[312] at randomSplit at
<console>:44, MapPartitionsRDD[313] at randomSplit at <console>:44)
scala> val training = splits(0).cache()
training: org.apache.spark.rdd.RDD[org.apache.spark.mllib.regression.
LabeledPoint] = MapPartitionsRDD[312] at randomSplit at <console>:44
scala> val test = splits(1)
test: org.apache.spark.rdd.RDD[org.apache.spark.mllib.regression.
LabeledPoint] = MapPartitionsRDD[313] at randomSplit at <console>:44
scala> val numIterations = 100
numIterations: Int = 100
scala> val model = SVMWithSGD.train(training, numIterations)
model: org.apache.spark.mllib.classification.SVMModel = org.apache.
spark.mllib.classification.SVMModel: intercept = 0.0, numFeatures = 2,
numClasses = 2, threshold = 0.0
scala> model.clearThreshold()
res30: model.type = org.apache.spark.mllib.classification.SVMModel:
intercept = 0.0, numFeatures = 2, numClasses = 2, threshold = None
scala> val scoreAndLabels = test.map { point =>
     |    val score = model.predict(point.features)
     |    (score, point.label)
     | }
scoreAndLabels: org.apache.spark.rdd.RDD[(Double, Double)] =
MapPartitionsRDD[517] at map at <console>:54
scala> val metrics = new BinaryClassificationMetrics(scoreAndLabels)
```

```
metrics: org.apache.spark.mllib.evaluation.BinaryClassificationMetrics =
org.apache.spark.mllib.evaluation.BinaryClassificationMetrics@27f49b8c

scala> val auROC = metrics.areaUnderROC()
auROC: Double = 1.0
scala> println("Area under ROC = " + auROC)
Area under ROC = 1.0
```

Here, we reduced the original four-dimensional problem to two-dimensional. Like averaging, computing linear combinations of input attributes and selecting only those that describe most of the variance helps to reduce noise.

Summary

In this chapter, we looked at supervised and unsupervised learning and a few examples of how to run them in Spark/Scala. We considered SVM, logistic regression, decision tree, and k-means in the example of UCI Iris dataset. This is in no way a complete guide, and many other libraries either exist or are being made as we speak, but I would bet that you can solve 99% of the immediate data analysis problems just with these tools.

This will give you a very fast shortcut on how to start being productive with a new dataset. There are many other ways to look at the datasets, but before we get into more advanced topics, let's discuss regression and classification in the next chapter, that is, how to predict continuous and discrete labels.

Regression and Classification 5

In the previous chapter, we got familiar with supervised and unsupervised learning. Another standard taxonomy of the machine learning methods is based on the label is from continuous or discrete space. Even if the discrete labels are ordered, there is a significant difference, particularly how the goodness of fit metrics is evaluated.

In this chapter, we will cover the following topics:

- Learning about the origin of the word regression
- Learning metrics for evaluating the goodness of fit in continuous and discrete space
- Discussing how to write simple code in Scala for linear and logistic regression
- Learning about advanced concepts such as regularization, multiclass predictions, and heteroscedasticity
- Discussing an example of MLlib application for regression tree analysis
- Learning about the different ways of evaluating classification models

What regression stands for?

While the word classification is intuitively clear, the word regression does not seem to imply a predictor of a continuous label. According to the Webster dictionary, regression is:

"a return to a former or less developed state."

It does also mention a special definition for statistics as *a measure of the relation between the mean value of one variable (for example, output) and corresponding values of other variables (for example, time and cost)*, which is actually correct these days. However, historically, the regression coefficient was meant to signify the hereditability of certain characteristics, such as weight and size, from one generation to another, with the hint of planned gene selection, including humans (http://www.amstat.org/publications/jse/v9n3/stanton.html). More specifically, in 1875, Galton, a cousin of Charles Darwin and an accomplished 19th-century scientist in his own right, which was also widely criticized for the promotion of eugenics, had distributed packets of sweet pea seeds to seven friends. Each friend received seeds of uniform weight, but with substantial variation across the seven packets. Galton's friends were supposed to harvest the next generation seeds and ship them back to him. Galton then proceeded to analyze the statistical properties of the seeds within each group, and one of the analysis was to plot the regression line, which always appeared to have the slope less than one—the specific number cited was 0.33 (Galton, F. (1894), Natural Inheritance (5th ed.), New York: Macmillan and Company), as opposed to either *0*, in the case of no correlation and no inheritance; or *1*, in the case the total replication of the parent's characteristics in the descendants. We will discuss why the coefficient of the regression line should always be less than *1* in the presence of noise in the data, even if the correlation is perfect. However, beyond the discussion and details, the origin of the term regression is partly due to planned breeding of plants and humans. Of course, Galton did not have access to PCA, Scala, or any other computing machinery at the time, which might shed more light on the differences between correlation and the slope of the regression line.

Continuous space and metrics

As most of this chapter's content will be dealing with trying to predict or optimize continuous variables, let's first understand how to measure the difference in a continuous space. Unless a drastically new discovery is made pretty soon, the space we live in is a three-dimensional Euclidian space. Whether we like it or not, this is the world we are mostly comfortable with today. We can completely specify our location with three continuous numbers. The difference in locations is usually measured by distance, or a metric, which is a function of a two arguments that returns a single positive real number. Naturally, the distance, $d^2(X,Y)$, between X and Y should always be equal or smaller than the sum of distances between X and Z and Y and Z:

$$d^2(X,Y) \leq d^2(X,Z) + d^2(Y,Z)$$

For any X, Y, and Z, which is also called triangle inequality. The two other properties of a metric is symmetry:

$$d^2(X,Y) = d^2(Y,X)$$

Non-negativity of distance:

$$d^2(X,Y) > 0 \text{ if } X \neq Y$$

$$d^2(X,Y) = 0 \text{ if } X = Y$$

Here, the metric is 0 if, and only if, $X=Y$. The L_2 distance is the distance as we understand it in everyday life, the square root of the sum of the squared differences along each of the dimensions. A generalization of our physical distance is p-norm ($p = 2$ for the L_2 distance):

$$d^p(X,Y) = \left(\sum_{i=1}^{N} |X_i - Y_i|^p \right)^{1/p}$$

Here, the sum is the overall components of the X and Y vectors. If $p=1$, the 1-norm is the sum of absolute differences, or Manhattan distance, as if the only path from point X to point Y would be to move only along one of the components. This distance is also often referred to as L_1 distance:

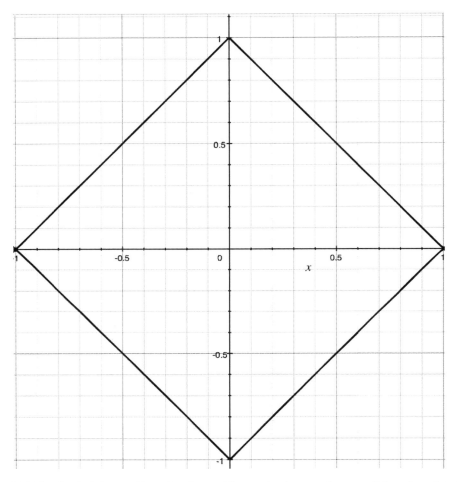

Figure 05-1. The L_1 circle in two-dimensional space (the set of points exactly one unit from the origin (0, 0))

Here is a representation of a circle in a two-dimensional space:

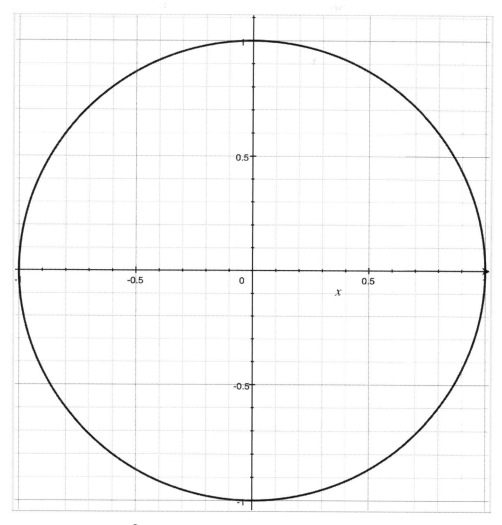

Figure 05-2. L_2 circle in two-dimensional space (the set of points equidistant
from the origin (0, 0)), which actually looks like a circle in our everyday understanding of distance.

Another frequently used special case is L_∞, the limit when $p \to \infty$, which is the maximum deviation along any of the components, as follows:

$$d^\infty(X,Y) = \max_i |X_i - Y_i|$$

The equidistant circle for the L_∞ distance is shown in *Figure 05-3*:

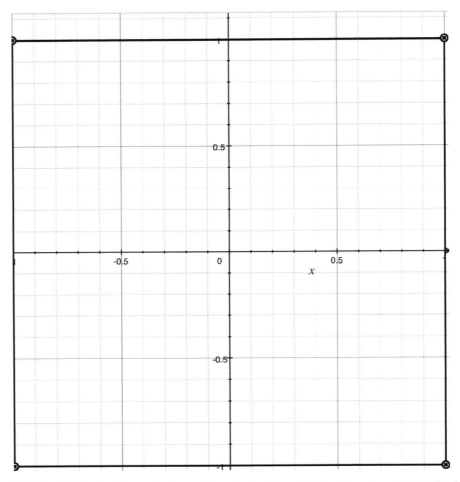

Figure 05-3. L_∞ circle in two-dimensional space (the set of points equidistant from the origin (0, 0)). This is a square as the L_∞ metric is the maximum distance along any of the components.

I'll consider the **Kullback-Leibler (KL)** distance later when I talk about classification, which measures the difference between two probability distributions, but it is an example of distance that is not symmetric and thus it is not a metric.

The metric properties make it easier to decompose the problem. Due to the triangle inequality, one can potentially reduce a difficult problem of optimizing a goal by substituting it by a set of problems by optimizing along a number of dimensional components of the problem separately.

Linear regression

As explained in *Chapter 2, Data Pipelines and Modeling,* most complex machine learning problems can be reduced to optimization as our final goal is to optimize the whole process where the machine is involved as an intermediary or the complete solution. The metric can be explicit, such as error rate, or more indirect, such as **Monthly Active Users (MAU)**, but the effectiveness of an algorithm is finally judged by how it improves some metrics and processes in our lives. Sometimes, the goals may consist of multiple subgoals, or other metrics such as maintainability and stability might eventually be considered, but essentially, we need to either maximize or minimize a continuous metric in one or other way.

For the rigor of the flow, let's show how the linear regression can be formulated as an optimization problem. The classical linear regression needs to optimize the cumulative L_2 error rate:

$$params = \underset{params}{\text{argmin}} \sum_{i=1}^{N}\left(y_i - \hat{y}\right)^2$$

Here, $\hat{y}$ is the estimate given by a model, which, in the case of linear regression, is as follows:

$$\hat{y} = a\,x_i + b$$

(Other potential **loss functions** have been enumerated in *Chapter 3, Working with Spark and MLlib*). As the L_2 metric is a differentiable convex function of a, b, the extreme value can be found by equating the derivative of the cumulative error rate to 0:

$$0 = \frac{\partial d^2}{\partial a} = \frac{\partial d^2}{\partial b}$$

Computing the derivatives is straightforward in this case and leads to the following equation:

$$0 = \frac{\partial \sum_{i=1}^{N}(y_i - ax_i - b)^2}{\partial a} = 2\sum_{i=1}^{N}(ax_i + b - y_i)\ x\_i$$

$$0 = \frac{\partial \sum_{i=1}^{N}(y_i - ax_i - b)^2}{\partial b} = 2\sum_{i=1}^{N}(ax_i + b - y_i)$$

This can be solved to give:

$$a = \frac{avg(x_i y_i) - avg(x_i)avg(y_i)}{avg(x_i^2) - avg(x_i)^2}$$

$$b = avg(y_i) - a\,avg(x_i)$$

Here, *avg()* denotes the average overall input records. Note that if *avg(x)=0* the preceding equation is reduced to the following:

$$a = \frac{avg(xy)}{avg(x^2)}$$

$$b = avg(y)$$

So, we can quickly compute the linear regression coefficients using basic Scala operators (we can always make *avg(x)* to be zero by performing a $x \Rightarrow x - avg(x)$):

```
akozlov@Alexanders-MacBook-Pro$ scala
```

```
Welcome to Scala version 2.11.6 (Java HotSpot(TM) 64-Bit Server VM, Java
1.8.0_40).
```

```
Type in expressions to have them evaluated.
```

```
Type :help for more information.
```

```
scala> import scala.util.Random
```

```
import scala.util.Random

scala> val x = -5 to 5
x: scala.collection.immutable.Range.Inclusive = Range(-5, -4, -3, -2, -1,
0, 1, 2, 3, 4, 5)

scala> val y = x.map(_ * 2 + 4 + Random.nextGaussian)
y: scala.collection.immutable.IndexedSeq[Double] =
Vector(-4.317116812989753, -4.4056031270948015, -2.0376543660274713,
0.0184679796245639, 1.8356532746253016, 3.2322795591658644,
6.821999810895798, 7.7977904139852035, 10.288549406814154,
12.424126535332453, 13.611442206874917)

scala> val a = (x, y).zipped.map(_ * _).sum / x.map(x => x * x).sum
a: Double = 1.9498665133868092

scala> val b = y.sum / y.size
b: Double = 4.115448625564203
```

Didn't I inform you previously that Scala is a very concise language? We just did linear regression with five lines of code, three of which were just data-generation statements.

Although there are libraries written in Scala for performing (multivariate) linear regression, such as Breeze (`https://github.com/scalanlp/breeze`), which provides a more extensive functionality, it is nice to be able to use pure Scala functionality to get some simple statistical results.

Let's look at the problem of Mr. Galton, where he found that the regression line always has the slope of less than one, which implies that we should always regress to some predefined mean. I will generate the same points as earlier, but they will be distributed along the horizontal line with some predefined noise. Then, I will rotate the line by 45 degrees by doing a linear rotation transformation in the *xy*-space. Intuitively, it should be clear that if anything, *y* is strongly correlated with x and absent, the *y* noise should be nothing else but *x*:

```
[akozlov@Alexanders-MacBook-Pro]$ scala
Welcome to Scala version 2.11.7 (Java HotSpot(TM) 64-Bit Server VM, Java
1.8.0_40).
Type in expressions to have them evaluated.
```

```
Type :help for more information.


scala> import scala.util.Random.nextGaussian
import scala.util.Random.nextGaussian


scala> val x0 = Vector.fill(201)(100 * nextGaussian)
x0: scala.collection.immutable.IndexedSeq[Double] =
Vector(168.28831870102465, -40.56031270948016, -3.7654366027471324,
1.84679796245639, -16.43467253746984, -76.77204408341358,
82.19998108957988, -20.22095860147962, 28.854940681415442,
42.41265353324536, -38.85577931250823, -17.320873680820082,
64.19368427702135, -8.173507833084892, -198.6064655461397,
40.73700995880357, 32.36849515282444, 0.07758364225363915,
-101.74032407199553, 34.789280276495646, 46.29624756866302,
35.54024768650289, 24.7867839701828, -11.931948933554782,
72.12437623460166, 30.51440227306552, -80.20756177356768,
134.2380548346385, 96.14401034937691, -205.48142161773896,
-73.48186022765427, 2.7861465340245215, 39.49041527572774,
12.262899592863906, -118.30408039749234, -62.727048950163855,
-40.58557796128219, -23.42...
scala> val y0 = Vector.fill(201)(30 * nextGaussian)
y0: scala.collection.immutable.IndexedSeq[Double] =
Vector(-51.675658534203876, 20.230770706186128, 32.47396891906855,
-29.35028743620815, 26.7392929946199, 49.85681312583139,
24.226102932450917, 31.19021547086266, 26.169544117916704,
-4.51435617676279, 5.6334117227063985, -59.641661744341775,
-48.83082934374863, 29.655750956280304, 26.000847703123497,
-17.43319605936741, 0.8354318740518344, 11.44787080976254,
-26.26312164695179, 88.63863939038357, 45.795968719043785,
88.12442528090506, -29.829048945601635, -1.0417034396751037,
-27.119245702417494, -14.055969115249258, 6.120344305721601,
6.102779172838027, -6.342516875566529, 0.06774080659895702,
46.364626315486014, -38.473161588561, -43.25262339890197,
19.77322736359687, -33.78364440355726, -29.085765762613683,
22.87698648100551, 30.53...
scala> val x1 = (x0, y0).zipped.map((a,b) => 0.5 * (a + b) )
```

```
x1: scala.collection.immutable.IndexedSeq[Double] =
Vector(58.30633008341039, -10.164771001647015, 14.354266158160707,
-13.75174473687588, 5.152310228575029, -13.457615478791094,
53.213042011015396, 5.484628434691521, 27.51224239966607,
18.949148678241286, -16.611183794900917, -38.48126771258093,
7.681427466636357, 10.741121561597705, -86.3028089215081,
11.651906949718079, 16.601963513438136, 5.7627272260080895,
-64.00172285947366, 61.71395983343961, 46.0461081438534,
61.83233648370397, -2.5211324877094174, -6.486826186614943,
22.50256526609208, 8.229216578908131, -37.04360873392304,
70.17041700373827, 44.90074673690519, -102.70684040557,
-13.558616956084126, -17.843507527268237, -1.8811040615871129,
16.01806347823039, -76.0438624005248, -45.90640735638877,
-8.85429574013834, 3.55536787...

scala> val y1 = (x0, y0).zipped.map((a,b) => 0.5 * (a - b) )

y1: scala.collection.immutable.IndexedSeq[Double] =
Vector(109.98198861761426, -30.395541707833143, -18.11970276090784,
15.598542699332269, -21.58698276604487, -63.31442860462248,
28.986939078564482, -25.70558703617114, 1.3426982817493691,
23.463504855004075, -22.244595517607316, 21.160394031760845,
56.51225681038499, -18.9146293946826, -112.3036566246316,
29.08510300908549, 15.7665316393863, -5.68514358375445,
-37.73860121252187, -26.924679556943964, 0.2501394248096176,
-26.292088797201085, 27.30791645789222, -5.445122746939839,
49.62181096850958, 22.28518569415739, -43.16395303964464,
64.06763783090022, 51.24326361247172, -102.77458121216895,
-59.92324327157014, 20.62965406129276, 41.37151933731485,
-3.755163885366482, -42.26021799696754, -16.820641593775086,
-31.73128222114385, -26.9...

scala> val a = (x1, y1).zipped.map(_ * _).sum / x1.map(x => x * x).sum

a: Double = 0.8119662470457414
```

The slope is only `0.81`! Note that if one runs PCA on the `x1` and `y1` data, the first principal component is correctly along the diagonal.

For completeness, I am giving a plot of (*x1, y1*) zipped here:

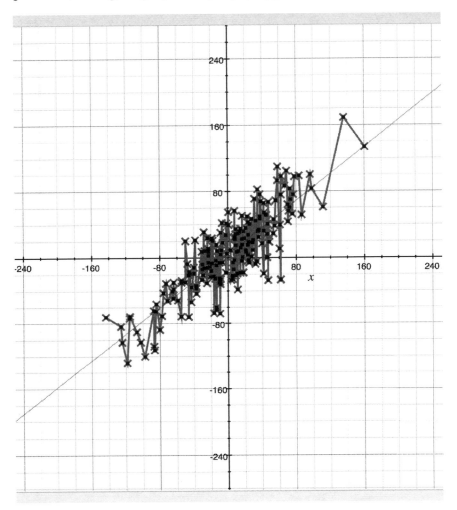

Figure 05-4. The regression curve slope of a seemingly perfectly correlated dataset is less than one. This has to do with the metric the regression problem optimizes (y-distance).

I will leave it to the reader to find the reason why the slope is less than one, but it has to do with the specific question the regression problem is supposed to answer and the metric it optimizes.

Logistic regression

Logistic regression optimizes the logit loss function with respect to w:

$$\ln\left(1 + \exp\left(-yw^{T}x\right)\right)$$

Here, y is binary (in this case plus or minus one). While there is no closed-form solution for the error minimization problem like there was in the previous case of linear regression, logistic function is differentiable and allows iterative algorithms that converge very fast.

The gradient is as follows:

$$\frac{\partial \ln(1 + \exp\left(-yw^{T}x\right))}{\partial w_{j}} = -\frac{\sum_{i=1}^{N} y_{i}x_{ij}}{\left(1 + \exp\left(yw^{T}x\right)\right)}$$

Again, we can quickly concoct a Scala program that uses the gradient to converge to the value, where $\sum_{i=1}^{N} \ln(1 + \exp\left(-y_{i}w^{T}x_{i}\right)) = 0$ (we use the MLlib `LabeledPoint` data structure only for convenience of reading the data):

```
$ bin/spark-shell
Welcome to


      ____              __
     / __/__  ___ _____/ /__
    _\ \/ _ \/ _ `/ __/  '_/
   /___/ .__/\_,_/_/ /_/\_\   version 1.6.1-SNAPSHOT
      /_/


Using Scala version 2.10.5 (Java HotSpot(TM) 64-Bit Server VM, Java
1.8.0_40)
Type in expressions to have them evaluated.
Type :help for more information.
Spark context available as sc.
SQL context available as sqlContext.


scala> import org.apache.spark.mllib.linalg.Vector
```

```
import org.apache.spark.mllib.linalg.Vector

scala> import org.apache.spark.util._
import org.apache.spark.util._

scala> import org.apache.spark.mllib.util._
import org.apache.spark.mllib.util._

scala> val data = MLUtils.loadLibSVMFile(sc, "data/iris/iris-libsvm.txt")
data: org.apache.spark.rdd.RDD[org.apache.spark.mllib.regression.
LabeledPoint] = MapPartitionsRDD[291] at map at MLUtils.scala:112

scala> var w = Vector.random(4)
w: org.apache.spark.util.Vector = (0.9515155226069267,
0.4901713461728122, 0.4308861351586426, 0.8030814804136821)

scala> for (i <- 1.to(10)) println { val gradient = data.map(p => ( -
p.label / (1+scala.math.exp(p.label*(Vector(p.features.toDense.values)
dot w))) * Vector(p.features.toDense.values) )).reduce(_+_); w -= 0.1 *
gradient; w }
(-24.056553839570114, -16.585585503253142, -6.881629923278653,
-0.4154730884796032)
(38.56344616042987, 12.134414496746864, 42.178370076721365,
16.344526911520397)
(13.533446160429868, -4.95558550325314, 34.858370076721364,
15.124526911520398)
(-11.496553839570133, -22.045585503253143, 27.538370076721364,
13.9045269115204)
(-4.002010810020908, -18.501520148476196, 32.506256310962314,
15.455945245916512)
(-4.002011353029471, -18.501520429824225, 32.50625615219947,
15.455945209971787)
(-4.002011896036225, -18.501520711171313, 32.50625599343715,
15.455945174027184)
(-4.002012439041171, -18.501520992517463, 32.506255834675365,
15.455945138082699)
(-4.002012982044308, -18.50152127386267, 32.50625567591411,
15.455945102138333)
```

```
(-4.002013525045636, -18.501521555206942, 32.506255517153384,
15.455945066194088)
```

```
scala> w *= 0.24 / 4
w: org.apache.spark.util.Vector = (-0.24012081150273815,
-1.110091293124165, 1.950375331029203, 0.9273567039716453)
```

The logistic regression was reduced to only one line of Scala code! The last line was to normalize the weights—only the relative values are important to define the separating plane—to compare them to the one obtained with the MLlib in previous chapter.

The **Stochastic Gradient Descent (SGD)** algorithm used in the actual implementation is essentially the same gradient descent, but optimized in the following ways:

- The actual gradient is computed on a subsample of records, which may lead to faster conversion due to less rounding noise and avoid local minima.

- The step—a fixed *0.1* in our case—is a monotonically decreasing function of the iteration as $\frac{1}{\sqrt{(i)}}$, which might also lead to better conversion.

- It incorporates regularization; instead of minimizing just the loss function, you minimize the sum of the loss function, plus some penalty metric, which is a function of model complexity. I will discuss this in the following section.

Regularization

The regularization was originally developed to cope with ill-poised problems, where the problem was underconstrained—allowed multiple solutions given the data—or the data and the solution that contained too much noise (*A.N. Tikhonov, A.S. Leonov, A.G. Yagola. Nonlinear Ill-Posed Problems, Chapman and Hall, London, Weinhe*). Adding additional penalty function that skews a solution if it does not have a desired property, such as the smoothness in curve fitting or spectral analysis, usually solves the problem.

The choice of the penalty function is somewhat arbitrary, but it should reflect a desired skew in the solution. If the penalty function is differentiable, it can be incorporated into the gradient descent process; ridge regression is an example where the penalty is the L_2 metric for the weights or the sum of squares of the coefficients.

MLlib currently implements L_2, L_1, and a mixture thereof called **Elastic Net**, as was shown in *Chapter 3, Working with Spark and MLlib*. The L_1 regularization effectively penalizes for the number of non-zero entries in the regression weights, but has been known to have slower convergence. **Least Absolute Shrinkage and Selection Operator (LASSO)** uses the L_1 regularization.

Another way to reduce the uncertainty in underconstrained problems is to take the prior information that may be coming from domain experts into account. This can be done using Bayesian analysis and introducing additional factors into the posterior probability — the probabilistic rules are generally expressed as multiplication rather than sum. However, since the goal is often minimizing the log likelihood, the Bayesian correction can often be expressed as standard regularizer as well.

Multivariate regression

It is possible to minimize multiple metrics at the same time. While Spark only has a few multivariate analysis tools, other more traditional well-established packages come with **Multivariate Analysis of Variance (MANOVA)**, a generalization of **Analysis of Variance (ANOVA)** method. I will cover ANOVA and MANOVA in *Chapter 7, Working with Graph Algorithms*.

For a practical analysis, we first need to understand if the target variables are correlated, for which we can use the PCA Spark implementation covered in *Chapter 3, Working with Spark and MLlib*. If the dependent variables are strongly correlated, maximizing one leads to maximizing the other, and we can just maximize the first principal component (and potentially build a regression model on the second component to understand what drives the difference).

If the targets are uncorrelated, building a separate model for each of them can pinpoint the important variables that drive either and whether these two sets are disjoint. In the latter case, we could build two separate models to predict each of the targets independently.

Heteroscedasticity

One of the fundamental assumptions in regression approach is that the target variance is not correlated with either independent (attributes) or dependent (target) variables. An example where this assumption might break is counting data, which is generally described by **Poisson distribution**. For Poisson distribution, the variance is proportional to the expected value, and the higher values can contribute more to the final variance of the weights.

While heteroscedasticity may or may not significantly skew the resulting weights, one practical way to compensate for heteroscedasticity is to perform a log transformation, which will compensate for it in the case of Poisson distribution:

$$y' = \log(y)$$

$$var(y') = \frac{var(y)}{y}$$

Some other (parametrized) transformations are the **Box-Cox transformation**:

$$y'_\lambda = \frac{y^\lambda - 1}{\lambda}$$

Here, λ is a parameter (the log transformation is a partial case, where $\lambda = 0$) and Tuckey's lambda transformation (for attributes between *0* and *1*):

$$y'_\lambda = 0.5^L \left(y^L - (1-y)^L \right) / L$$

These compensate for Poisson binomial distributed attributes or the estimates of the probability of success in a sequence of trails with potentially a mix of n Bernoulli distributions.

Heteroscedasticity is one of the main reasons that logistic function minimization works better than linear regression with L_2 minimization in a binary prediction problem. Let's consider discrete labels in more details.

Regression trees

We have seen classification trees in the previous chapter. One can build a recursive split-and-concur structure for a regression problem, where a split is chosen to minimize the remaining variance. Regression trees are less popular than decision trees or classical ANOVA analysis; however, let's provide an example of a regression tree here as a part of MLlib:

```
akozlov@Alexanders-MacBook-Pro$ bin/spark-shell
Welcome to


      ____              __
     / __/__  ___ _____/ /__
    _\ \/ _ \/ _ `/ __/  '_/
   /___/ .__/\_,_/_/ /_/\_\   version 1.6.1-SNAPSHOT
      /_/


Using Scala version 2.10.5 (Java HotSpot(TM) 64-Bit Server VM, Java
1.8.0_40)
Type in expressions to have them evaluated.
Type :help for more information.
Spark context available as sc.
SQL context available as sqlContext.


scala> import org.apache.spark.mllib.tree.DecisionTree
import org.apache.spark.mllib.tree.DecisionTree


scala> import org.apache.spark.mllib.tree.model.DecisionTreeModel
import org.apache.spark.mllib.tree.model.DecisionTreeModel


scala> import org.apache.spark.mllib.util.MLUtils
import org.apache.spark.mllib.util.MLUtils


scala> // Load and parse the data file.


scala> val data = MLUtils.loadLibSVMFile(sc, "data/mllib/sample_libsvm_
data.txt")
```

```
data: org.apache.spark.rdd.RDD[org.apache.spark.mllib.regression.
LabeledPoint] = MapPartitionsRDD[6] at map at MLUtils.scala:112


scala> // Split the data into training and test sets (30% held out for
testing)


scala> val Array(trainingData, testData) = data.randomSplit(Array(0.7,
0.3))
trainingData: org.apache.spark.rdd.RDD[org.apache.spark.mllib.regression.
LabeledPoint] = MapPartitionsRDD[7] at randomSplit at <console>:26
testData: org.apache.spark.rdd.RDD[org.apache.spark.mllib.regression.
LabeledPoint] = MapPartitionsRDD[8] at randomSplit at <console>:26


scala> val categoricalFeaturesInfo = Map[Int, Int]()
categoricalFeaturesInfo: scala.collection.immutable.Map[Int,Int] = Map()


scala> val impurity = "variance"
impurity: String = variance


scala> val maxDepth = 5
maxDepth: Int = 5


scala> val maxBins = 32
maxBins: Int = 32


scala> val model = DecisionTree.trainRegressor(trainingData,
categoricalFeaturesInfo, impurity, maxDepth, maxBins)
model: org.apache.spark.mllib.tree.model.DecisionTreeModel =
DecisionTreeModel regressor of depth 2 with 5 nodes


scala> val labelsAndPredictions = testData.map { point =>
     |    val prediction = model.predict(point.features)
     |    (point.label, prediction)
     | }
labelsAndPredictions: org.apache.spark.rdd.RDD[(Double, Double)] =
MapPartitionsRDD[20] at map at <console>:36


scala> val testMSE = labelsAndPredictions.map{ case(v, p) => math.pow((v
- p), 2)}.mean()
```

```
testMSE: Double = 0.07407407407407407


scala> println(s"Test Mean Squared Error = $testMSE")
Test Mean Squared Error = 0.07407407407407407


scala> println("Learned regression tree model:\n" + model.toDebugString)
Learned regression tree model:
DecisionTreeModel regressor of depth 2 with 5 nodes
  If (feature 378 <= 71.0)
   If (feature 100 <= 165.0)
    Predict: 0.0
   Else (feature 100 > 165.0)
    Predict: 1.0
  Else (feature 378 > 71.0)
   Predict: 1.0
```

The splits at each level are made to minimize the variance, as follows:

$$var(x) = \sum_{k} N_k \left(\sum_{i=1}^{N_k} |x_i - avg(x)|^2 / N_k \right)^{1/2}$$

which is equivalent to minimizing the L_2 distances between the label values and their mean within each leaf summed over all the leaves of the node.

Classification metrics

If the label is discrete, the prediction problem is called classification. In general, the target can take only one of the values for each record (even though multivalued targets are possible, particularly for text classification problems to be considered in *Chapter 6, Working with Unstructured Data*).

If the discrete values are ordered and the ordering makes sense, such as *Bad*, *Worse*, *Good*, the discrete labels can be cast into integer or double, and the problem is reduced to regression (we believe if you are between *Bad* and *Worse*, you are definitely farther away from being *Good* than *Worse*).

A generic metric to optimize is the misclassification rate is as follows:

$$error = 1 - \sum_{i=1}^{N} if \ y_i = \overline{y_i \ then \ 1 \ else \ 0}$$

However, if the algorithm can predict the distribution of possible values for the target, a more general metric such as the KL divergence or Manhattan can be used.

KL divergence is a measure of information loss when probability distribution P_1 is used to approximate probability distribution P_2:

$$d^{KL}(P_1, P_2) = \sum P_1(i) \log\left(P_1(i) \middle/ P_2(i)\right)$$

It is closely related to entropy gain split criteria used in the decision tree induction, as the latter is the sum of KL divergences of the node probability distribution to the leaf probability distribution over all leaf nodes.

Multiclass problems

If the number of possible outcomes for target is larger than two, in general, we have to predict either the expected probability distribution of the target values or at least the list of ordered values—hopefully augmented by a rank variable, which can be used for additional analysis.

While some algorithms, such as decision trees, can natively predict multivalued attributes. A common technique is to reduce the prediction of one of the K target values to *(K-1)* binary classification problems by choosing one of the values as the base and building *(K-1)* binary classifiers. It is usually a good idea to select the most populated level as the base.

Perceptron

In the early days of machine learning, researchers were trying to imitate the functionality of the human brain. At the beginning of the 20th century, people thought that the human brain consisted entirely of cells that are called neurons—cells with long appendages called axons that were able to transmit signals by means of electric impulses. The AI researchers were trying to replicate the functionality of neurons by a perceptron, which is a function that is firing, based on a linearly-weighted sum of its input values:

$$y = \begin{cases} 1 \, if \ w^T x > b \\ 0 \, otherwise \end{cases}$$

This is a very simplistic representation of the processes in the human brain—biologists have since then discovered other ways in which information is transferred besides electric impulses such as chemical ones. Moreover, they have found over 300 different types of cells that may be classified as neurons (`http://neurolex.org/wiki/Category:Neuron`). Also, the process of neuron firing is more complex than just linear transmission of voltages as it involves complex time patterns as well. Nevertheless, the concept turned out to be very productive, and multiple algorithms and techniques were developed for neural nets, or the sets of perceptions connected to each other in layers. Specifically, it can be shown that the neural network, with certain modification, where the step function is replaced by a logistic function in the firing equation, can approximate an arbitrary differentiable function with any desired precision.

MLlib implements **Multilayer Perceptron Classifier (MLCP)** as an `org.apache.spark.ml.classification.MultilayerPerceptronClassifier` class:

```
$ bin/spark-shell
Welcome to


      ____              __
     / __/__  ___ _____/ /__
    _\ \/ _ \/ _ `/ __/  '_/
   /___/ .__/\_,_/_/ /_/\_\   version 1.6.1-SNAPSHOT
      /_/

Using Scala version 2.10.5 (Java HotSpot(TM) 64-Bit Server VM, Java
1.8.0_40)
Type in expressions to have them evaluated.
```

```
Type :help for more information.

Spark context available as sc.

SQL context available as sqlContext.


scala> import org.apache.spark.ml.classification.
MultilayerPerceptronClassifier
import org.apache.spark.ml.classification.MultilayerPerceptronClassifier


scala> import org.apache.spark.ml.evaluation.
MulticlassClassificationEvaluator
import org.apache.spark.ml.evaluation.MulticlassClassificationEvaluator


scala> import org.apache.spark.mllib.util.MLUtils
import org.apache.spark.mllib.util.MLUtils


scala>


scala> val data = MLUtils.loadLibSVMFile(sc, "iris-libsvm-3.txt").toDF()
data: org.apache.spark.sql.DataFrame = [label: double, features: vector]


scala>


scala> val Array(train, test) = data.randomSplit(Array(0.6, 0.4), seed =
13L)
train: org.apache.spark.sql.DataFrame = [label: double, features: vector]
test: org.apache.spark.sql.DataFrame = [label: double, features: vector]


scala> // specify layers for the neural network:


scala> // input layer of size 4 (features), two intermediate of size 5
and 4 and output of size 3 (classes)


scala> val layers = Array(4, 5, 4, 3)
layers: Array[Int] = Array(4, 5, 4, 3)


scala> // create the trainer and set its parameters
```

```
scala> val trainer = new MultilayerPerceptronClassifier().
setLayers(layers).setBlockSize(128).setSeed(13L).setMaxIter(100)
trainer: org.apache.spark.ml.classification.
MultilayerPerceptronClassifier = mlpc_b5f2c25196f9


scala> // train the model


scala> val model = trainer.fit(train)
model: org.apache.spark.ml.classification.
MultilayerPerceptronClassificationModel = mlpc_b5f2c25196f9


scala> // compute precision on the test set


scala> val result = model.transform(test)
result: org.apache.spark.sql.DataFrame = [label: double, features:
vector, prediction: double]


scala> val predictionAndLabels = result.select("prediction", "label")
predictionAndLabels: org.apache.spark.sql.DataFrame = [prediction:
double, label: double]


scala> val evaluator = new MulticlassClassificationEvaluator().
setMetricName("precision")
evaluator: org.apache.spark.ml.evaluation.
MulticlassClassificationEvaluator = mcEval_55757d35e3b0


scala> println("Precision = " + evaluator.evaluate(predictionAndLabels))
Precision = 0.9375
```

Generalization error and overfitting

So, how do we know that the model we have discussed is good? One obvious and ultimate criterion is its performance in practice.

One common problem that plagues the more complex models, such as decision trees and neural nets, is overfitting. The model can minimize the desired metric on the provided data, but does a very poor job on a slightly different dataset in practical deployments, Even a standard technique, when we split the dataset into training and test, the training for deriving the model and test for validating that the model works well on a hold-out data, may not capture all the changes that are in the deployments. For example, linear models such as ANOVA, logistic, and linear regression are usually relatively stable and less of a subject to overfitting. However, you might find that any particular technique either works or doesn't work for your specific domain.

Another case when generalization may fail is time-drift. The data may change over time significantly so that the model trained on the old data no longer generalizes on the new data in a deployment. In practice, it is always a good idea to have several models in production and constantly monitor their relative performance.

I will consider standard ways to avoid overfitting such as hold out datasets and cross-validation in *Chapter 7, Working with Graph Algorithms* and model monitoring in *Chapter 9, NLP in Scala*.

Summary

We now have all the necessary tools to look at more complex problems that are more commonly called the big data problems. Armed with standard statistical algorithms—I understand that I have not covered many details and I am completely ready to accept the criticism—there is an entirely new ground to explore where we do not have clearly defined records, the variables in the datasets may be sparse and nested, and we have to cover a lot of ground and do a lot of preparatory work just to get to the stage where we can apply the standard statistical models. This is where Scala shines best.

In the next chapter, we will look more at working with unstructured data.

6
Working with Unstructured Data

I am very excited to introduce you to this chapter. Unstructured data is what, in reality, makes big data different from the old data, it also makes Scala to be the new paradigm for processing the data. To start with, unstructured data at first sight seems a lot like a derogatory term. Notwithstanding, every sentence in this book is unstructured data: it does not have the traditional record / row / column semantics. For most people, however, this is the easiest thing to read rather than the book being presented as a table or spreadsheet.

In practice, the unstructured data means nested and complex data. An XML document or a photograph are good examples of unstructured data, which have very rich structure to them. My guess is that the originators of the term meant that the new data, the data that engineers at social interaction companies such as Google, Facebook, and Twitter saw, had a different structure to it as opposed to a traditional flat table that everyone used to see. These indeed did not fit the traditional RDBMS paradigm. Some of them can be flattened, but the underlying storage would be too inefficient as the RDBMSs were not optimized to handle them and also be hard to parse not only for humans, but for the machines as well.

A lot of techniques introduced in this chapter were created as an emergency Band-Aid to deal with the need to just process the data.

In this chapter, we will cover the following topics:

- Learning about the serialization, popular serialization frameworks, and language in which the machines talk to each other
- Learning about Avro-Parquet encoding for nested data
- Learning how RDBMs try to incorporate nested structures in modern SQL-like languages to work with them

- Learning how you can start working with nested structures in Scala
- Seeing a practical example of sessionization—one of the most frequent use cases for unstructured data
- Seeing how Scala traits and match/case statements can simplify path analysis
- Learning where the nested structures can benefit your analysis

Nested data

You already saw unstructured data in the previous chapters, the data was an array of **LabeledPoint**, which is a tuple **(label: Double, features: Vector)**. The label is just a number of type **Double**. **Vector** is a sealed trait with two subclasses: **SparseVector** and **DenseVector**. The class diagram is as follows:

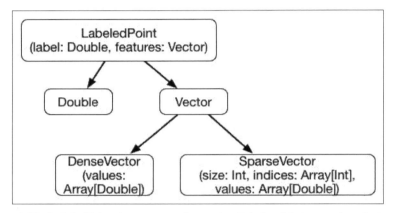

Figure 1: The LabeledPoint class structure is a tuple of label and features, where features is a trait with two inherited subclasses {Dense,Sparse}Vector. DenseVector is an array of double, while SparseVector stores only size and non-default elements by index and value.

Each observation is a tuple of label and features, and features can be sparse. Definitely, if there are no missing values, the whole row can be represented as vector. A dense vector representation requires (*8 x size + 8*) bytes. If most of the elements are missing—or equal to some default value—we can store only the non-default elements. In this case, we would require (*12 x non_missing_size + 20*) bytes, with small variations depending on the JVM implementation. So, the threshold for switching between one or another, from the storage point of view, is when the size is greater than *1.5 x (non_missing_size + 1)*, or if roughly at least 30% of elements are non-default. While the computer languages are good at representing the complex structures via pointers, we need some convenient form to exchange these data between JVMs or machines. First, let's see first how Spark/Scala does it, specifically persisting the data in the Parquet format:

```
akozlov@Alexanders-MacBook-Pro$ bin/spark-shell
Welcome to


      ____              __
     / __/__  ___ _____/ /__
    _\ \/ _ \/ _ `/ __/  '_/
   /___/ .__/\_,_/_/ /_/\_\   version 1.6.1-SNAPSHOT
      /_/


Using Scala version 2.11.7 (Java HotSpot(TM) 64-Bit Server VM, Java
1.8.0_40)
Type in expressions to have them evaluated.
Type :help for more information.
Spark context available as sc.
SQL context available as sqlContext.


scala> import org.apache.spark.mllib.regression.LabeledPoint
import org.apache.spark.mllib.regression.LabeledPoint


scala> import org.apache.spark.mllib.linalg.Vectors
import org.apache.spark.mllib.linalg.Vectors
Wha
scala>


scala> val points = Array(
```

```
    |     LabeledPoint(0.0, Vectors.sparse(3, Array(1), Array(1.0))),
    |     LabeledPoint(1.0, Vectors.dense(0.0, 2.0, 0.0)),
    |     LabeledPoint(2.0, Vectors.sparse(3, Array((1, 3.0)))),
    |     LabeledPoint.parse("(3.0,[0.0,4.0,0.0])"));
pts: Array[org.apache.spark.mllib.regression.LabeledPoint] =
Array((0.0,(3,[1],[1.0])), (1.0,[0.0,2.0,0.0]), (2.0,(3,[1],[3.0])),
(3.0,[0.0,4.0,0.0]))
scala>


scala> val rdd = sc.parallelize(points)
rdd: org.apache.spark.rdd.RDD[org.apache.spark.mllib.regression.
LabeledPoint] = ParallelCollectionRDD[0] at parallelize at <console>:25


scala>


scala> val df = rdd.repartition(1).toDF
df: org.apache.spark.sql.DataFrame = [label: double, features: vector]


scala> df.write.parquet("points")
```

What we did was create a new RDD dataset from command line, or we could use org.apache.spark.mllib.util.MLUtils to load a text file, converted it to a DataFrames and create a serialized representation of it in the Parquet file under the points directory.

What Parquet stands for?

Apache Parquet is a columnar storage format, jointly developed by Cloudera and Twitter for big data. Columnar storage allows for better compression of values in the datasets and is more efficient if only a subset of columns need to be retrieved from the disk. Parquet was built from the ground up with complex nested data structures in mind and uses the record shredding and assembly algorithm described in the Dremel paper (`https://blog.twitter.com/2013/dremel-made-simple-with-parquet`). Dremel/Parquet encoding uses definition/repetition fields to denote the level in the hierarchy the data is coming from, which covers most of the immediate encoding needs, as it is sufficient to store optional fields, nested arrays, and maps. Parquet stores the data by chunks, thus probably the name Parquet, which means flooring composed of wooden blocks arranged in a geometric pattern. Parquet can be optimized for reading only a subset of blocks from disk, depending on the subset of columns to be read and the index used (although it very much depends on whether the specific implementation is aware of these features). The values in the columns can use dictionary and **Run-Length Encoding (RLE)**, which provides exceptionally good compression for columns with many duplicate entries, a frequent use case in big data.

Parquet file is a binary format, but you might look at the information in it using `parquet-tools`, which are downloadable from `http://archive.cloudera.com/cdh5/cdh/5`:

```
akozlov@Alexanders-MacBook-Pro$ wget -O - http://archive.cloudera.com/
cdh5/cdh/5/parquet-1.5.0-cdh5.5.0.tar.gz | tar xzvf -

akozlov@Alexanders-MacBook-Pro$ cd parquet-1.5.0-cdh5.5.0/parquet-tools

akozlov@Alexanders-MacBook-Pro$ tar xvf xvf parquet-1.5.0-cdh5.5.0/
parquet-tools/target/parquet-tools-1.5.0-cdh5.5.0-bin.tar.gz

akozlov@Alexanders-MacBook-Pro$ cd parquet-tools-1.5.0-cdh5.5.0

akozlov@Alexanders-MacBook-Pro $ ./parquet-schema ~/points/*.parquet
message spark_schema {
  optional double label;
  optional group features {
    required int32 type (INT_8);
    optional int32 size;
```

```
    optional group indices (LIST) {
      repeated group list {
        required int32 element;
      }
    }
    optional group values (LIST) {
      repeated group list {
        required double element;
      }
    }
  }
}
```

Let's look at the schema, which is very close to the structure depicted in *Figure 1*: first member is the label of type double and the second and last one is features of composite type. The keyword optional is another way of saying that the value can be null (absent) in the record for one or another reason. The lists or arrays are encoded as a repeated field. As the whole array may be absent (it is possible for all features to be absent), it is wrapped into optional groups (indices and values). Finally, the type encodes whether it is a sparse or dense representation:

```
akozlov@Alexanders-MacBook-Pro $ ./parquet-dump ~/points/*.parquet

row group 0

--------------------------------------------------------------------------
--------------------------------------------------------------------------
-------------------

label:        DOUBLE GZIP DO:0 FPO:4 SZ:78/79/1.01 VC:4 ENC:BIT_
PACKED,PLAIN,RLE

features:

.type:        INT32 GZIP DO:0 FPO:82 SZ:101/63/0.62 VC:4 ENC:BIT_
PACKED,PLAIN_DICTIONARY,RLE

.size:        INT32 GZIP DO:0 FPO:183 SZ:97/59/0.61 VC:4 ENC:BIT_
PACKED,PLAIN_DICTIONARY,RLE

.indices:

..list:

...element:  INT32 GZIP DO:0 FPO:280 SZ:100/65/0.65 VC:4 ENC:PLAIN_
DICTIONARY,RLE

.values:

..list:
```

```
...element:  DOUBLE GZIP DO:0 FPO:380 SZ:125/111/0.89 VC:8 ENC:PLAIN_
DICTIONARY,RLE


     label TV=4 RL=0 DL=1
     ------------------------------------------------------------------
------------------------------------------------------------------------
--------------------
     page 0:                                        DLE:RLE RLE:BIT_
PACKED VLE:PLAIN SZ:38 VC:4


     features.type TV=4 RL=0 DL=1 DS:             2 DE:PLAIN_
DICTIONARY
     ------------------------------------------------------------------
------------------------------------------------------------------------
--------------------
     page 0:                                        DLE:RLE RLE:BIT_
PACKED VLE:PLAIN_DICTIONARY SZ:9 VC:4


     features.size TV=4 RL=0 DL=2 DS:             1 DE:PLAIN_
DICTIONARY
     ------------------------------------------------------------------
------------------------------------------------------------------------
--------------------
     page 0:                                        DLE:RLE RLE:BIT_
PACKED VLE:PLAIN_DICTIONARY SZ:9 VC:4


     features.indices.list.element TV=4 RL=1 DL=3 DS: 1 DE:PLAIN_
DICTIONARY
     ------------------------------------------------------------------
------------------------------------------------------------------------
--------------------
     page 0:                                        DLE:RLE RLE:RLE
VLE:PLAIN_DICTIONARY SZ:15 VC:4


     features.values.list.element TV=8 RL=1 DL=3 DS:  5 DE:PLAIN_
DICTIONARY
     ------------------------------------------------------------------
------------------------------------------------------------------------
--------------------
```

```
      page 0:                                          DLE:RLE RLE:RLE
VLE:PLAIN_DICTIONARY SZ:17 VC:8


DOUBLE label
------------------------------------------------------------------------
------------------------------------------------------------------------
-------------------
*** row group 1 of 1, values 1 to 4 ***
value 1: R:0 D:1 V:0.0
value 2: R:0 D:1 V:1.0
value 3: R:0 D:1 V:2.0
value 4: R:0 D:1 V:3.0


INT32 features.type
------------------------------------------------------------------------
------------------------------------------------------------------------
-------------------
*** row group 1 of 1, values 1 to 4 ***
value 1: R:0 D:1 V:0
value 2: R:0 D:1 V:1
value 3: R:0 D:1 V:0
value 4: R:0 D:1 V:1


INT32 features.size
------------------------------------------------------------------------
------------------------------------------------------------------------
-------------------
*** row group 1 of 1, values 1 to 4 ***
value 1: R:0 D:2 V:3
value 2: R:0 D:1 V:<null>
value 3: R:0 D:2 V:3
value 4: R:0 D:1 V:<null>


INT32 features.indices.list.element
------------------------------------------------------------------------
------------------------------------------------------------------------
-------------------
*** row group 1 of 1, values 1 to 4 ***
```

```
value 1: R:0 D:3 V:1
value 2: R:0 D:1 V:<null>
value 3: R:0 D:3 V:1
value 4: R:0 D:1 V:<null>


DOUBLE features.values.list.element
---------------------------------------------------------------------------
---------------------------------------------------------------------------
-------------------
*** row group 1 of 1, values 1 to 8 ***
value 1: R:0 D:3 V:1.0
value 2: R:0 D:3 V:0.0
value 3: R:1 D:3 V:2.0
value 4: R:1 D:3 V:0.0
value 5: R:0 D:3 V:3.0
value 6: R:0 D:3 V:0.0
value 7: R:1 D:3 V:4.0
value 8: R:1 D:3 V:0.0
```

You are probably a bit confused about the R: and D: in the output. These are the repetition and definition levels as described in the Dremel paper and they are necessary to efficiently encode the values in the nested structures. Only repeated fields increment the repetition level and only non-required fields increment the definition level. Drop in R signifies the end of the list(array). For every non-required level in the hierarchy tree, one needs a new definition level. Repetition and definition level values are small by design and can be efficiently stored in a serialized form.

What is best, if there are many duplicate entries, they will all be placed together. The case for which the compression algorithm (by default, it is gzip) are optimized. Parquet also implements other algorithms exploiting repeated values such as dictionary encoding or RLE compression.

This is a simple and efficient serialization out of the box. We have been able to write a set of complex objects to a file, each column stored in a separate block, representing all values in the records and nested structures.

Let's now read the file and recover RDD. The Parquet format does not know anything about the LabeledPoint class, so we'll have to do some typecasting and trickery here. When we read the file, we'll see a collection of org.apache.spark.sql.Row:

```
akozlov@Alexanders-MacBook-Pro$ bin/spark-shell
Welcome to
      ____              __
     / __/__  ___ _____/ /__
    _\ \/ _ \/ _ `/ __/  '_/
   /___/ .__/\_,_/_/ /_/\_\   version 1.6.1-SNAPSHOT
      /_/

Using Scala version 2.11.7 (Java HotSpot(TM) 64-Bit Server VM, Java
1.8.0_40)
Type in expressions to have them evaluated.
Type :help for more information.
Spark context available as sc.
SQL context available as sqlContext.


scala> val df = sqlContext.read.parquet("points")
df: org.apache.spark.sql.DataFrame = [label: double, features: vector]


scala> val df = sqlContext.read.parquet("points").collect
df: Array[org.apache.spark.sql.Row] = Array([0.0,(3,[1],[1.0])],
[1.0,[0.0,2.0,0.0]], [2.0,(3,[1],[3.0])], [3.0,[0.0,4.0,0.0]])


scala> val rdd = df.map(x => LabeledPoint(x(0).asInstanceOf[scala.
Double], x(1).asInstanceOf[org.apache.spark.mllib.linalg.Vector]))
rdd: org.apache.spark.rdd.RDD[org.apache.spark.mllib.regression.
LabeledPoint] = MapPartitionsRDD[16] at map at <console>:25


scala> rdd.collect
res12: Array[org.apache.spark.mllib.regression.LabeledPoint] =
Array((0.0,(3,[1],[1.0])), (1.0,[0.0,2.0,0.0]), (2.0,(3,[1],[3.0])),
(3.0,[0.0,4.0,0.0]))


scala> rdd.filter(_.features(1) <= 2).collect
res13: Array[org.apache.spark.mllib.regression.LabeledPoint] =
Array((0.0,(3,[1],[1.0])), (1.0,[0.0,2.0,0.0]))
```

Personally, I think that this is pretty cool: without any compilation, we can encode and decide complex objects. One can easily create their own objects in REPL. Let's consider that we want to track user's behavior on the web:

```
akozlov@Alexanders-MacBook-Pro$ bin/spark-shell
Welcome to


      ____              __
     / __/__  ___ _____/ /__
    _\ \/ _ \/ _ `/ __/  '_/
   /___/ .__/\_,_/_/ /_/\_\   version 1.6.1-SNAPSHOT
      /_/


Using Scala version 2.11.7 (Java HotSpot(TM) 64-Bit Server VM, Java
1.8.0_40)
Type in expressions to have them evaluated.
Type :help for more information.
Spark context available as sc.
SQL context available as sqlContext.


scala> case class Person(id: String, visits: Array[String]) { override
def toString: String = { val vsts = visits.mkString(","); s"($id ->
$vsts)" } }
defined class Person


scala> val p1 = Person("Phil", Array("http://www.google.com", "http://
www.facebook.com", "http://www.linkedin.com", "http://www.homedepot.
com"))

p1: Person = (Phil -> http://www.google.com,http://www.facebook.
com,http://www.linkedin.com,http://www.homedepot.com)


scala> val p2 = Person("Emily", Array("http://www.victoriassecret.com",
"http://www.pacsun.com", "http://www.abercrombie.com/shop/us", "http://
www.orvis.com"))

p2: Person = (Emily -> http://www.victoriassecret.com,http://www.pacsun.
com,http://www.abercrombie.com/shop/us,http://www.orvis.com)


scala> sc.parallelize(Array(p1,p2)).repartition(1).toDF.write.
parquet("history")


scala> import scala.collection.mutable.WrappedArray
```

```
import scala.collection.mutable.WrappedArray


scala> val df = sqlContext.read.parquet("history")
df: org.apache.spark.sql.DataFrame = [id: string, visits: array<string>]


scala> val rdd = df.map(x => Person(x(0).asInstanceOf[String], x(1).asIns
tanceOf[WrappedArray[String]].toArray[String]))
rdd: org.apache.spark.rdd.RDD[Person] = MapPartitionsRDD[27] at map at
<console>:28


scala> rdd.collect
res9: Array[Person] = Array((Phil -> http://www.google.com,http://www.
facebook.com,http://www.linkedin.com,http://www.homedepot.com), (Emily
-> http://www.victoriassecret.com,http://www.pacsun.com,http://www.
abercrombie.com/shop/us,http://www.orvis.com))
```

As a matter of good practice, we need to register the newly created classes with the `Kryo serializer`—Spark will use another serialization mechanism to pass the objects between tasks and executors. If the class is not registered, Spark will use default Java serialization, which might be up to *10 x* slower:

```
scala> :paste
// Entering paste mode (ctrl-D to finish)


import com.esotericsoftware.kryo.Kryo
import org.apache.spark.serializer.{KryoSerializer, KryoRegistrator}


class MyKryoRegistrator extends KryoRegistrator {
  override def registerClasses(kryo: Kryo) {
    kryo.register(classOf[Person])
  }
}


object MyKryoRegistrator {
  def register(conf: org.apache.spark.SparkConf) {
    conf.set("spark.serializer", classOf[KryoSerializer].getName)
    conf.set("spark.kryo.registrator", classOf[MyKryoRegistrator].
getName)
  }
```

```
}
^D
```

```
// Exiting paste mode, now interpreting.
```

```
import com.esotericsoftware.kryo.Kryo
import org.apache.spark.serializer.{KryoSerializer, KryoRegistrator}
defined class MyKryoRegistrator
defined module MyKryoRegistrator
```

```
scala>
```

If you are deploying the code on a cluster, the recommendation is to put this code in a jar on the classpath.

I've certainly seen examples of up to 10 level deep nesting in production. Although this might be an overkill for performance reasons, nesting is required in more and more production business use cases. Before we go into the specifics of constructing a nested object in the example of sessionization, let's get an overview of serialization in general.

Other serialization formats

I do recommend the Parquet format for storing the data. However, for completeness, I need to at least mention other serialization formats, some of them like Kryo will be used implicitly for you during Spark computations without your knowledge and there is obviously a default Java serialization.

Object-oriented approach versus functional approach

Objects in object-oriented approach are characterized by state and behavior. Objects are the cornerstone of object-oriented programming. A class is a template for objects with fields that represent the state, and methods that may represent the behavior. Abstract method implementation may depend on the instance of the class. In functional approach, the state is usually frowned upon; in pure programming languages, there should be no state, no side effects, and every invocation should return the same result. The behaviors may be expressed though additional function parameters and higher order functions (functions over functions, such as currying), but should be explicit unlike the abstract methods. Since Scala is a mix of object-oriented and functional language, some of the preceding constraints are violated, but this does not mean that you have to use them unless absolutely necessary. It is best practice to store the code in jar packages while storing the data, particularly for the big data, separate from code in data files (in a serialized form); but again, people often store data/configurations in jar files, and it is less common, but possible to store code in the data files.

The serialization has been an issue since the need to persist data on disk or transfer object from one JVM or machine to another over network appeared. Really, the purpose of serialization is to make complex nested objects be represented as a series of bytes, understandable by machines, and as you can imagine, this might be language-dependent. Luckily, serialization frameworks converge on a set of common data structures they can handle.

One of the most popular serialization mechanisms, but not the most efficient, is to dump an object in an ASCII file: CSV, XML, JSON, YAML, and so on. They do work for more complex nested data like structures, arrays, and maps, but are inefficient from the storage space perspective. For example, a Double represents a continuous number with 15-17 significant digits that will, without rounding or trivial ratios, take 15-17 bytes to represent in US ASCII, while the binary representation takes only 8 bytes. Integers may be stored even more efficiently, particularly if they are small, as we can compress/remove zeroes.

One advantage of text encoding is that they are much easier to visualize with simple command-line tools, but any advanced serialization framework now comes with a set of tools to work with raw records such as `avro-` or `parquet-tools`.

The following table provides an overview for most common serialization frameworks:

Serialization Format	When developed	Comments
XML, JSON, YAML	This was a direct response to the necessity to encode nested structures and exchange the data between machines.	While grossly inefficient, these are still used in many places, particularly in web services. The only advantage is that they are relatively easy to parse without machines.
Protobuf	Developed by Google in the early 2000s. This implements the Dremel encoding scheme and supports multiple languages (Scala is not officially supported yet, even though some code exists).	The main advantage is that Protobuf can generate native classes in many languages. C++, Java, and Python are officially supported. There are ongoing projects in C, C#, Haskell, Perl, Ruby, Scala, and more. Run-time can call native code to inspect/serialize/deserialize the objects and binary representations.
Avro	Avro was developed by Doug Cutting while he was working at Cloudera. The main objective was to separate the encoding from a specific implementation and language, allowing better schema evolution.	While the arguments whether Protobuf or Avro are more efficient are still ongoing, Avro supports a larger number of complex structures, say unions and maps out of the box, compared to Protobuf. Scala support is still to be strengthened to the production level. Avro files have schema encoded with every file, which has its pros and cons.

Serialization Format	When developed	Comments
Thrift	The Apache Thrift was developed at Facebook for the same purpose Protobuf was developed. It probably has the widest selection of supported languages: C++, Java, Python, PHP, Ruby, Erlang, Perl, Haskell, C#, Cocoa, JavaScript, Node.js, Smalltalk, OCaml, Delphi, and other languages. Again, Twitter is hard at work for making the Thrift code generation in Scala (`https://twitter.github.io/scrooge/`).	Apache Thrift is often described as a framework for cross-language services development and is most frequently used as **Remote Procedure Call** (**RPC**). Even though it can be used directly for serialization/deserialization, other frameworks just happen to be more popular.
Parquet	Parquet was developed in a joint effort between Twitter and Cloudera. Compared to the Avro format, which is row-oriented, Parquet is columnar storage that results in better compression and performance if only a few columns are to be selected. The interval encoding is Dremel or Protobuf-based, even though the records are presented as Avro records; thus, it is often called **AvroParquet**.	Advances features such as indices, dictionary encoding, and RLE compression potentially make it very efficient for pure disk storage. Writing the files may be slower as Parquet requires some preprocessing and index building before it can be committed to the disk.
Kryo	This is a framework for encoding arbitrary classes in Java. However, not all built-in Java collection classes can be serialized.	If one avoids non-serializable exceptions, such as priority queues, Kryo can be very efficient. Direct support in Scala is also under way.

Certainly, Java has a built-in serialization framework, but as it has to support all Java cases, and therefore is overly general, the Java serialization is far less efficient than any of the preceding methods. I have certainly seen other companies implement their own proprietary serialization earlier, which would beat any of the preceding serialization for the specific cases. Nowadays, it is no longer necessary, as the maintenance costs definitely overshadow the converging inefficiency of the existing frameworks.

Hive and Impala

One of the design considerations for a new framework is always the compatibility with the old frameworks. For better or worse, most data analysts still work with SQL. The roots of the SQL go to an influential relational modeling paper (*Codd, Edgar F (June 1970). A Relational Model of Data for Large Shared Data Banks. Communications of the ACM (Association for Computing Machinery) 13 (6): 377–87*). All modern databases implement one or another version of SQL.

While the relational model was influential and important for bringing the database performance, particularly for **Online Transaction Processing** (**OLTP**) to the competitive levels, the significance of normalization for analytic workloads, where one needs to perform aggregations, and for situations where relations themselves change and are subject to analysis, is less critical. This section will cover the extensions of standard SQL language for analysis engines traditionally used for big data analytics: Hive and Impala. Both of them are currently Apache licensed projects. The following table summarizes the complex types:

Type	Hive support since version	Impala support since version	Comments
ARRAY	This is supported since 0.1.0, but the use of non-constant index expressions is allowed only as of 0.14.	This is supported since 2.3.0 (only for Parquet tables).	This can be an array of any type, including complex. The index is int in Hive (bigint in Impala) and access is via array notation, for example, element[1] only in Hive (array.pos and item pseudocolumns in Impala).
MAP	This is supported since 0.1.0, but the use of non-constant index expressions is allowed only as of 0.14.	This is supported since 2.3.0 (only for Parquet tables).	The key should be of primitive type. Some libraries support keys of the string type only. Fields are accessed using array notation, for example, map["key"] only in Hive (map key and value pseudocolumns in Impala).
STRUCT	This is supported since 0.5.0.	This is supported since 2.3.0 (only for Parquet tables).	Access is using dot notation, for example, struct.element.

Type	Hive support since version	Impala support since version	Comments
UNIONTYPE	This is supported since 0.7.0.	This is not supported in Impala.	Support is incomplete: queries that reference UNIONTYPE fields in JOIN (HIVE-2508), WHERE, and GROUP BY clauses will fail, and Hive does not define the syntax to extract the tag or value fields of UNIONTYPE. This means that UNIONTYPEs are effectively look-at-only.

While Hive/Impala tables can be created on top of many underlying file formats (Text, Sequence, ORC, Avro, Parquet, and even custom format) and multiple serializations, in most practical instances, Hive is used to read lines of text in ASCII files. The underlying serialization/deserialization format is LazySimpleSerDe (**Serialization/Deserialization (SerDe)**). The format defines several levels of separators, as follows:

```
row_format
    : DELIMITED [FIELDS TERMINATED BY char [ESCAPED BY char]]
      [COLLECTION ITEMS TERMINATED BY char]
      [MAP KEYS TERMINATED BY char]  [LINES TERMINATED BY char]
      [NULL DEFINED AS char]
```

The default for separators are '\001' or ^A, '\002' or ^B, and '\003' or ^B. In other words, it's using the new separator at each level of the hierarchy as opposed to the definition/repetition indicator in the Dremel encoding. For example, to encode the LabeledPoint table that we used before, we need to create a file, as follows:

```
$ cat data
0^A1^B1^D1.0$
2^A1^B1^D3.0$
1^A0^B0.0^C2.0^C0.0$
3^A0^B0.0^C4.0^C0.0$
```

Download Hive from `http://archive.cloudera.com/cdh5/cdh/5/hive-1.1.0-cdh5.5.0.tar.gz` and perform the follow:

```
$ tar xf hive-1.1.0-cdh5.5.0.tar.gz
$ cd hive-1.1.0-cdh5.5.0
$ bin/hive
...

hive> CREATE TABLE LABELED_POINT ( LABEL INT, VECTOR
UNIONTYPE<ARRAY<DOUBLE>, MAP<INT,DOUBLE>> ) STORED AS TEXTFILE;
OK
Time taken: 0.453 seconds
hive> LOAD DATA LOCAL INPATH './data' OVERWRITE INTO TABLE LABELED_POINT;
Loading data to table alexdb.labeled_point
Table labeled_point stats: [numFiles=1, numRows=0, totalSize=52,
rawDataSize=0]
OK
Time taken: 0.808 seconds
hive> select * from labeled_point;
OK
0   {1:{1:1.0}}
2   {1:{1:3.0}}
1   {0:[0.0,2.0,0.0]}
3   {0:[0.0,4.0,0.0]}
Time taken: 0.569 seconds, Fetched: 4 row(s)
hive>
```

In Spark, select from a relational table is supported via the `sqlContext.sql` method, but unfortunately the Hive union types are not directly supported as of Spark 1.6.1; it does support maps and arrays though. The supportability of complex objects in other BI and data analysis tools still remains the biggest obstacle to their adoption. Supporting everything as a rich data structure in Scala is one of the options to converge on nested data representation.

Sessionization

I will demonstrate the use of the complex or nested structures in the example of sessionization. In sessionization, we want to find the behavior of an entity, identified by some ID over a period of time. While the original records may come in any order, we want to summarize the behavior over time to derive trends.

We already analyzed web server logs in *Chapter 1, Exploratory Data Analysis*. We found out how often different web pages are accessed over a period of time. We could dice and slice this information, but without analyzing the sequence of pages visited, it would be hard to understand each individual user interaction with the website. In this chapter, I would like to give this analysis more individual flavor by tracking the user navigation throughout the website. Sessionization is a common tool for website personalization and advertising, IoT tracking, telemetry, and enterprise security, in fact anything to do with entity behavior.

Let's assume the data comes as tuples of three elements (fields 1, 5, 11 in the original dataset in *Chapter 1, Exploratory Data Analysis*):

```
(id, timestamp, path)
```

Here, id is a unique entity ID, timestamp is an event timestamp (in any sortable format: Unix timestamp or an ISO8601 date format), and path is some indication of the location on the web server page hierarchy.

For people familiar with SQL, sessionization, or at least a subset of it, is better known as a windowing analytics function:

```
SELECT id, timestamp, path
  ANALYTIC_FUNCTION(path) OVER (PARTITION BY id ORDER BY
    timestamp) AS agg
FROM log_table;
```

Here ANALYTIC_FUNCTION is some transformation on the sequence of paths for a given id. While this approach works for a relatively simple function, such as first, last, lag, average, expressing a complex function over a sequence of paths is usually very convoluted (for example, nPath from Aster Data (https://www.nersc.gov/assets/Uploads/AnalyticsFoundation5.0previewfor4.6.x-Guide.pdf)). Besides, without additional preprocessing and partitioning, these approaches usually result in big data transfers across multiple nodes in a distributed setting.

While in a pure functional approach, one would just have to design a function—or a sequence of function applications—to produce the desired answers from the original set of tuples, I will create two helper objects that will help us to simplify working with the concept of a user session. As an additional benefit, the new nested structures can be persisted on a disk to speed up getting answers on additional questions.

Let's see how it's done in Spark/Scala using case classes:

```
akozlov@Alexanders-MacBook-Pro$ bin/spark-shell
Welcome to


    / __/__  ___ _____/ /__
   _\ \/ _ \/ _ `/ __/  '_/
  /___/ .__/\_,_/_/ /_/\_\   version 1.6.1-SNAPSHOT
     /_/


Using Scala version 2.11.7 (Java HotSpot(TM) 64-Bit Server VM, Java
1.8.0_40)
Type in expressions to have them evaluated.
Type :help for more information.
Spark context available as sc.
SQL context available as sqlContext.


scala> :paste
// Entering paste mode (ctrl-D to finish)

import java.io._

// a basic page view structure
@SerialVersionUID(123L)
case class PageView(ts: String, path: String) extends Serializable with
Ordered[PageView] {
  override def toString: String = {
    s"($ts :$path)"
  }
  def compare(other: PageView) = ts compare other.ts
}

// represent a session
```

```
@SerialVersionUID(456L)
case class Session[A  <: PageView](id: String, visits: Seq[A]) extends
Serializable {
  override def toString: String = {
    val vsts = visits.mkString("[", ",", "]")
    s"($id -> $vsts)"
  }
}^D
// Exiting paste mode, now interpreting.


import java.io._
defined class PageView
defined class Session
```

The first class will represent a single page view with a timestamp, which, in this case, is an ISO8601 `String`, while the second a sequence of page views. Could we do it by encoding both members as a `String` with a object separator? Absolutely, but representing the fields as members of a class gives us nice access semantics, together with offloading some of the work that we need to perform on the compiler, which is always nice.

Let's read the previously described log files and construct the objects:

```
scala> val rdd = sc.textFile("log.csv").map(x => { val z =
x.split(",",3); (z(1), new PageView(z(0), z(2))) } ).groupByKey.map( x =>
{ new Session(x._1, x._2.toSeq.sorted) } ).persist
rdd: org.apache.spark.rdd.RDD[Session] = MapPartitionsRDD[14] at map at
<console>:31


scala> rdd.take(3).foreach(println)
(189.248.74.238 -> [(2015-08-23 23:09:16 :mycompanycom>homepa
ge),(2015-08-23 23:11:00 :mycompanycom>homepage),(2015-08-23 23:11:02
:mycompanycom>running:slp),(2015-08-23 23:12:01 :mycompanycom>running
:slp),(2015-08-23 23:12:03 :mycompanycom>running>stories>2013>04>them
ycompanyfreestore:cdp),(2015-08-23 23:12:08 :mycompanycom>running>sto
ries>2013>04>themycompanyfreestore:cdp),(2015-08-23 23:12:08 :mycomp
anycom>running>stories>2013>04>themycompanyfreestore:cdp),(2015-08-23
23:12:42 :mycompanycom>running:slp),(2015-08-23 23:13:25 :mycompanyc
om>homepage),(2015-08-23 23:14:00 :mycompanycom>homepage),(2015-08-23
23:14:06 :mycompanycom:mobile>mycompany photoid>landing),(2015-08-23
23:14:56 :mycompanycom>men>shoes:segmentedgrid),(2015-08-23 23:15:10
:mycompanycom>homepage)])

(82.166.130.148 -> [(2015-08-23 23:14:27 :mycompanycom>homepage)])
```

```
(88.234.248.111 -> [(2015-08-23 22:36:10 :mycompanycom>plus>ho
me),(2015-08-23 22:36:20 :mycompanycom>plus>home),(2015-08-23 22:36:28
:mycompanycom>plus>home),(2015-08-23 22:36:30 :mycompanycom>plus>
onepluspdp>sport band),(2015-08-23 22:36:52 :mycompanycom>onsite
search>results found),(2015-08-23 22:37:19 :mycompanycom>plus>onepluspd
p>sport band),(2015-08-23 22:37:21 :mycompanycom>plus>home),(2015-08-23
22:37:39 :mycompanycom>plus>home),(2015-08-23 22:37:43 :mycompanyc
om>plus>home),(2015-08-23 22:37:46 :mycompanycom>plus>onepluspdp>s
port watch),(2015-08-23 22:37:50 :mycompanycom>gear>mycompany+ sp
ortwatch:standardgrid),(2015-08-23 22:38:14 :mycompanycom>homepa
ge),(2015-08-23 22:38:35 :mycompanycom>homepage),(2015-08-23 22:38:37
:mycompanycom>plus>products landing),(2015-08-23 22:39:01 :mycompanyc
om>homepage),(2015-08-23 22:39:24 :mycompanycom>homepage),(2015-08-23
22:39:26 :mycompanycom>plus>whatismycompanyfuel)])
```

Bingo! We have an RDD of Sessions, one per each unique IP address. The IP `189.248.74.238` has a session that lasted from `23:09:16` to `23:15:10`, and seemingly ended after browsing for men's shoes. The session for IP `82.166.130.148` contains only one hit. The last session concentrated on sports watch and lasted for over three minutes from `2015-08-23 22:36:10` to `2015-08-23 22:39:26`. Now, we can easily ask questions involving specific navigation path patterns. For example, we want analyze all the sessions that resulted in checkout (the path contains `checkout`) and see the number of hits and the distribution of times after the last hit on homepage:

```
scala> import java.time.ZoneOffset
import java.time.ZoneOffset

scala> import java.time.LocalDateTime
import java.time.LocalDateTime

scala> import java.time.format.DateTimeFormatter
import java.time.format.DateTimeFormatter

scala>
scala> def toEpochSeconds(str: String) : Long = { LocalDateTime.
parse(str, DateTimeFormatter.ofPattern("yyyy-MM-dd HH:mm:ss")).
toEpochSecond(ZoneOffset.UTC) }
toEpochSeconds: (str: String)Long

scala> val checkoutPattern = ".*>checkout.*".r.pattern
```

```
checkoutPattern: java.util.regex.Pattern = .*>checkout.*


scala> val lengths = rdd.map(x => { val pths = x.visits.map(y => y.path);
val pchs = pths.indexWhere(checkoutPattern.matcher(_).matches); (x.id,
x.visits.map(y => y.ts).min, x.visits.map(y => y.ts).max, x.visits.
lastIndexWhere(_ match { case PageView(ts, "mycompanycom>homepage")
=> true; case _ => false }, pchs), pchs, x.visits) } ).filter(_._4>0).
filter(t => t._5>t._4).map(t => (t._5 - t._4, toEpochSeconds(t._6(t._5).
ts) - toEpochSeconds(t._6(t._4).ts))))


scala> lengths.toDF("cnt", "sec").agg(avg($"cnt"),min($"cnt"),max($"cnt")
,avg($"sec"),min($"sec"),max($"sec")).show

+-----------------+--------+--------+------------------+--------+-------
-+


|        avg(cnt) |min(cnt)|max(cnt)|
avg(sec)|min(sec)|max(sec)|

+-----------------+--------+--------+------------------+--------+-------
-+

|19.77570093457944|       1|     121|366.06542056074767|      15|
2635|

+-----------------+--------+--------+------------------+--------+-------
-+


scala> lengths.map(x => (x._1,1)).reduceByKey(_+_).sortByKey().collect
res18: Array[(Int, Int)] = Array((1,1), (2,8), (3,2), (5,6), (6,7),
(7,9), (8,10), (9,4), (10,6), (11,4), (12,4), (13,2), (14,3), (15,2),
(17,4), (18,6), (19,1), (20,1), (21,1), (22,2), (26,1), (27,1), (30,2),
(31,2), (35,1), (38,1), (39,2), (41,1), (43,2), (47,1), (48,1), (49,1),
(65,1), (66,1), (73,1), (87,1), (91,1), (103,1), (109,1), (121,1))
```

The sessions last from 1 to 121 hits with a mode at 8 hits and from 15 to 2653 seconds (or about 45 minutes). Why would you be interested in this information? Long sessions might indicate that there was a problem somewhere in the middle of the session: a long delay or non-responsive call. It does not have to be: the person might just have taken a long lunch break or a call to discuss his potential purchase, but there might be something of interest here. At least one should agree that this is an outlier and needs to be carefully analyzed.

Let's talk about persisting this data to the disk. As you've seen, our transformation is written as a long pipeline, so there is nothing in the result that one could not compute from the raw data. This is a functional approach, the data is immutable. Moreover, if there is an error in our processing, let's say I want to change the homepage to some other anchor page, I can always modify the function as opposed to data. You may be content or not with this fact, but there is absolutely no additional piece of information in the result—transformations only increase the disorder and entropy. They might make it more palatable for humans, but this is only because humans are a very inefficient data-processing apparatus.

Why rearranging the data makes the analysis faster?

Sessionization seems just a simple rearranging of data—we just put the pages that were accessed in sequence together. Yet, in many cases, it makes practical data analysis run 10 to 100 times faster. The reason is data locality. The analysis, like filtering or path matching, most often tends to happen on the pages in one session at a time. Deriving user features requires all page views or interactions of the user to be in one place on disk and memory. This often beats other inefficiencies such as the overhead of encoding/decoding the nested structures as this can happen in local L1/L2 cache as opposed to data transfers from RAM or disk, which are much more expensive in modern multithreaded CPUs. This very much depends on the complexity of the analysis, of course.

There is a reason to persist the new data to the disk, and we can do it with either CSV, Avro, or Parquet format. The reason is that we do not want to reprocess the data if we want to look at them again. The new representation might be more compact and more efficient to retrieve and show to my manager. Really, humans like side effects and, fortunately, Scala/Spark allows you to do this as was described in the previous section.

Well, well, well...will say the people familiar with sessionization. This is only a part of the story. We want to split the path sequence into multiple sessions, run path analysis, compute conditional probabilities for page transitions, and so on. This is exactly where the functional paradigm shines. Write the following function:

```
def splitSession(session: Session[PageView]) :
  Seq[Session[PageView]] = { … }
```

Then run the following code:

```
val newRdd = rdd.flatMap(splitSession)
```

Bingo! The result is the session's split. I intentionally left the implementation out; it's the implementation that is user-dependent, not the data, and every analyst might have it's own way to split the sequence of page visits into sessions.

Another use case to apply the function is feature generation for applying machine learning...well, this is already hinting at the side effect: we want to modify the state of the world to make it more personalized and user-friendly. I guess one cannot avoid it after all.

Working with traits

As we saw, case classes significantly simplify handling of new nested data structures that we want to construct. The case class definition is probably the most convincing reason to move from Java (and SQL) to Scala. Now, what about the methods? How do we quickly add methods to a class without expensive recompilation? Scala allows you to do this transparently with traits!

A fundamental feature of functional programming is that functions are a first class citizen on par with objects. In the previous section, we defined the two `EpochSeconds` functions that transform the ISO8601 format to epoch time in seconds. We also suggested the `splitSession` function that provides a multi-session view for a given IP. How do we associate this or other behavior with a given class?

First, let's define a desired behavior:

```
scala> trait Epoch {
     |    this: PageView =>
     |    def epoch() : Long = { LocalDateTime.parse(ts,
DateTimeFormatter.ofPattern("yyyy-MM-dd HH:mm:ss")).
toEpochSecond(ZoneOffset.UTC) }
     | }
defined trait Epoch
```

This basically creates a `PageView`-specific function that converts a string representation for datetime to epoch time in seconds. Now, if we just make the following transformation:

```
scala> val rddEpoch = rdd.map(x => new Session(x.id, x.visits.map(x =>
new PageView(x.ts, x.path) with Epoch)))

rddEpoch: org.apache.spark.rdd.RDD[Session[PageView with Epoch]] =
MapPartitionsRDD[20] at map at <console>:31
```

We now have a new RDD of page views with additional behavior. For example, if we want to find out what is the time spent on each individual page in a session is, we will run a pipeline, as follows:

```
scala> rddEpoch.map(x => (x.id, x.visits.zip(x.visits.tail).map(x =>
(x._2.path, x._2.epoch - x._1.epoch)).mkString("[", ",", "]"))).take(3).
foreach(println)
```

```
(189.248.74.238,[(mycompanycom>homepage,104),(mycompanycom>running:slp,2)
,(mycompanycom>running:slp,59),(mycompanycom>running>stories>2013>04>them
ycompanyfreestore:cdp,2),(mycompanycom>running>stories>2013>04>themycompa
nyfreestore:cdp,5),(mycompanycom>running>stories>2013>04>themycompanyfree
store:cdp,0),(mycompanycom>running:slp,34),(mycompanycom>homepage,43),(my
companycom>homepage,35),(mycompanycom:mobile>mycompany photoid>landing,6)
,(mycompanycom>men>shoes:segmentedgrid,50),(mycompanycom>homepage,14)])
```

```
(82.166.130.148,[])
```

```
(88.234.248.111,[(mycompanycom>plus>home,10),(mycompanycom>plus>home
,8),(mycompanycom>plus>onepluspdp>sport band,2),(mycompanycom>onsite
search>results found,22),(mycompanycom>plus>onepluspdp>sport band,27),(my
companycom>plus>home,2),(mycompanycom>plus>home,18),(mycompanycom>plus>h
ome,4),(mycompanycom>plus>onepluspdp>sport watch,3),(mycompanycom>gear>my
company+ sportwatch:standardgrid,4),(mycompanycom>homepage,24),(mycompany
com>homepage,21),(mycompanycom>plus>products landing,2),(mycompanycom>hom
epage,24),(mycompanycom>homepage,23),(mycompanycom>plus>whatismycompanyfu
el,2)])
```

Multiple traits can be added at the same time without affecting either the original class definitions or original data. No recompilation is required.

Working with pattern matching

No Scala book would be complete without mentioning the match/case statements. Scala has a very rich pattern-matching mechanism. For instance, let's say we want to find all instances of a sequence of page views that start with a homepage followed by a products page—we really want to filter out the determined buyers. This may be accomplished with a new function, as follows:

```
scala> def findAllMatchedSessions(h: Seq[Session[PageView]], s:
Session[PageView]) : Seq[Session[PageView]] = {
    |       def matchSessions(h: Seq[Session[PageView]], id: String, p:
Seq[PageView]) : Seq[Session[PageView]] = {
    |          p match {
    |            case Nil => Nil
    |            case PageView(ts1, "mycompanycom>homepage") ::
PageView(ts2, "mycompanycom>plus>products landing") :: tail =>
    |              matchSessions(h, id, tail).+:(new Session(id, p))
    |            case _ => matchSessions(h, id, p.tail)
    |          }
    |       }
    |     matchSessions(h, s.id, s.visits)
    | }
```

```
findAllSessions: (h: Seq[Session[PageView]], s: Session[PageView])
Seq[Session[PageView]]
```

Note that we explicitly put `PageView` constructors in the case statement! Scala will traverse the `visits` sequence and generate new sessions that match the specified two `PageViews`, as follows:

```
scala> rdd.flatMap(x => findAllMatchedSessions(Nil, x)).take(10).
foreach(println)
```

(88.234.248.111 -> [(2015-08-23 22:38:35 :mycompanycom>homepa
ge),(2015-08-23 22:38:37 :mycompanycom>plus>products landing),(2015-08-23
22:39:01 :mycompanycom>homepage),(2015-08-23 22:39:24 :mycompanycom>homep
age),(2015-08-23 22:39:26 :mycompanycom>plus>whatismycompanyfuel)])

(148.246.218.251 -> [(2015-08-23 22:52:09 :mycompanycom>homepa
ge),(2015-08-23 22:52:16 :mycompanycom>plus>products landing),(2015-08-23
22:52:23 :mycompanycom>homepage),(2015-08-23 22:52:32 :mycompanycom>homep
age),(2015-08-23 22:52:39 :mycompanycom>running:slp)])

(86.30.116.229 -> [(2015-08-23 23:15:00 :mycompanycom>homepa
ge),(2015-08-23 23:15:02 :mycompanycom>plus>products landing),(2015-08-23
23:15:12 :mycompanycom>plus>products landing),(2015-08-23
23:15:18 :mycompanycom>language tunnel>load),(2015-08-23 23:15:23
:mycompanycom>language tunnel>geo selected),(2015-08-23 23:15:24
:mycompanycom>homepage),(2015-08-23 23:15:27 :mycompanycom>homepa
ge),(2015-08-23 23:15:30 :mycompanycom>basketball:slp),(2015-08-23
23:15:38 :mycompanycom>basketball>lebron-10:cdp),(2015-08-23 23:15:50
:mycompanycom>basketball>lebron-10:cdp),(2015-08-23 23:16:05 :my
companycom>homepage),(2015-08-23 23:16:09 :mycompanycom>homepa
ge),(2015-08-23 23:16:11 :mycompanycom>basketball:slp),(2015-08-23
23:16:29 :mycompanycom>onsite search>results found),(2015-08-23 23:16:39
:mycompanycom>onsite search>no results)])

(204.237.0.130 -> [(2015-08-23 23:26:23 :mycompanycom>homepa
ge),(2015-08-23 23:26:27 :mycompanycom>plus>products landing),(2015-08-23
23:26:35 :mycompanycom>plus>fuelband activity>summary>wk)])

(97.82.221.34 -> [(2015-08-23 22:36:24 :mycompanycom>homepa
ge),(2015-08-23 22:36:32 :mycompanycom>plus>products landing),(2015-08-23
22:37:09 :mycompanycom>plus>plus activity>summary>wk),(2015-08-23
22:37:39 :mycompanycom>plus>products landing),(2015-08-23 22:44:17
:mycompanycom>plus>home),(2015-08-23 22:44:33 :mycompanycom>plus>ho
me),(2015-08-23 22:44:34 :mycompanycom>plus>home),(2015-08-23 22:44:36
:mycompanycom>plus>home),(2015-08-23 22:44:43 :mycompanycom>plus>home)])

(24.230.204.72 -> [(2015-08-23 22:49:58 :mycompanycom>homepa
ge),(2015-08-23 22:50:00 :mycompanycom>plus>products landing),(2015-08-23
22:50:30 :mycompanycom>homepage),(2015-08-23 22:50:38 :mycompa
nycom>homepage),(2015-08-23 22:50:41 :mycompanycom>training:c
dp),(2015-08-23 22:51:56 :mycompanycom>training:cdp),(2015-08-23
22:51:59 :mycompanycom>store locator>start),(2015-08-23 22:52:28
:mycompanycom>store locator>landing)])

(62.248.72.18 -> [(2015-08-23 23:14:27 :mycompanycom>homepa
ge),(2015-08-23 23:14:30 :mycompanycom>plus>products landing),(2015-08-23
23:14:33 :mycompanycom>plus>products landing),(2015-08-23
23:14:40 :mycompanycom>plus>products landing),(2015-08-23 23:14:47
:mycompanycom>store homepage),(2015-08-23 23:14:50 :mycompanycom>store
homepage),(2015-08-23 23:14:55 :mycompanycom>men:clp),(2015-08-23
23:15:08 :mycompanycom>men:clp),(2015-08-23 23:15:15 :mycompanyco
m>men:clp),(2015-08-23 23:15:16 :mycompanycom>men:clp),(2015-08-23
23:15:24 :mycompanycom>men>sportswear:standardgrid),(2015-08-23
23:15:41 :mycompanycom>pdp>mycompany blazer low premium vintage
suede men's shoe),(2015-08-23 23:15:45 :mycompanycom>pdp>mycompany
blazer low premium vintage suede men's shoe),(2015-08-23 23:15:45
:mycompanycom>pdp>mycompany blazer low premium vintage suede
men's shoe),(2015-08-23 23:15:49 :mycompanycom>pdp>mycompany
blazer low premium vintage suede men's shoe),(2015-08-23 23:15:50
:mycompanycom>pdp>mycompany blazer low premium vintage suede men's
shoe),(2015-08-23 23:15:56 :mycompanycom>men>sportswear:standardgr
id),(2015-08-23 23:18:41 :mycompanycom>pdp>mycompany bruin low men's
shoe),(2015-08-23 23:18:42 :mycompanycom>pdp>mycompany bruin low
men's shoe),(2015-08-23 23:18:53 :mycompanycom>pdp>mycompany bruin low
men's shoe),(2015-08-23 23:18:55 :mycompanycom>pdp>mycompany bruin
low men's shoe),(2015-08-23 23:18:57 :mycompanycom>pdp>mycompany
bruin low men's shoe),(2015-08-23 23:19:04 :mycompanycom>men>sport
swear:standardgrid),(2015-08-23 23:20:12 :mycompanycom>men>sportsw
ear>silver:standardgrid),(2015-08-23 23:28:20 :mycompanycom>onsite
search>no results),(2015-08-23 23:28:33 :mycompanycom>onsite
search>no results),(2015-08-23 23:28:36 :mycompanycom>pdp>mycompany
blazer low premium vintage suede men's shoe),(2015-08-23 23:28:40
:mycompanycom>pdp>mycompany blazer low premium vintage suede
men's shoe),(2015-08-23 23:28:41 :mycompanycom>pdp>mycompany
blazer low premium vintage suede men's shoe),(2015-08-23 23:28:43
:mycompanycom>pdp>mycompany blazer low premium vintage suede men's
shoe),(2015-08-23 23:28:43 :mycompanycom>pdp>mycompany blazer low premium
vintage suede men's shoe),(2015-08-23 23:29:00 :mycompanycom>pdp:mycompan
yid>mycompany blazer low id shoe)])

(46.5.127.21 -> [(2015-08-23 22:58:00 :mycompanycom>homepage),(2015-08-23
22:58:01 :mycompanycom>plus>products landing)])

(200.45.228.1 -> [(2015-08-23 23:07:33 :mycompanycom>homepa
ge),(2015-08-23 23:07:39 :mycompanycom>plus>products landing),(2015-08-23
23:07:42 :mycompanycom>plus>products landing),(2015-08-23 23:07:45
:mycompanycom>language tunnel>load),(2015-08-23 23:07:59 :mycompanyco
m>homepage),(2015-08-23 23:08:15 :mycompanycom>homepage),(2015-08-23
23:08:26 :mycompanycom>onsite search>results found),(2015-08-23
23:08:43 :mycompanycom>onsite search>no results),(2015-08-23
23:08:49 :mycompanycom>onsite search>results found),(2015-08-23
23:08:53 :mycompanycom>language tunnel>load),(2015-08-23 23:08:55
:mycompanycom>plus>products landing),(2015-08-23 23:09:04 :mycompanycom>h
omepage),(2015-08-23 23:11:34 :mycompanycom>running:slp)])

```
(37.78.203.213 -> [(2015-08-23 23:18:10 :mycompanycom>homepa
ge),(2015-08-23 23:18:12 :mycompanycom>plus>products landing),(2015-08-23
23:18:14 :mycompanycom>plus>products landing),(2015-08-23 23:18:22
:mycompanycom>plus>products landing),(2015-08-23 23:18:25
:mycompanycom>store homepage),(2015-08-23 23:18:31 :mycompanycom>store
homepage),(2015-08-23 23:18:34 :mycompanycom>men:clp),(2015-08-23
23:18:50 :mycompanycom>store homepage),(2015-08-23 23:18:51 :mycompanyc
om>footwear:segmentedgrid),(2015-08-23 23:19:12 :mycompanycom>men>footwe
ar:segmentedgrid),(2015-08-23 23:19:12 :mycompanycom>men>footwear:segmen
tedgrid),(2015-08-23 23:19:26 :mycompanycom>men>footwear>new releases:st
andardgrid),(2015-08-23 23:19:26 :mycompanycom>men>footwear>new releases
:standardgrid),(2015-08-23 23:19:35 :mycompanycom>pdp>mycompany cheyenne
2015 men's shoe),(2015-08-23 23:19:40 :mycompanycom>men>footwear>new
releases:standardgrid)])
```

I leave it to the reader to write a function that also filters only those sessions where the user spent less than 10 seconds before going to the products page. The epoch trait or the previously defined to the `EpochSeconds` function may be useful.

The match/case function can be also used for feature generation and return a vector of features over a session.

Other uses of unstructured data

The personalization and device diagnostic obviously are not the only uses of unstructured data. The preceding case is a good example as we started from structured record and quickly converged on the need to construct an unstructured data structure to simplify the analysis.

In fact, there are many more unstructured data than there are structured; it is just the convenience of having the flat structure for the traditional statistical analysis that makes us to present the data as a set of records. Text, images, and music are the examples of semi-structured data.

One example of non-structured data is denormalized data. Traditionally the record data are normalized mostly for performance reasons as the RDBMSs have been optimized to work with structured data. This leads to foreign key and lookup tables, but these are very hard to maintain if the dimensions change. Denormalized data does not have this problem as the lookup table can be stored with each record — it is just an additional table object associated with a row, but may be less storage-efficient.

Probabilistic structures

Another use case is the probabilistic structures. Usually people assume that answering a question is deterministic. As I showed in *Chapter 2, Data Pipelines and Modeling*, in many cases, the true answer has some uncertainty associated with it. One of the most popular ways to encode uncertainty is probability, which is a frequentist approach, meaning that the simple count of when the answer does happen to be the true answer, divided by the total number of attempts—the probability also can encode our beliefs. I will touch on probabilistic analysis and models in the following chapters, but probabilistic analysis requires storing each possible outcome with some measure of probability, which happens to be a nested structure.

Projections

One way to deal with high dimensionality is projections on a lower dimensional space. The fundamental basis for why projections might work is Johnson-Lindenstrauss lemma. The lemma states that a small set of points in a high-dimensional space can be embedded into a space of much lower dimension in such a way that distances between the points are nearly preserved. We will touch on random and other projections when we talk about NLP in *Chapter 9, NLP in Scala*, but the random projections work well for nested structures and functional programming language, as in many cases, generating a random projection is the question of applying a function to a compactly encoded data rather than flattening the data explicitly. In other words, the Scala definition for a random projection may look like functional paradigm shines. Write the following function:

```
def randomeProjecton(data: NestedStructure) : Vector = { … }
```

Here, `Vector` is in low dimensional space.

The map used for embedding is at least Lipschitz, and can even be taken to be an orthogonal projection.

Summary

In this chapter, we saw examples of how to represent and work with complex and nested data in Scala. Obviously, it would be hard to cover all the cases as the world of unstructured data is much larger than the nice niche of structured row-by-row simplification of the real world and is still under construction. Pictures, music, and spoken and written language have a lot of nuances that are hard to capture in a flat representation.

While for ultimate data analysis, we eventually convert the datasets to the record-oriented flat representation, at least at the time of collection, one needs to be careful to store that data as it is and not throw away useful information that might be contained in data or metadata. Extending the databases and storage with a way to record this useful information is the first step. The next one is to use languages that can effectively analyze this information; which is definitely Scala.

In the next chapter we'll look at somewhat related topic of working with graphs, a specific example of non-structured data.

7
Working with Graph Algorithms

In this chapter, I'll delve into graph libraries and algorithm implementations in Scala. In particular, I will introduce Graph for Scala (`http://www.scala-graph.org`), an open source project that was started in 2011 in the EPFL Scala incubator. Graph for Scala does not support distributed computing yet—the distributed computing aspects of popular graph algorithms is available in GraphX, which is a part of MLlib library that is part of Spark project (`http://spark.apache.org/docs/latest/mllib-guide.html`). Both, Spark and MLlib were started as class projects at UC Berkeley around or after 2009. I considered Spark in *Chapter 3, Working with Spark and MLlib* and introduced an RDD. In GraphX, a graph is a pair of RDDs, each of which is partitioned among executors and tasks, represents vertices and edges in a graph.

In this chapter, we will cover the following topics:

- Configuring **Simple Build Tool** (**SBT**) to use the material in this chapter interactively
- Learning basic operations on graphs supported by Graph for Scala
- Learning how to enforce graph constraints
- Learning how to import/export graphs in JSON
- Performing connected components, triangle count, and strongly connected components running on Enron e-mail data
- Performing PageRank computations on Enron e-mail data
- Learning how to use SVD++

A quick introduction to graphs

What is a graph? A graph is a set of **vertices** where some pairs of these vertices are linked with **edges**. If every vertex is linked with every other vertex, we say the graph is a complete graph. On the contrary, if it has no edges, the graph is said to be empty. These are, of course, extremes that are rarely encountered in practice, as graphs have varying degrees of density; the more edges it has proportional to the number of vertices, the more dense we say it is.

Depending on what algorithms we intend to run on a graph and how dense is it expected to be, we can choose how to appropriately represent the graph in memory. If the graph is really dense, it pays off to store it as a square $N \times N$ matrix, where 0 in the nth row and mth column means that the n vertex is not connected to the m vertex. A diagonal entry expresses a node connection to itself. This representation is called the adjacency matrix.

If there are not many edges and we need to traverse the whole edge set without distinction, often it pays off to store it as a simple container of pairs. This structure is called an **edge list**.

In practice, we can model many real-life situations and events as graphs. We could imagine cities as vertices and plane routes as edges. If there is no flight between two cities, there is no edge between them. Moreover, if we add the numerical costs of plane tickets to the edges, we say that the graph is **weighted**. If there are some edges where only travels in one direction exist, we can represent that by making a graph directed as opposed to an undirected graph. So, for an undirected graph, it is true that the graph is symmetric, that is, if A is connected to B, then B is also connected to A — that is not necessarily true for a directed graph.

Graphs without cycles are called acyclic. Multigraph can contain multiple edges, potentially of different type, between the nodes. Hyperedges can connect arbitrary number of nodes.

The most popular algorithm on the undirected graphs is probably **connected components**, or partitioning of a graph into subgraph, in which any two vertices are connected to each other by paths. Partitioning is important to parallelize the operations on the graphs.

Google and other search engines made PageRank popular. According to Google, PageRank estimates of how important the website is by counting the number and quality of links to a page. The underlying assumption is that more important websites are likely to receive more links from other websites, especially more highly ranked ones. PageRank can be applied to many problems outside of websites ranking and is equivalent to finding eigenvectors and the most significant eigenvalue of the connectivity matrix.

The most basic, nontrivial subgraph, consists of three nodes. Triangle counting finds all the possible fully connected (or complete) triples of nodes and is another well-known algorithm used in community detection and CAD.

A **clique** is a fully connected subgraph. A strongly connected component is an analogous notion for a directed graph: every vertex in a subgraph is reachable from every other vertex. GraphX provides an implementation for both.

Finally, a recommender graph is a graph connecting two types of nodes: users and items. The edges can additionally contain the strength of a recommendation or a measure of satisfaction. The goal of a recommender is to predict the satisfaction for potentially missing edges. Multiple algorithms have been developed for a recommendation engine, such as SVD and SVD++, which are considered at the end of this chapter.

SBT

Everyone likes Scala REPL. REPL is the command line for Scala. It allows you to type Scala expressions that are evaluated immediately and try and explore things. As you saw in the previous chapters, one can simply type `scala` at the command prompt and start developing complex data pipelines. What is even more convenient is that one can press *tab* to have auto-completion, a required feature of any fully developed modern IDE (such as Eclipse or IntelliJ, *Ctrl +.* or *Ctrl + Space*) by keeping track of the namespace and using reflection mechanisms. Why would we need one extra tool or framework for builds, particularly that other builds management frameworks such as Ant, Maven, and Gradle exist in addition to IDEs? As the SBT authors argue, even though one might compile Scala using the preceding tools, all of them have inefficiencies, as it comes to interactivity and reproducibility of Scala builds (*SBT in Action* by *Joshua Suereth* and *Matthew Farwell*, Nov 2015).

One of the main SBT features for me is interactivity and the ability to seamlessly work with multiple versions of Scala and dependent libraries. In the end, what is critical for software development is the speed with which one can prototype and test new ideas. I used to work on mainframes using punch cards, where the programmers were waiting to execute their programs and ideas, sometimes for hours and days. The efficiency of the computers mattered more, as this was the bottleneck. These days are gone, and a personal laptop is probably having more computing power than rooms full of servers a few decades back. To take advantage of this efficiency, we need to utilize human time more efficiently by speeding up the program development cycle, which also means interactivity and more versions in the repositories.

Apart from the ability to handle multiple versions and REPL, SBT's main features are as follows:

- Native support for compiling Scala code and integrating with many test frameworks, including JUnit, ScalaTest, and Selenium
- Build descriptions written in Scala using a DSL
- Dependency management using Ivy (which also supports Maven-format repositories)
- Continuous execution, compilation, testing, and deployment
- Integration with the Scala interpreter for rapid iteration and debugging
- Support for mixed Java/Scala projects
- Support for testing and deployment frameworks
- Ability to complement the tool with custom plugins
- Parallel execution of tasks

SBT is written in Scala and uses SBT to build itself (bootstrapping or dogfooding). SBT became the de facto build tool for the Scala community, and is used by the **Lift** and **Play** frameworks.

While you can download SBT directly from `http://www.scala-sbt.org/download`, the easiest way to install SBT on Mac is to run MacPorts:

```
$ port install sbt
```

You can also run Homebrew:

```
$ brew install sbt
```

While other tools exist to create SBT projects, the most straightforward way is to run the `bin/create_project.sh` script in the GitHub book project repository provided for each chapter:

```
$ bin/create_project.sh
```

This will create main and test source subdirectories (but not the code). The project directory contains project-wide settings (refer to `project/build.properties`). The target will contain compiled classes and build packages (the directory will contain different subdirectories for different versions of Scala, for example, 2.10 and 2.11). Finally, any jars or libraries put into the `lib` directory will be available across the project (I personally recommend using the `libraryDependencies` mechanism in the `build.sbt` file, but not all libraries are available via centralized repositories). This is the minimal setup, and the directory structure may potentially contain multiple subprojects. The Scalastyle plugin will even check the syntax for you (http://www.scalastyle.org/sbt.html). Just add `project/plugin.sbt`:

```
$ cat >> project.plugin.sbt << EOF
addSbtPlugin("org.scalastyle" %% "scalastyle-sbt-plugin" % "0.8.0")
EOF
```

Finally, the SBT creates Scaladoc documentation with the `sdbt doc` command.

> **Blank lines and other settings in build.sbt**
>
> Probably most of the `build.sbt` files out there are double spaced: this is a remnant of old versions. You no longer need them. As of version 0.13.7, the definitions do not require extra lines.
>
> There are many other settings that you can use on `build.sbt` or `build.properties`, the up-to-date documentation is available at http://www.scala-sbt.org/documentation.html.

When run from the command line, the tool will automatically download and use the dependencies, in this case, `graph-{core,constrained,json}` and `lift-json`. In order to run the project, simply type `sbt run`.

In continuous mode, SBT will automatically detect changes to the source file and rerun the command(s). In order to continuously compile and run the code, type `~~ run` after starting REPL with `sbt`.

To get help on the commands, run the following command:

```
$ sbt
 [info] Loading global plugins from /Users/akozlov/.sbt/0.13/plugins
[info] Set current project to My Graph Project (in build file:/Users/akozlov/Scala/graph/)
> help

  help                                    Displays this help message or
prints detailed help on requested commands (run 'help <command>').
```

For example, `sbt package` will build a Java jar, as follows:

```
$ sbt package
[info] Loading global plugins from /Users/akozlov/.sbt/0.13/plugins
[info] Loading project definition from /Users/akozlov/Scala/graph/project
[info] Set current project to My Graph Project (in build file:/Users/
akozlov/Scala/graph/)
[info] Updating {file:/Users/akozlov/Scala/graph/}graph...
[info] Resolving jline#jline;2.12.1 ...
[info] Done updating.
$ ls -1 target/scala-2.11/
classes
my-graph-project_2.11-1.0.jar
```

While SBT will be sufficient for our use even with a simple editor such as **vi** or **Emacs**, the `sbteclipse` project at `https://github.com/typesafehub/sbteclipse` will create the necessary project files to work with your Eclipse IDE.

Graph for Scala

For this project, I will create a `src/main/scala/InfluenceDiagram.scala` file. For demo purpose, I will just recreate the graph from *Chapter 2, Data Pipelines and Modeling*:

```scala
import scalax.collection.Graph
import scalax.collection.edge._
import scalax.collection.GraphPredef._
import scalax.collection.GraphEdge._

import scalax.collection.edge.Implicits._

object InfluenceDiagram extends App {
  var g = Graph[String, LDiEdge](("'Weather'"~+>"'Weather Forecast'")
("Forecast"), ("'Weather Forecast'"~+>"'Vacation Activity'")
("Decision"), ("'Vacation Activity'"~+>"'Satisfaction'")
("Deterministic"), ("'Weather'"~+>"'Satisfaction'")("Deterministic"))
  println(g.mkString(";"))
  println(g.isDirected)
  println(g.isAcyclic)
}
```

The `~+>` operator is used to create a directed labeled edge between two nodes defined in `scalax/collection/edge/Implicits.scala`, which, in our case, are of the `String` type. The list of other edge types and operators is provided in the following table:

The following table shows graph edges from `scalax.collection.edge.Implicits` (from `http://www.scala-graph.org/guides/core-initializing.html`)

Edge Class	Shortcut/Operator	Description
Hyperedges		
HyperEdge	~	hyperedge
WHyperEdge	~%	weighted hyperedge
WkHyperEdge	~%#	key-weighted hyperedge
LHyperEdge	~+	labeled hyperedge
LkHyperEdge	~+#	key-labeled hyperedge
WLHyperEdge	~%+	weighted labeled hyperedge
WkLHyperEdge	~%#+	key-weighted labeled hyperedge
WLkHyperEdge	~%+#	weighted key-labeled hyperedge
WkLkHyperEdge	~%#+#	key-weighted key-labeled hyperedge
Directed hyperedges		
DiHyperEdge	~>	directed hyperedge
WDiHyperEdge	~%>	weighted directed hyperedge
WkDiHyperEdge	~%#>	key-weighted directed hyperedge
LDiHyperEdge	~+>	labeled directed hyperedge
LkDiHyperEdge	~+#>	key-labeled directed hyperedge
WLDiHyperEdge	~%+>	weighted labeled directed hyperedge
WkLDiHyperEdge	~%#+>	key-weighted labeled directed hyperedge
WLkDiHyperEdge	~%+#>	weighted key-labeled directed hyperedge
WkLkDiHyperEdge	~%#+#>	key-weighted key-labeled directed hyperedge
Undirected edges		
UnDiEdge	~	undirected edge
WUnDiEdge	~%	weighted undirected edge
WkUnDiEdge	~%#	key-weighted undirected edge
LUnDiEdge	~+	labeled undirected edge
LkUnDiEdge	~+#	key-labeled undirected edge
WLUnDiEdge	~%+	weighted labeled undirected edge

Edge Class	Shortcut/Operator	Description
WkLUnDiEdge	~%#+	key-weighted labeled undirected edge
WLkUnDiEdge	~%+#	weighted key-labeled undirected edge
WkLkUnDiEdge	~%#+#	key-weighted key-labeled undirected edge
Directed edges		
DiEdge	~>	directed edge
WDiEdge	~%>	weighted directed edge
WkDiEdge	~%#>	key-weighted directed edge
LDiEdge	~+>	labeled directed edge
LkDiEdge	~+#>	key-labeled directed edge
WLDiEdge	~%+>	weighted labeled directed edge
WkLDiEdge	~%#+>	key-weighted labeled directed edge
WLkDiEdge	~%+#>	weighted key-labeled directed edge
WkLkDiEdge	~%#+#>	key-weighted key-labeled directed edge

You saw the power of graph for Scala: the edges can be weighted and we may potentially construct a multigraph (key-labeled edges allow multiple edges for a pair of source and destination nodes).

If you run SBT on the preceding project with the Scala file in the src/main/scala directory, the output will be as follows:

```
[akozlov@Alexanders-MacBook-Pro chapter07(master)]$ sbt

[info] Loading project definition from /Users/akozlov/Src/Book/ml-in-scala/chapter07/project

[info] Set current project to Working with Graph Algorithms (in build file:/Users/akozlov/Src/Book/ml-in-scala/chapter07/)

> run

[warn] Multiple main classes detected.  Run 'show discoveredMainClasses' to see the list


Multiple main classes detected, select one to run:

 [1] org.akozlov.chapter07.ConstranedDAG

 [2] org.akozlov.chapter07.EnronEmail

 [3] org.akozlov.chapter07.InfluenceDiagram
```

```
[4]  org.akozlov.chapter07.InfluenceDiagramToJson
```

```
Enter number: 3
```

```
[info]  Running org.akozlov.chapter07.InfluenceDiagram
'Weather';'Vacation Activity';'Satisfaction';'Weather
Forecast';'Weather'~>'Weather Forecast' 'Forecast;'Weather'~>'S
atisfaction' 'Deterministic;'Vacation Activity'~>'Satisfaction'
'Deterministic;'Weather Forecast'~>'Vacation Activity' 'Decision
```

```
Directed: true
```

```
Acyclic: true
```

```
'Weather';'Vacation Activity';'Satisfaction';'Recommend to a
Friend';'Weather Forecast';'Weather'~>'Weather Forecast' 'Forecast;'Wea
ther'~>'Satisfaction' 'Deterministic;'Vacation Activity'~>'Satisfaction'
'Deterministic;'Satisfaction'~>'Recommend to a Friend'
'Probabilistic;'Weather Forecast'~>'Vacation Activity' 'Decision
```

```
Directed: true
```

```
Acyclic: true
```

If continuous compilation is enabled, the main method will be run as soon as SBT detects that the file has changed (in the case of multiple classes having the main method, SBT will ask you which one to run, which is not great for interactivity; so you might want to limit the number of executable classes).

I will cover different output formats in a short while, but let's first see how to perform simple operations on the graph.

Adding nodes and edges

First, we already know that the graph is directed and acyclic, which is a required property for all decision diagrams so that we know we did not make a mistake. Let's say that I want to make the graph more complex and add a node that will indicate the likelihood of me recommending a vacation in Portland, Oregon to another person. The only thing I need to add is the following line:

```
g += ("'Satisfaction'" ~+> "'Recommend to a Friend'")("Probabilistic")
```

If you have continuous compilation/run enabled, you will immediately see the changes after pressing the **Save File** button:

```
'Weather';'Vacation Activity';'Satisfaction';'Recommend to a
Friend';'Weather Forecast';'Weather'~>'Weather Forecast' 'Forecast;'Wea
ther'~>'Satisfaction' 'Deterministic;'Vacation Activity'~>'Satisfaction'
'Deterministic;'Satisfaction'~>'Recommend to a Friend'
'Probabilistic;'Weather Forecast'~>'Vacation Activity' 'Decision

Directed: true

Acyclic: true
```

Now, if we want to know the parents of the newly introduced node, we can simply run the following code:

```
println((g get "'Recommend to a Friend'").incoming)

Set('Satisfaction'~>'Recommend to a Friend' 'Probabilistic)
```

This will give us a set of parents for a specific node — and thus drive the decision making process. If we add a cycle, the acyclic method will automatically detect it:

```
g += ("'Satisfaction'" ~+> "'Weather'")("Cyclic")
println(g.mkString(";")) println("Directed: " + g.isDirected)
println("Acyclic: " + g.isAcyclic)

'Weather';'Vacation Activity';'Satisfaction';'Recommend to a
Friend';'Weather Forecast';'Weather'~>'Weather Forecast' 'Fo
recast;'Weather'~>'Satisfaction' 'Deterministic;'Vacation
Activity'~>'Satisfaction' 'Deterministic;'Satisfaction'~>'Recommend to
a Friend' 'Probabilistic;'Satisfaction'~>'Weather' 'Cyclic;'Weather
Forecast'~>'Vacation Activity' 'Decision
Directed: true
Acyclic: false
```

Note that you can create the graphs completely programmatically:

```
var n, m = 0; val f = Graph.fill(45){ m = if (m < 9) m + 1 else { n =
if (n < 8) n + 1 else 8; n + 1 }; m ~ n }

println(f.nodes)
println(f.edges)
println(f)

println("Directed: " + f.isDirected)
println("Acyclic: " + f.isAcyclic)

NodeSet(0, 9, 1, 5, 2, 6, 3, 7, 4, 8)
```

```
EdgeSet(9~0, 9~1, 9~2, 9~3, 9~4, 9~5, 9~6, 9~7, 9~8, 1~0, 5~0, 5~1,
5~2, 5~3, 5~4, 2~0, 2~1, 6~0, 6~1, 6~2, 6~3, 6~4, 6~5, 3~0, 3~1, 3~2,
7~0, 7~1, 7~2, 7~3, 7~4, 7~5, 7~6, 4~0, 4~1, 4~2, 4~3, 8~0, 8~1, 8~2,
8~3, 8~4, 8~5, 8~6, 8~7)
Graph(0, 1, 2, 3, 4, 5, 6, 7, 8, 9, 1~0, 2~0, 2~1, 3~0, 3~1, 3~2, 4~0,
4~1, 4~2, 4~3, 5~0, 5~1, 5~2, 5~3, 5~4, 6~0, 6~1, 6~2, 6~3, 6~4, 6~5,
7~0, 7~1, 7~2, 7~3, 7~4, 7~5, 7~6, 8~0, 8~1, 8~2, 8~3, 8~4, 8~5, 8~6,
8~7, 9~0, 9~1, 9~2, 9~3, 9~4, 9~5, 9~6, 9~7, 9~8)
Directed: false
Acyclic: false
```

Here, the element computation provided as the second parameter to the fill method is repeated 45 times (the first parameter). The graph connects every node to all of its predecessors, which is also known as a clique in the graph theory.

Graph constraints

Graph for Scala enables us to set constraints that cannot be violated by any future graph update. This comes in handy when we want to preserve some detail in the graph structure. For example, a **Directed Acyclic Graph (DAG)** should not contain cycles. Two constraints are currently implemented as a part of the scalax. collection.constrained.constraints package—connected and acyclic, as follows:

```
package org.akozlov.chapter07

import scalax.collection.GraphPredef._, scalax.collection.GraphEdge._
import scalax.collection.constrained.{Config, ConstraintCompanion,
Graph => DAG}
import scalax.collection.constrained.constraints.{Connected, Acyclic}

object AcyclicWithSideEffect extends ConstraintCompanion[Acyclic] {
  def apply [N, E[X] <: EdgeLikeIn[X]] (self: DAG[N,E]) =
    new Acyclic[N,E] (self) {
      override def onAdditionRefused(refusedNodes: Iterable[N],
        refusedEdges: Iterable[E[N]],
        graph:          DAG[N,E]) = {
        println("Addition refused: " + "nodes = " + refusedNodes
          + ", edges = " + refusedEdges)
        true
      }
    }
}

object ConnectedWithSideEffect extends ConstraintCompanion[Connected]
{
```

```
def apply [N, E[X] <: EdgeLikeIn[X]] (self: DAG[N,E]) =
  new Connected[N,E] (self) {
    override def onSubtractionRefused(refusedNodes:
      Iterable[DAG[N,E]#NodeT],
      refusedEdges: Iterable[DAG[N,E]#EdgeT],
      graph:        DAG[N,E]) = {
        println("Subtraction refused: " + "nodes = " +
        refusedNodes + ", edges = " + refusedEdges)
        true
      }
    }
}

class CycleException(msg: String) extends
IllegalArgumentException(msg)
object ConstranedDAG extends App {
  implicit val conf: Config = ConnectedWithSideEffect &&
AcyclicWithSideEffect
  val g = DAG(1~>2, 1~>3, 2~>3, 3~>4) // Graph()
  println(g ++ List(1~>4, 3~>1))
  println(g - 2~>3)
  println(g - 2)
  println((g + 4~>5) - 3)
}
```

Here is the command to run the program that tries to add or remove nodes that violate the constraints:

```
[akozlov@Alexanders-MacBook-Pro chapter07(master)]$ sbt "run-main org.
akozlov.chapter07.ConstranedDAG"

[info] Loading project definition from /Users/akozlov/Src/Book/ml-in-
scala/chapter07/project

[info] Set current project to Working with Graph Algorithms (in build
file:/Users/akozlov/Src/Book/ml-in-scala/chapter07/)

[info] Running org.akozlov.chapter07.ConstranedDAG

Addition refused: nodes = List(), edges = List(1~>4, 3~>1)

Graph(1, 2, 3, 4, 1~>2, 1~>3, 2~>3, 3~>4)

Subtraction refused: nodes = Set(), edges = Set(2~>3)

Graph(1, 2, 3, 4, 1~>2, 1~>3, 2~>3, 3~>4)

Graph(1, 3, 4, 1~>3, 3~>4)

Subtraction refused: nodes = Set(3), edges = Set()

Graph(1, 2, 3, 4, 5, 1~>2, 1~>3, 2~>3, 3~>4, 4~>5)

[success] Total time: 1 s, completed May 1, 2016 1:53:42 PM
```

Adding or subtracting nodes that violate one of the constraints is rejected. The programmer can also specify a side effect if an attempt to add or subtract a node that violates the condition is made.

JSON

Graph for Scala supports importing/exporting graphs to JSON, as follows:

```
object InfluenceDiagramToJson extends App {

  val g = Graph[String,LDiEdge](("'Weather'" ~+> "'Weather Forecast'")
("Forecast"), ("'Weather Forecast'" ~+> "'Vacation Activity'")
("Decision"), ("'Vacation Activity'" ~+> "'Satisfaction'")
("Deterministic"), ("'Weather'" ~+> "'Satisfaction'")
("Deterministic"), ("'Satisfaction'" ~+> "'Recommend to a Friend'")
("Probabilistic"))

  import scalax.collection.io.json.descriptor.predefined.{LDi}
  import scalax.collection.io.json.descriptor.StringNodeDescriptor
  import scalax.collection.io.json._

  val descriptor = new Descriptor[String](
    defaultNodeDescriptor = StringNodeDescriptor,
    defaultEdgeDescriptor = LDi.descriptor[String,String]("Edge")
  )

  val n = g.toJson(descriptor)
  println(n)
  import net.liftweb.json._
  println(Printer.pretty(JsonAST.render(JsonParser.parse(n))))
}
```

To produce a JSON representation for a sample graph, run:

```
[kozlov@Alexanders-MacBook-Pro chapter07(master)]$ sbt "run-main org.
akozlov.chapter07.InfluenceDiagramToJson"

[info] Loading project definition from /Users/akozlov/Src/Book/ml-in-
scala/chapter07/project

[info] Set current project to Working with Graph Algorithms (in build
file:/Users/akozlov/Src/Book/ml-in-scala/chapter07/)

[info] Running org.akozlov.chapter07.InfluenceDiagramToJson
{
  "nodes":[["'Recommend to a Friend'"],["'Satisfaction'"],["'Vacation
Activity'"],["'Weather Forecast'"],["'Weather'"]],
```

```
  "edges":[{
    "n1":"'Weather'",
    "n2":"'Weather Forecast'",
    "label":"Forecast"
  },{
    "n1":"'Vacation Activity'",
    "n2":"'Satisfaction'",
    "label":"Deterministic"
  },{
    "n1":"'Weather'",
    "n2":"'Satisfaction'",
    "label":"Deterministic"
  },{
    "n1":"'Weather Forecast'",
    "n2":"'Vacation Activity'",
    "label":"Decision"
  },{
    "n1":"'Satisfaction'",
    "n2":"'Recommend to a Friend'",
    "label":"Probabilistic"
  }]
}
[success] Total time: 1 s, completed May 1, 2016 1:55:30 PM
```

For more complex structures, one might need to write custom descriptors, serializers, and deserializers (refer to http://www.scala-graph.org/api/json/api/#scalax.collection.io.json.package).

GraphX

While graph for Scala may be considered a DSL for graph operations and querying, one should go to GraphX for scalability. GraphX is build on top of a powerful Spark framework. As an example of Spark/GraphX operations, I'll use the CMU Enron e-mail dataset (about 2 GB). The actual semantic analysis of the e-mail content is not going to be important to us until the next chapters. The dataset can be downloaded from the CMU site. It has e-mail from mailboxes of 150 users, primarily Enron managers, and about 517,401 e-mails between them. The e-mails may be considered as an indication of a relation (edge) between two people: Each email is an edge between a source (From:) and a destination (To:) vertices.

Since GraphX requires the data in RDD format, I'll have to do some preprocessing. Luckily, it is extremely easy with Scala — this is why Scala is the perfect language for semi-structured data. Here is the code:

```scala
package org.akozlov.chapter07

import scala.io.Source

import scala.util.hashing.{MurmurHash3 => Hash}
import scala.util.matching.Regex

import java.util.{Date => javaDateTime}

import java.io.File
import net.liftweb.json._
import Extraction._
import Serialization.{read, write}

object EnronEmail {

  val emailRe = """[a-zA-Z0-9_.+\-]+@enron.com""".r.unanchored

  def emails(s: String) = {
    for (email <- emailRe findAllIn s) yield email
  }

  def hash(s: String) = {
    java.lang.Integer.MAX_VALUE.toLong + Hash.stringHash(s)
```

```scala
  }

  val messageRe =
    """(?:Message-ID:\s+)(<[A-Za-z0-9_.+\-@]+>)(?s)(?:.*?)(?m)
      |(?:Date:\s+)(.*?)$(?:.*?)
      |(?:From:\s+)([a-zA-Z0-9_.+\-]+@enron.com)(?:.*?)
      |(?:Subject: )(.*?)$""".stripMargin.r.unanchored

  case class Relation(from: String, fromId: Long, to: String, toId:
Long, source: String, messageId: String, date: javaDateTime, subject:
String)

  implicit val formats = Serialization.formats(NoTypeHints)

  def getFileTree(f: File): Stream[File] =
    f #:: (if (f.isDirectory) f.listFiles().toStream.
flatMap(getFileTree) else Stream.empty)

  def main(args: Array[String]) {
    getFileTree(new File(args(0))).par.map {
      file => {
        "\\.$".r findFirstIn file.getName match {
          case Some(x) =>
          try {
            val src = Source.fromFile(file, "us-ascii")
            val message = try src.mkString finally src.close()
            message match {
              case messageRe(messageId, date, from , subject) =>
              val fromLower = from.toLowerCase
              for (to <- emails(message).filter(_ !=
                fromLower).toList.distinct)
              println(write(Relation(fromLower, hash(fromLower),
                to, hash(to), file.toString, messageId, new
                javaDateTime(date), subject)))
              case _ =>
            }
          } catch {
            case e: Exception => System.err.println(e)
          }
          case _ =>
        }
      }
    }
  }
}
```

First, we use the `MurmurHash3` class to generate node IDs, which are of type `Long`, as they are required for each node in GraphX. The `emailRe` and `messageRe` are used to match the file content to find the required content. Scala allows you to parallelize the programs without much work.

Note the `par` call on line 50, `getFileTree(new File(args(0))).par.map`. This will make the loop parallel. If processing the whole Enron dataset can take up to an hour even on 3 GHz processor, adding parallelization reduces it by about 8 minutes on a 32-core Intel Xeon E5-2630 2.4 GHz CPU Linux machine (it took 15 minutes on an Apple MacBook Pro with 2.3 GHz Intel Core i7).

Running the code will produce a set of JSON records that can be loaded into Spark (to run it, you'll need to put **joda-time** and **lift-json** library jars on the classpath), as follows:

```
# (mkdir Enron; cd Enron; wget -O - http://www.cs.cmu.edu/~./enron/enron_mail_20150507.tgz | tar xzvf -)
...
# sbt --error "run-main org.akozlov.chapter07.EnronEmail Enron/maildir" > graph.json

# spark --driver-memory 2g --executor-memory 2g
...
scala> val df = sqlContext.read.json("graph.json")
df: org.apache.spark.sql.DataFrame = [[date: string, from: string, fromId: bigint, messageId: string, source: string, subject: string, to: string, toId: bigint]
```

Nice! Spark was able to figure out the fields and types on it's own. If Spark was not able to parse all the records, one would have a `_corrupt_record` field containing the unparsed records (one of them is the `[success]` line at the end of the dataset, which can be filtered out with a `grep -Fv [success]`). You can see them with the following command:

```
scala> df.select("_corrupt_record").collect.foreach(println)
...
```

The nodes (people) and edges (relations) datasets can be extracted with the following commands:

```
scala> import org.apache.spark._
...
scala> import org.apache.spark.graphx._
...
```

```
scala> import org.apache.spark.rdd.RDD

...

scala> val people: RDD[(VertexId, String)] = df.select("fromId", "from").
unionAll(df.select("toId", "to")).na.drop.distinct.map( x => (x.get(0).
toString.toLong, x.get(1).toString))
people: org.apache.spark.rdd.RDD[(org.apache.spark.graphx.VertexId,
String)] = MapPartitionsRDD[146] at map at <console>:28


scala> val relationships = df.select("fromId", "toId", "messageId",
"subject").na.drop.distinct.map( x => Edge(x.get(0).toString.toLong,
x.get(1).toString.toLong, (x.get(2).toString, x.get(3).toString)))
relationships: org.apache.spark.rdd.RDD[org.apache.spark.graphx.
Edge[(String, String)]] = MapPartitionsRDD[156] at map at <console>:28


scala> val graph = Graph(people, relationships).cache
graph: org.apache.spark.graphx.Graph[String,(String, String)] = org.
apache.spark.graphx.impl.GraphImpl@7b59aa7b
```

Node IDs in GraphX

As we saw in Graph for Scala, specifying the edges is sufficient for defining the nodes and the graph. In Spark/GraphX, nodes need to be extracted explicitly, and each node needs to be associated with *n* id of the Long type. While this potentially limits the flexibility and the number of unique nodes, it enhances the efficiency. In this particular example, generating node ID as a hash of the e-mail string was sufficient as no collisions were detected, but the generation of unique IDs is usually a hard problem to parallelize.

The first GraphX graph is ready!! It took a bit more work than Scala for Graph, but now it's totally ready for distributed processing. A few things to note: first, we needed to explicitly convert the fields to Long and String as the Edge constructor needed help in figuring out the types. Second, Spark might need to optimize the number of partitions (likely, it created too many):

```
scala> graph.vertices.getNumPartitions
res1: Int = 200


scala> graph.edges.getNumPartitions
res2: Int = 200
```

To repartition, there are two calls: repartition and coalesce. The latter tries to avoid shuffle, as follows:

```
scala> val graph = Graph(people.coalesce(6), relationships.coalesce(6))
graph: org.apache.spark.graphx.Graph[String,(String, String)] = org.
apache.spark.graphx.impl.GraphImpl@5dc7d016


scala> graph.vertices.getNumPartitions
res10: Int = 6


scala> graph.edges.getNumPartitions
res11: Int = 6
```

However, this might limit parallelism if one performs computations over a large cluster. Finally, it's a good idea to use `cache` method that pins the data structure in memory:

```
scala> graph.cache
res12: org.apache.spark.graphx.Graph[String,(String, String)] = org.
apache.spark.graphx.impl.GraphImpl@5dc7d016
```

It took a few more commands to construct a graph in Spark, but four is not too bad. Let's compute some statistics (and show the power of Spark/GraphX, in the following table:

Computing basic statistics on Enron e-mail graph.

Statistics	Spark command	Value for Enron
Total # of relations (pairwise communications)	`graph.numEdges`	3,035,021
Number of e-mails (message IDs)	`graph.edges.map( e => e.attr._1 ).distinct.count`	371,135
Number of connected pairs	`graph.edges.flatMap( e => List((e.srcId, e.dstId), (e.dstId, e.srcId))). distinct.count / 2`	217,867
Number of one-way communications	`graph.edges.flatMap( e => List((e.srcId, e.dstId), (e.dstId, e.srcId))). distinct.count - graph. edges.map( e => (e.srcId, e.dstId)).distinct.count`	193,183

Statistics	Spark command	Value for Enron
Number of distinct subject lines	`graph.edges.map( e => e.attr._2 ).distinct.count`	110,273
Total # of nodes	`graph.numVertices`	23,607
Number of destination-only nodes	`graph. numVertices - graph. edges.map( e => e.srcId). distinct.count`	17,264
Number of source-only nodes	`graph. numVertices - graph. edges.map( e => e.dstId). distinct.count`	611

Who is getting e-mails?

One of the most straightforward ways to estimate people's importance in an organization is to look at the number of connections or the number of incoming and outgoing communicates. The GraphX graph has built-in `inDegrees` and `outDegrees` methods. To rank the emails with respect to the number of incoming emails, run:

```
scala> people.join(graph.inDegrees).sortBy(_._2._2, ascending=false).
take(10).foreach(println)
(268746271,(richard.shapiro@enron.com,18523))
(1608171805,(steven.kean@enron.com,15867))
(1578042212,(jeff.dasovich@enron.com,13878))
(960683221,(tana.jones@enron.com,13717))
(3784547591,(james.steffes@enron.com,12980))
(1403062842,(sara.shackleton@enron.com,12082))
(2319161027,(mark.taylor@enron.com,12018))
(969899621,(mark.guzman@enron.com,10777))
(1362498694,(geir.solberg@enron.com,10296))
(4151996958,(ryan.slinger@enron.com,10160))
```

To rank the emails with respect to the number of egressing emails, run:

```
scala> people.join(graph.outDegrees).sortBy(_._2._2, ascending=false).
take(10).foreach(println)
(1578042212,(jeff.dasovich@enron.com,139786))
(2822677534,(veronica.espinoza@enron.com,106442))
(3035779314,(pete.davis@enron.com,94666))
(2346362132,(rhonda.denton@enron.com,90570))
(861605621,(cheryl.johnson@enron.com,74319))
```

```
(14078526,(susan.mara@enron.com,58797))

(2058972224,(jae.black@enron.com,58718))

(871077839,(ginger.dernehl@enron.com,57559))

(3852770211,(lorna.brennan@enron.com,50106))

(241175230,(mary.hain@enron.com,40425))
```

...

Let's apply some more complex algorithms to the Enron dataset.

Connected components

Connected components determine whether the graph is naturally partitioned into
several parts. In the Enron relationship graph, this would mean that two or several
groups communicate mostly between each other:

```
scala> val groups = org.apache.spark.graphx.lib.ConnectedComponents.
run(graph).vertices.map(_._2).distinct.cache

groups: org.apache.spark.rdd.RDD[org.apache.spark.graphx.VertexId] =
MapPartitionsRDD[2404] at distinct at <console>:34


scala> groups.count
res106: Long = 18


scala> people.join(groups.map( x => (x, x))).map(x => (x._1, x._2._1)).
sortBy(_._1).collect.foreach(println)

(332133,laura.beneville@enron.com)

(81833994,gpg.me-q@enron.com)

(115247730,dl-ga-enron_debtor@enron.com)

(299810291,gina.peters@enron.com)

(718200627,techsupport.notices@enron.com)

(847455579,paul.de@enron.com)

(919241773,etc.survey@enron.com)

(1139366119,enron.global.services.-.us@enron.com)

(1156539970,shelley.ariel@enron.com)

(1265773423,dl-ga-all_ews_employees@enron.com)

(1493879606,chairman.ees@enron.com)

(1511379835,gary.allen.-.safety.specialist@enron.com)

(2114016426,executive.robert@enron.com)

(2200225669,ken.board@enron.com)
```

```
(2914568776,ge.americas@enron.com)
```

```
(2934799198,yowman@enron.com)
```

```
(2975592118,tech.notices@enron.com)
```

```
(3678996795,mail.user@enron.com)
```

We see 18 groups. Each one of the groups can be counted and extracted by filtering the ID. For instance, the group associated with `etc.survey@enron.com` can be found by running a SQL query on DataFrame:

```
scala> df.filter("fromId = 919241773 or toId = 919241773").select("date",
"from","to","subject","source").collect.foreach(println)
```
```
[2000-09-19T18:40:00.000Z,survey.test@enron.com,etc.survey@enron.com,NO
ACTION REQUIRED - TEST,Enron/maildir/dasovich-j/all_documents/1567.]
```
```
[2000-09-19T18:40:00.000Z,survey.test@enron.com,etc.survey@enron.com,NO
ACTION REQUIRED - TEST,Enron/maildir/dasovich-j/notes_inbox/504.]
```

This group is based on a single e-mail sent on September 19, 2000, from `survey.test@enron.com` to `etc.survey@enron`. The e-mail is listed twice, only because it ended up in two different folders (and has two distinct message IDs). Only the first group, the largest subgraph, contains more than two e-mail addresses in the organization.

Triangle counting

The triangle counting algorithm is relatively straightforward and can be computed in the following three steps:

1. Compute the set of neighbors for each vertex.

2. For each edge, compute the intersection of the sets and send the count to both vertices.

3. Compute the sum at each vertex and divide by two, as each triangle is counted twice.

We need to convert the multigraph to an undirected graph with `srcId < dstId`, which is a precondition for the algorithm:

```
scala> val unedges = graph.edges.map(e => if (e.srcId < e.dstId)
(e.srcId, e.dstId) else (e.dstId, e.srcId)).map( x => Edge(x._1, x._2,
1)).cache
```
```
unedges: org.apache.spark.rdd.RDD[org.apache.spark.graphx.Edge[Int]] =
MapPartitionsRDD[87] at map at <console>:48
```

```
scala> val ungraph = Graph(people, unedges).partitionBy(org.apache.spark.
graphx.PartitionStrategy.EdgePartition1D, 10).cache
```

```
ungraph: org.apache.spark.graphx.Graph[String,Int] = org.apache.spark.
graphx.impl.GraphImpl@77274fff

scala> val triangles = org.apache.spark.graphx.lib.TriangleCount.
run(ungraph).cache

triangles: org.apache.spark.graphx.Graph[Int,Int] = org.apache.spark.
graphx.impl.GraphImpl@6aec6da1

scala> people.join(triangles.vertices).map(t => (t._2._2,t._2._1)).
sortBy(_._1, ascending=false).take(10).foreach(println)
(31761,sally.beck@enron.com)

(24101,louise.kitchen@enron.com)

(23522,david.forster@enron.com)

(21694,kenneth.lay@enron.com)

(20847,john.lavorato@enron.com)

(18460,david.oxley@enron.com)

(17951,tammie.schoppe@enron.com)

(16929,steven.kean@enron.com)

(16390,tana.jones@enron.com)

(16197,julie.clyatt@enron.com)
```

While there is no direct relationship between the triangle count and the importance of people in the organization, the people with higher triangle count arguably are more social—even though a clique or a strongly connected component count might be a better measure.

Strongly connected components

In the mathematical theory of directed graphs, a subgraph is said to be strongly connected if every vertex is reachable from every other vertex. It could happen that the whole graph is just one strongly connected component, but on the other end of the spectrum, each vertex could be its own connected component.

If you contract each connected component to a single vertex, you get a new directed graph that has a property to be without cycles—acyclic.

The algorithm for SCC detection is already built into GraphX:

```scala
scala> val components = org.apache.spark.graphx.lib.
StronglyConnectedComponents.run(graph, 100).cache

components: org.apache.spark.graphx.Graph[org.apache.spark.
graphx.VertexId,(String, String)] = org.apache.spark.graphx.impl.
GraphImpl@55913bc7


scala> components.vertices.map(_._2).distinct.count

res2: Long = 17980


scala> people.join(components.vertices.map(_._2).distinct.map( x => (x,
x))).map(x => (x._1, x._2._1)).sortBy(_._1).collect.foreach(println)

(332133,laura.beneville@enron.com)

(466265,medmonds@enron.com)

(471258,.jane@enron.com)

(497810,.kimberly@enron.com)

(507806,aleck.dadson@enron.com)

(639614,j..bonin@enron.com)

(896860,imceanotes-hbcamp+40aep+2ecom+40enron@enron.com)

(1196652,enron.legal@enron.com)

(1240743,thi.ly@enron.com)

(1480469,ofdb12a77a.a6162183-on86256988.005b6308@enron.com)

(1818533,fran.i.mayes@enron.com)

(2337461,michael.marryott@enron.com)

(2918577,houston.resolution.center@enron.com)
```

There are 18,200 strongly connected components with only an average 23,787/18,200 = 1.3 users per group.

PageRank

The PageRank algorithm gives us an estimate of how important a person by analysing the links, which are the emails in this case. For example, let's run PageRank on Enron email graph:

```
scala> val ranks = graph.pageRank(0.001).vertices

ranks: org.apache.spark.graphx.VertexRDD[Double] = VertexRDDImpl[955] at
RDD at VertexRDD.scala:57


scala> people.join(ranks).map(t => (t._2._2,t._2._1)).sortBy(_._1,
ascending=false).take(10).foreach(println)


scala> val ranks = graph.pageRank(0.001).vertices

ranks: org.apache.spark.graphx.VertexRDD[Double] = VertexRDDImpl[955] at
RDD at VertexRDD.scala:57


scala> people.join(ranks).map(t => (t._2._2,t._2._1)).sortBy(_._1,
ascending=false).take(10).foreach(println)
(32.073722548483325,tana.jones@enron.com)
(29.086568868043248,sara.shackleton@enron.com)
(28.14656912897315,louise.kitchen@enron.com)
(26.57894933459292,vince.kaminski@enron.com)
(25.865486865014493,sally.beck@enron.com)
(23.86746232662471,john.lavorato@enron.com)
(22.489814482022275,jeff.skilling@enron.com)
(21.968039409295585,mark.taylor@enron.com)
(20.903053536275547,kenneth.lay@enron.com)
(20.39124651779771,gerald.nemec@enron.com)
```

Ostensibly, these are the go-to people. PageRank tends to emphasize the incoming edges, and Tana Jones returns to the top of the list compared to the 9th place in the triangle counting.

SVD++

SVD++ is a recommendation engine algorithm, developed specifically for Netflix competition by Yahuda Koren and team in 2008 — the original paper is still out there in the public domain and can be Googled as `kdd08koren.pdf`. The specific implementation comes from the .NET *MyMediaLite* library by ZenoGarther (`https://github.com/zenogantner/MyMediaLite`), who granted Apache 2 license to the Apache Foundation. Let's assume I have a set of users (on the left) and items (on the right):

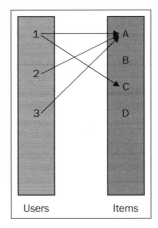

Figure 07-1. A graphical representation of a recommendation problem as a bipartite graph.

The preceding diagram is a graphical representation of the recommendation problem. The nodes on the left represent users. The nodes on the right represent items. User **1** recommends items **A** and **C**, while users **2** and **3** recommend only a single item **A**. The rest of the edges are missing. The common question is to find recommendation ranking of the rest of the items, the edges may also have a weight or recommendation strength attached to them. The graph is usually sparse. Such graph is also often called bipartite, as the edges only go from one set of nodes to another set of nodes (the user does not recommend another user).

For the recommendation engine, we typically need two types of nodes — users and items. The recommendations are based on the rating matrix of (user, item, and rating) tuples. One of the implementation of the recommendation algorithm is based on **Singular Value Decomposition (SVD)** of the preceding matrix. The final scoring has four components: the baseline, which is the sum of average for the whole matrix, average for the users, and average for the items, as follows:

$$r_{\{u,i\}} = \mu + b_u + b_i$$

Here, the μ, b_u, and b_i can be understood as the averages for the whole population, user (among all user recommendations), and item (among all the users). The final part is the Cartesian product of two rows:

$$r_{\{i,j\}} = \mu + b_u + b_i u + p_u^T q_i$$

The problem is posed as a minimization problem (refer to *Chapter 4, Supervised and Unsupervised Learning*):

$$\min_{p*,q*,b*} \sum_{u,i} \left(r_{ui} - \mu + b_u + b_i + p_u^T q_i \right) + \lambda_3 \left(\left\| p_u \right\|^2 + \left\| q_i \right\|^2 + b_u^2 + b_i^2 \right)$$

Here, λ_3 is a regularization coefficient also discussed in *Chapter 4, Supervised and Unsupervised Learning*. So, each user is associated with a set of numbers $((b_u, p_u)$, and each item with b_i, q_i. In this particlar implementation, the optimal coefficients are found by gradient descent. This is the basic of SVD optimization. In linear algebra, SVD takes an arbitrary $m \times n$ matrix A and represents it as a product of an orthogonal $m \times n$ matrix U, a diagonal $m \times n$ matrix Σ, and a $m \times n$ unitary matrix V, for example, the columns are mutually orthogonal. Arguably, if one takes the largest r entries of the Σ matrix, the product is reduced to the product of a very tall $m \times r$ matrix and a wide $r \times n$ matric, where r is called the rank of decomposition. If the remaining values are small, the new $(m+n) \times r$ numbers approximate the original $m \times n$ numbers for the relation, A. If m and n are large to start with, and in practical online shopping situations, m is the items and can be in hundreds of thousands, and n is the users and can be hundreds of millions, the saving can be substantial. For example, for $r=10$, $m=100,000$, and $n=100,000,000$, the savings are as follows:

$$\frac{m \times n}{(m+n) \times r} = \frac{10,000,000,000,000}{1,001,000,000} \sim 10,000$$

SVD can also be viewed as PCA for matrices with $m \neq n$. In the Enron case, we can treat senders as users and recipients as items (we'll need to reassign the node IDs), as follows:

```
scala> val rgraph = graph.partitionBy(org.apache.spark.graphx.
PartitionStrategy.EdgePartition1D, 10).mapEdges(e => 1).groupEdges(_+_).
cache

rgraph: org.apache.spark.graphx.Graph[String,Int] = org.apache.spark.
graphx.impl.GraphImpl@2c1a48d6


scala> val redges = rgraph.edges.map( e => Edge(-e.srcId, e.dstId, Math.
log(e.attr.toDouble)) ).cache

redges: org.apache.spark.rdd.RDD[org.apache.spark.graphx.Edge[Double]] =
MapPartitionsRDD[57] at map at <console>:36


scala> import org.apache.spark.graphx.lib.SVDPlusPlus

import org.apache.spark.graphx.lib.SVDPlusPlus


scala> implicit val conf = new SVDPlusPlus.Conf(10, 50, 0.0, 10.0, 0.007,
0.007, 0.005, 0.015)

conf: org.apache.spark.graphx.lib.SVDPlusPlus.Conf = org.apache.spark.
graphx.lib.SVDPlusPlus$Conf@15cdc117


scala> val (svd, mu) = SVDPlusPlus.run(redges, conf)

svd: org.apache.spark.graphx.Graph[(Array[Double], Array[Double], Double,
Double),Double] = org.apache.spark.graphx.impl.GraphImpl@3050363d

mu: Double = 1.3773578970633769


scala> val svdRanks = svd.vertices.filter(_._1 > 0).map(x => (x._2._3,
x._1))

svdRanks: org.apache.spark.rdd.RDD[(Double, org.apache.spark.graphx.
VertexId)] = MapPartitionsRDD[1517] at map at <console>:31


scala> val svdRanks = svd.vertices.filter(_._1 > 0).map(x => (x._1,
x._2._3))

svdRanks: org.apache.spark.rdd.RDD[(org.apache.spark.graphx.VertexId,
Double)] = MapPartitionsRDD[1520] at map at <console>:31


scala> people.join(svdRanks).sortBy(_._2._2, ascending=false).map(x =>
(x._2._2, x._2._1)).take(10).foreach(println)
```

```
(8.864218804309887,jbryson@enron.com)

(5.935146713012661,dl-ga-all_enron_worldwide2@enron.com)

(5.740242927715701,houston.report@enron.com)

(5.441934324464593,a478079f-55e1f3b0-862566fa-612229@enron.com)

(4.910272928389445,pchoi2@enron.com)

(4.701529779800544,dl-ga-all_enron_worldwide1@enron.com)

(4.4046392452058045,eligible.employees@enron.com)

(4.374738019256556,all_ena_egm_eim@enron.com)

(4.303078586979311,dl-ga-all_enron_north_america@enron.com)

(3.8295412053860867,the.mailout@enron.com)
```

The `svdRanks` is the user-part of the $\mu + b_i$ prediction. The distribution lists take a priority as this is usually used for mass e-mailing. To get the user-specific part, we need to provide the user ID:

```
scala> import com.github.fommil.netlib.BLAS.{getInstance => blas}

scala> def topN(uid: Long, num: Int) = {
     |       val usr = svd.vertices.filter(uid == -_._1).collect()(0)._2
     |       val recs = svd.vertices.filter(_._1 > 0).map( v => (v._1, mu +
usr._3 + v._2._3 + blas.ddot(usr._2.length, v._2._1, 1, usr._2, 1)))
     |       people.join(recs).sortBy(_._2._2, ascending=false).map(x =>
(x._2._2, x._2._1)).take(num)
     | }
topN: (uid: Long, num: Int)Array[(Double, String)]

scala> def top5(x: Long) : Array[(Double, String)] = topN(x, 5)
top5: (x: Long)Array[(Double, String)]


scala> people.join(graph.inDegrees).sortBy(_._2._2, ascending=false).
map(x => (x._1, x._2._1)).take(10).toList.map(t => (t._2, top5(t._1).
toList)).foreach(println)
(richard.shapiro@enron.com,List((4.866184418005094E66,anne.
bertino@enron.com), (3.9246829664352734E66,kgustafs@enron.com),
(3.9246829664352734E66,gweiss@enron.com), (3.871029763863491E66,hill@
enron.com), (3.743135924382312E66,fraser@enron.com)))
(steven.kean@enron.com,List((2.445163626935533E66,an
ne.bertino@enron.com), (1.9584692804232504E66,hill@
enron.com), (1.9105427465629028E66,kgustafs@enron.com),
(1.9105427465629028E66,gweiss@enron.com), (1.8931872324048717E66,fraser@
enron.com)))
```

```
(jeff.dasovich@enron.com,List((2.8924566115596135E66,
anne.bertino@enron.com), (2.3157345904446663E66,hill@
enron.com), (2.2646318970030287E66,gweiss@enron.
com), (2.2646318970030287E66,kgustafs@enron.com),
(2.2385865127706285E66,fraser@enron.com)))

(tana.jones@enron.com,List((6.1758464471309754E66,elizabeth.
sager@enron.com), (5.279291610047078E66,tana.jones@enron.com),
(4.967589820856654E66,tim.belden@enron.com), (4.909283344915057E66,jeff.
dasovich@enron.com), (4.869177440115682E66,mark.taylor@enron.com)))

(james.steffes@enron.com,List((5.7702834706832735E66,anne.
bertino@enron.com), (4.703038082326939E66,gweiss@enron.com),
(4.703038082326939E66,kgustafs@enron.com), (4.579565962089777E66,hill@
enron.com), (4.4298763869135494E66,george@enron.com)))

(sara.shackleton@enron.com,List((9.198688613290757E67,loui
se.kitchen@enron.com), (8.078107057848099E67,john.lavorato@
enron.com), (6.922806078209984E67,greg.whalley@enron.
com), (6.787266892881456E67,elizabeth.sager@enron.com),
(6.420473603137515E67,sally.beck@enron.com)))

(mark.taylor@enron.com,List((1.302856119148208E66,anne.
bertino@enron.com), (1.0678968544568682E66,hill@enron.com),
(1.031255083546722E66,fraser@enron.com), (1.009319696608474E66,george@
enron.com), (9.901391892701356E65,brad@enron.com)))

(mark.guzman@enron.com,List((9.770393472845669E65,anne.
bertino@enron.com), (7.97370292724488E65,kgustafs@enron.com),
(7.97370292724488E65,gweiss@enron.com), (7.751983820970696E65,hill@enron.
com), (7.500175024539423E65,george@enron.com)))

(geir.solberg@enron.com,List((6.856103529420811E65,anne.
bertino@enron.com), (5.611272903720188E65,gweiss@enron.com),
(5.611272903720188E65,kgustafs@enron.com), (5.436280144720843E65,hill@
enron.com), (5.2621103015001885E65,george@enron.com)))

(ryan.slinger@enron.com,List((5.0579114162531735E65,anne.
bertino@enron.com), (4.136838933824579E65,kgustafs@enron.com),
(4.136838933824579E65,gweiss@enron.com), (4.0110663808847004E65,hill@
enron.com), (3.8821438267917902E65,george@enron.com)))


scala> people.join(graph.outDegrees).sortBy(_._2._2, ascending=false).
map(x => (x._1, x._2._1)).take(10).toList.map(t => (t._2, top5(t._1).
toList)).foreach(println)

(jeff.dasovich@enron.com,List((2.8924566115596135E66,
anne.bertino@enron.com), (2.3157345904446663E66,hill@
enron.com), (2.2646318970030287E66,gweiss@enron.
com), (2.2646318970030287E66,kgustafs@enron.com),
(2.2385865127706285E66,fraser@enron.com)))
```

```
(veronica.espinoza@enron.com,List((3.135142195254243E65,gw
eiss@enron.com), (3.135142195254243E65,kgustafs@enron.com),
(2.773512892785554E65,anne.bertino@enron.com), (2.350799070225962E65,marc
ia.a.linton@enron.com), (2.2055288158758267E65,robert@enron.com)))

(pete.davis@enron.com,List((5.773492048248794E66,louise.
kitchen@enron.com), (5.067434612038159E66,john.lavorato@
enron.com), (4.389028076992449E66,greg.whalley@enron.
com), (4.179171984241975E66,sally.beck@enron.com),
(4.009544764149938E66,elizabeth.sager@enron.com)))

(rhonda.denton@enron.com,List((2.834710591578977E68,louise.
kitchen@enron.com), (2.488253676819922E68,john.lavorato@
enron.com), (2.1516048969715738E68,greg.whalley@enron.com),
(2.0405329247770104E68,sally.beck@enron.com), (1.9877213034021861E68,eliz
abeth.sager@enron.com)))

(cheryl.johnson@enron.com,List((3.453167402163105E64,ma
ry.dix@enron.com), (3.208849221485621E64,theresa.byrne@
enron.com), (3.208849221485621E64,sandy.olofson@enron.com),
(3.037427009315 7086E64,hill@enron.com), (2.886581252384442E64,fraser@
enron.com)))

(susan.mara@enron.com,List((5.1729089729525785E66,anne.
bertino@enron.com), (4.220843848723133E66,kgustafs@enron.com),
(4.220843848723133E66,gweiss@enron.com), (4.1044435240204605E66,hill@
enron.com), (3.9709951893268635E66,george@enron.com)))

(jae.black@enron.com,List((2.513139130001457E65,anne.bertino@enron.com),
(2.1037756300035247E65,hill@enron.com), (2.0297519350719265E65,fraser@
enron.com), (1.9587139280519927E65,george@enron.com),
(1.947164483486155E65,brad@enron.com)))

(ginger.dernehl@enron.com,List((4.516267307013845E66,anne.
bertino@enron.com), (3.653408921875843E66,gweiss@enron.com),
(3.653408921875843E66,kgustafs@enron.com), (3.590298037045689E66,hill@
enron.com), (3.471781765250177E66,fraser@enron.com)))

(lorna.brennan@enron.com,List((2.0719309635087482E66,anne.
bertino@enron.com), (1.732651408857978E66,kgustafs@enron.com),
(1.732651408857978E66,gweiss@enron.com), (1.6348480059915056E66,hill@
enron.com), (1.5880693846486309E66,george@enron.com)))

(mary.hain@enron.com,List((5.596589595417286E66,anne.bertino@enron.com),
(4.559474243930487E66,kgustafs@enron.com), (4.559474243930487E66,gweiss@
enron.com), (4.4421474044331
```

Here, we computed the top five recommended e-mail-to list for top in-degree and out-degree users.

SVD has only 159 lines of code in Scala and can be the basis for some further improvements. SVD++ includes a part based on implicit user feedback and item similarity information. Finally, the Netflix winning solution had also taken into consideration the fact that user preferences are time-dependent, but this part has not been implemented in GraphX yet.

Summary

While one can easily create their own data structures for graph problems, Scala's support for graphs comes from both semantic layer—Graph for Scala is effectively a convenient, interactive, and expressive language for working with graphs—and scalability via Spark and distributed computing. I hope that some of the material exposed in this chapter will be useful for implementing algorithms on top of Scala, Spark, and GraphX. It is worth mentioning that bot libraries are still under active development.

In the next chapter, we'll step down from from our flight in the the skies and look at Scala integration with traditional data analysis frameworks such as statistical language R and Python, which are often used for data munching. Later, in *Chapter 9, NLP in Scala*. I'll look at NLP Scala tools, which leverage complex data structures extensively.

8

Integrating Scala with R and Python

While Spark provides MLlib as a library for machine learning, in many practical situations, R or Python present a more familiar and time-tested interface for statistical computations. In particular, R's extensive statistical library includes very popular ANOVA/MANOVA methods of analyzing variance and variable dependencies/independencies, sets of statistical tests, and random number generators that are not currently present in MLlib. The interface from R to Spark is available under SparkR project. Finally, data analysts know Python's NumPy and SciPy linear algebra implementations for their efficiency as well as other time-series, optimization, and signal processing packages. With R/Python integration, all these familiar functionalities can be exposed to Scala/Spark users until the Spark/MLlib interfaces stabilize and the libraries make their way into the new framework while benefiting the users with Spark's ability to execute workflows in a distributed way across multiple machines.

When people program in R or Python, or with any statistical or linear algebra packages for this matter, they are usually not specifically focusing on the functional programming aspects. As I mentioned in *Chapter 1*, *Exploratory Data Analysis*, Scala should be treated as a high-level language and this is where it shines. Integration with highly efficient C and Fortran implementations, for example, of the freely available **Basic Linear Algebra Subprograms (BLAS)**, **Linear Algebra Package (LAPACK)**, and **Arnoldi Package (ARPACK)**, is known to find its way into Java and thus Scala (`http://www.netlib.org`, `https://github.com/fommil/netlib-java`). I would like to leave Scala at what it's doing best. In this chapter, however, I will focus on how to use these languages with Scala/Spark.

I will use the publicly available United States Department of Transportation flights dataset for this chapter (`http://www.transtats.bts.gov`).

In this chapter, we will cover the following topics:

- Installing R and configuring SparkR if you haven't done so yet
- Learning about R (and Spark) DataFrames
- Performing linear regression and ANOVA analysis with R
- Performing **Generalized Linear Model** (**GLM**) modeling with SparkR
- Installing Python if you haven't done so yet
- Learning how to use PySpark and call Python from Scala

Integrating with R

As with many advanced and carefully designed technologies, people usually either love or hate R as a language. One of the reason being that R was one of the first language implementations that tries to manipulate complex objects, even though most of them turn out to be just a list as opposed to struct or map as in more mature modern implementations. R was originally created at the University of Auckland by Ross Ihaka and Robert Gentleman around 1993, and had its roots in the S language developed at Bell Labs around 1976, when most of the commercial programming was still done in Fortran. While R incorporates some functional features such as passing functions as a parameter and map/apply, it conspicuously misses some others such as lazy evaluation and list comprehensions. With all this said, R has a very good help system, and if someone says that they never had to go back to the `help(...)` command to figure out how to run a certain data transformation or model better, they are either lying or just starting in R.

Setting up R and SparkR

To run SparkR, you'll need R version 3.0 or later. Follow the given instructions for the installation, depending on you operating system.

Linux

On a Linux system, detailed installation documentation is available at `https://cran.r-project.org/bin/linux`. However, for example, on a Debian system, one installs it by running the following command:

```
# apt-get update
...
# apt-get install r-base r-base-dev
...
```

To list installed/available packages on the Linux repository site, perform the following command:

```
# apt-cache search "^r-.*" | sort
...
```

R packages, which are a part of `r-base` and `r-recommended`, are installed into the `/usr/lib/R/library` directory. These can be updated using the usual package maintenance tools such as `apt-get` or aptitude. The other R packages available as precompiled Debian packages, `r-cran-*` and `r-bioc-*`, are installed into `/usr/lib/R/site-library`. The following command shows all packages that depend on `r-base-core`:

```
# apt-cache rdepends r-base-core
```

This comprises of a large number of contributed packages from CRAN and other repositories. If you want to install R packages that are not provided as package, or if you want to use newer versions, you need to build them from source that requires the `r-base-dev` development package that can be installed by the following command:

```
# apt-get install r-base-dev
```

This pulls in the basic requirements to compile R packages, such as the development tools group install. R packages may then be installed by the local user/admin from the CRAN source packages, typically from inside R using the `R> install.packages()` function or `R CMD INSTALL`. For example, to install the R `ggplot2` package, run the following command:

```
> install.packages("ggplot2")
--- Please select a CRAN mirror for use in this session ---
also installing the dependencies 'stringi', 'magrittr', 'colorspace',
'Rcpp', 'stringr', 'RColorBrewer', 'dichromat', 'munsell', 'labeling',
'digest', 'gtable', 'plyr', 'reshape2', 'scales'
```

This will download and optionally compile the package and its dependencies from one of the available sites. Sometime R is confused about the repositories; in this case, I recommend creating a `~/.Rprofile` file in the home directory pointing to the closest CRAN repository:

```
$ cat >> ~/.Rprofile << EOF
r = getOption("repos") # hard code the Berkeley repo for CRAN
r["CRAN"] = "http://cran.cnr.berkeley.edu"
options(repos = r)
rm(r)

EOF
```

~/.Rprofile contains commands to customize your sessions. One of the commands I recommend to put in there is options (prompt="R> ") to be able to distinguish the shell you are working in by the prompt, following the tradition of most tools in this book. The list of known mirrors is available at https://cran.r-project.org/mirrors.html.

Also, it is good practice to specify the directory to install system/site/user packages via the following command, unless your OS setup does it already by putting these commands into ~/.bashrc or system /etc/profile:

```
$ export R_LIBS_SITE=${R_LIBS_SITE:-/usr/local/lib/R/site-library:/usr/
lib/R/site-library:/usr/lib/R/library}
```

```
$ export R_LIBS_USER=${R_LIBS_USER:-$HOME/R/$(uname -i)-library/$( R
--version | grep -o -E [0-9]+\.[0-9]+ | head -1)}
```

Mac OS

R for Mac OS can be downloaded, for example, from http://cran.r-project.org/bin/macosx. The latest version at the time of the writing is 3.2.3. Always check the consistency of the downloaded package. To do so, run the following command:

```
$ pkgutil --check-signature R-3.2.3.pkg

Package "R-3.2.3.pkg":

   Status: signed by a certificate trusted by Mac OS X

   Certificate Chain:

    1. Developer ID Installer: Simon Urbanek

        SHA1 fingerprint: B7 EB 39 5E 03 CF 1E 20 D1 A6 2E 9F D3 17 90 26
D8 D6 3B EF

        ----------------------------------------------------------------
----------

    2. Developer ID Certification Authority

        SHA1 fingerprint: 3B 16 6C 3B 7D C4 B7 51 C9 FE 2A FA B9 13 56 41
E3 88 E1 86

        ----------------------------------------------------------------
----------

    3. Apple Root CA

        SHA1 fingerprint: 61 1E 5B 66 2C 59 3A 08 FF 58 D1 4A E2 24 52 D1
98 DF 6C 60
```

The environment settings in the preceding subsection also apply to the Mac OS setup.

Windows

R for Windows can be downloaded from `https://cran.r-project.org/bin/windows/` as an exe installer. Run this executable as an administrator to install R.

One can usually edit the environment setting for **System/User** by following the **Control Panel | System and Security | System | Advanced system settings | Environment Variables** path from the Windows menu.

Running SparkR via scripts

To run SparkR, one needs to run install the `R/install-dev.sh` script that comes with the Spark git tree. In fact, one only needs the shell script and the content of the `R/pkg` directory, which is not always included with the compiled Spark distributions:

```
$ git clone https://github.com/apache/spark.git
Cloning into 'spark'...
remote: Counting objects: 301864, done.
...
$ cp -r R/{install-dev.sh,pkg) $SPARK_HOME/R
...
$ cd $SPARK_HOME
$ ./R/install-dev.sh
* installing *source* package 'SparkR' ...
** R
** inst
** preparing package for lazy loading
Creating a new generic function for 'colnames' in package 'SparkR'
...
$ bin/sparkR


R version 3.2.3 (2015-12-10) -- "Wooden Christmas-Tree"
Copyright (C) 2015 The R Foundation for Statistical Computing
Platform: x86_64-redhat-linux-gnu (64-bit)


R is free software and comes with ABSOLUTELY NO WARRANTY.
You are welcome to redistribute it under certain conditions.
```

```
Type 'license()' or 'licence()' for distribution details.

  Natural language support but running in an English locale

R is a collaborative project with many contributors.
Type 'contributors()' for more information and
'citation()' on how to cite R or R packages in publications.

Type 'demo()' for some demos, 'help()' for on-line help, or
'help.start()' for an HTML browser interface to help.
Type 'q()' to quit R.

Launching java with spark-submit command /home/alex/spark-1.6.1-bin-
hadoop2.6/bin/spark-submit   "sparkr-shell" /tmp/RtmpgdTfmU/backend_
port22446d0391e8


  Welcome to

     ____              __
    / __/__  ___ _____/ /__
   _\ \/ _ \/ _ `/ __/  '_/
  /___/ .__/\_,_/_/ /_/\_\   version  1.6.1
     /_/


  Spark context is available as sc, SQL context is available as sqlContext
>
```

Running Spark via R's command line

Alternatively, we can also initialize Spark from the R command line directly (or from
RStudio at http://rstudio.org/) using the following commands:

```
R> library(SparkR, lib.loc = c(file.path(Sys.getenv("SPARK_HOME"), "R",
"lib")))
...
R> sc <- sparkR.init(master = Sys.getenv("SPARK_MASTER"), sparkEnvir =
list(spark.driver.memory="1g"))
...
R> sqlContext <- sparkRSQL.init(sc)
```

As described previously in *Chapter 3, Working with Spark and MLlib*, the SPARK_HOME environment variable needs to point to your local Spark installation directory and SPARK_MASTER and YARN_CONF_DIR to the desired cluster manager (local, standalone, mesos, and YARN) and YARN configuration directory if one is using Spark with the YARN cluster manager.

Although most all of the distributions come with a UI, in the tradition of this book and for the purpose of this chapter I'll use the command line.

DataFrames

The DataFrames originally came from R and Python, so it is natural to see them in SparkR.

 Please note that the implementation of DataFrames in SparkR is on top of RDDs, so they work differently than the R DataFrames.

The question of when and where to store and apply the schema and other metadata like types has been a topic of active debate recently. On one hand, providing the schema early with the data enables thorough data validation and potentially optimization. On the other hand, it may be too restrictive for the original data ingest, whose goal is just to capture as much data as possible and perform data formatting/cleansing later on, the approach often referred as schema on read. The latter approach recently won more ground with the tools to work with evolving schemas such as Avro and automatic schema discovery tools, but for the purpose of this chapter, I'll assume that we have done the schema discovery part and can start working with a DataFrames.

Let's first download and extract a flight delay dataset from the United States Department of Transportation, as follows:

```
$ wget http://www.transtats.bts.gov/Download/On_Time_On_Time_
Performance_2015_7.zip

--2016-01-23 15:40:02--  http://www.transtats.bts.gov/Download/On_Time_
On_Time_Performance_2015_7.zip

Resolving www.transtats.bts.gov... 204.68.194.70

Connecting to www.transtats.bts.gov|204.68.194.70|:80... connected.

HTTP request sent, awaiting response... 200 OK

Length: 26204213 (25M) [application/x-zip-compressed]
```

```
Saving to: "On_Time_On_Time_Performance_2015_7.zip"


100%[=======================================================================
========================================================================
===================================>] 26,204,213   966K/s   in 27s


2016-01-23 15:40:29 (956 KB/s) - "On_Time_On_Time_Performance_2015_7.zip"
saved [26204213/26204213]


$ unzip -d flights On_Time_On_Time_Performance_2015_7.zip
Archive:  On_Time_On_Time_Performance_2015_7.zip
  inflating: flights/On_Time_On_Time_Performance_2015_7.csv
  inflating: flights/readme.html
```

If you have Spark running on the cluster, you want to copy the file in HDFS:

```
$ hadoop fs -put flights .
```

The `flights/readme.html` files gives you detailed metadata information, as shown in the following image:

BACKGROUND

The data contained in the compressed file has been extracted from the On-Time Performance data table of the "On-Time" database from the TranStats data library. The time period is indicated in the name of the compressed file; for example, XXX_XXXXX_2001_1 contains data of the first month of the year 2001.

RECORD LAYOUT

Below are fields in the order that they appear on the records:

Year	Year
Quarter	Quarter (1-4)
Month	Month
DayofMonth	Day of Month
DayOfWeek	Day of Week
FlightDate	Flight Date (yyyymmdd)
UniqueCarrier	Unique Carrier Code. When the same code has been used by multiple carriers, a numeric suffix is used for earlier users, for example, PA, PA(1), PA(2). Use this field for analysis across a range of years.
AirlineID	An identification number assigned by US DOT to identify a unique airline (carrier). A unique airline (carrier) is defined as one holding and reporting under the same DOT certificate regardless of its Code, Name, or holding company/corporation.
Carrier	Code assigned by IATA and commonly used to identify a carrier. As the same code may have been assigned to different carriers over time, the code is not always unique. For analysis, use the Unique Carrier Code.
TailNum	Tail Number
FlightNum	Flight Number
OriginAirportID	Origin Airport, Airport ID. An identification number assigned by US DOT to identify a unique airport. Use this field for airport analysis across a range of years because an airport can change its airport code and airport codes can be reused.
OriginAirportSeqID	Origin Airport, Airport Sequence ID. An identification number assigned by US DOT to identify a unique airport at a given point of time. Airport attributes, such as airport name or coordinates, may change over time.
OriginCityMarketID	Origin Airport, City Market ID. City Market ID is an identification number assigned by US DOT to identify a city market. Use this field to consolidate airports serving the same city market.
Origin	Origin Airport
OriginCityName	Origin Airport, City Name
OriginState	Origin Airport, State Code
OriginStateFips	Origin Airport, State Fips
OriginStateName	Origin Airport, State Name
OriginWac	Origin Airport, World Area Code

Figure 08-1: Metadata provided with the On-Time Performance dataset released by the US Department of Transportation (for demo purposes only)

Now, I want you to analyze the delays of SFO returning flights and possibly find the factors contributing to the delay. Let's start with the R `data.frame`:

```
$ bin/sparkR --master local[8]


R version 3.2.3 (2015-12-10) -- "Wooden Christmas-Tree"
Copyright (C) 2015 The R Foundation for Statistical Computing
Platform: x86_64-apple-darwin13.4.0 (64-bit)


R is free software and comes with ABSOLUTELY NO WARRANTY.
You are welcome to redistribute it under certain conditions.
Type 'license()' or 'licence()' for distribution details.


  Natural language support but running in an English locale


R is a collaborative project with many contributors.
Type 'contributors()' for more information and
'citation()' on how to cite R or R packages in publications.


Type 'demo()' for some demos, 'help()' for on-line help, or
'help.start()' for an HTML browser interface to help.
Type 'q()' to quit R.


[Previously saved workspace restored]


Launching java with spark-submit command /Users/akozlov/spark-1.6.1-
bin-hadoop2.6/bin/spark-submit   "--master" "local[8]" "sparkr-shell" /
var/folders/p1/y7ygx_4507q34vhd60q115p80000gn/T//RtmpD42eTz/backend_
port682e58e2c5db


  Welcome to
```

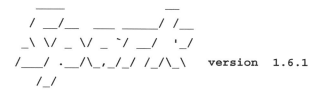

```
      ____              __
     / __/__  ___ _____/ /__
    _\ \/ _ \/ _ `/ __/  '_/
   /___/ .__/\_,_/_/ /_/\_\   version  1.6.1
      /_/


  Spark context is available as sc, SQL context is available as sqlContext
```

```
> flights <- read.table(unz("On_Time_On_Time_Performance_2015_7.zip",
"On_Time_On_Time_Performance_2015_7.csv"), nrows=1000000, header=T,
quote="\"", sep=",")
> sfoFlights <- flights[flights$Dest == "SFO", ]
> attach(sfoFlights)
> delays <- aggregate(ArrDelayMinutes ~ DayOfWeek + Origin +
UniqueCarrier, FUN=mean, na.rm=TRUE)
> tail(delays[order(delays$ArrDelayMinutes), ])
```

	DayOfWeek	Origin	UniqueCarrier	ArrDelayMinutes
220	4	ABQ	OO	67.60
489	4	TUS	OO	71.80
186	5	IAH	F9	77.60
696	3	RNO	UA	79.50
491	6	TUS	OO	168.25
84	7	SLC	AS	203.25

If you were flying from Salt Lake City on Sunday with Alaska Airlines in July 2015, consider yourself unlucky (we have only done simple analysis so far, so one shouldn't attach too much significance to this result). There may be multiple other random factors contributing to the delay.

Even though we ran the example in SparkR, we still used the R `data.frame`. If we want to analyze data across multiple months, we will need to distribute the load across multiple nodes. This is where the SparkR distributed DataFrame comes into play, as it can be distributed across multiple threads even on a single node. There is a direct way to convert the R DataFrame to SparkR DataFrame (and thus to RDD):

```
> sparkDf <- createDataFrame(sqlContext, flights)
```

If I run it on a laptop, I will run out of memory. The overhead is large due to the fact that I need to transfer the data between multiple threads/nodes, we want to filter it as soon as possible:

```
sparkDf <- createDataFrame(sqlContext, subset(flights, select =
c("ArrDelayMinutes", "DayOfWeek", "Origin", "Dest", "UniqueCarrier")))
```

This will run even on my laptop. There is, of course, a reverse conversion from Spark's DataFrame to R's `data.frame`:

```
> rDf <- as.data.frame(sparkDf)
```

Alternatively, I can use the `spark-csv` package to read it from the `.csv` file, which, if the original `.csv` file is in a distributed filesystem such as HDFS, will avoid shuffling the data over network in a cluster setting. The only drawback, at least currently, is that Spark cannot read from the `.zip` files directly:

```
> $ ./bin/sparkR --packages com.databricks:spark-csv_2.10:1.3.0 --master
local[8]


R version 3.2.3 (2015-12-10) -- "Wooden Christmas-Tree"
Copyright (C) 2015 The R Foundation for Statistical Computing
Platform: x86_64-redhat-linux-gnu (64-bit)


R is free software and comes with ABSOLUTELY NO WARRANTY.
You are welcome to redistribute it under certain conditions.
Type 'license()' or 'licence()' for distribution details.


  Natural language support but running in an English locale


R is a collaborative project with many contributors.
Type 'contributors()' for more information and
'citation()' on how to cite R or R packages in publications.


Type 'demo()' for some demos, 'help()' for on-line help, or
'help.start()' for an HTML browser interface to help.
Type 'q()' to quit R.


Warning: namespace 'SparkR' is not available and has been replaced
by .GlobalEnv when processing object 'sparkDf'
[Previously saved workspace restored]


Launching java with spark-submit command /home/alex/spark-1.6.1-bin-
hadoop2.6/bin/spark-submit   "--master" "local[8]" "--packages" "com.
databricks:spark-csv_2.10:1.3.0" "sparkr-shell" /tmp/RtmpfhcUXX/backend_
port1b066bea5a03
Ivy Default Cache set to: /home/alex/.ivy2/cache
The jars for the packages stored in: /home/alex/.ivy2/jars
:: loading settings :: url = jar:file:/home/alex/spark-1.6.1-bin-
hadoop2.6/lib/spark-assembly-1.6.1-hadoop2.6.0.jar!/org/apache/ivy/core/
settings/ivysettings.xml
```

```
com.databricks#spark-csv_2.10 added as a dependency
:: resolving dependencies :: org.apache.spark#spark-submit-parent;1.0
  confs: [default]
  found com.databricks#spark-csv_2.10;1.3.0 in central
  found org.apache.commons#commons-csv;1.1 in central
  found com.univocity#univocity-parsers;1.5.1 in central
:: resolution report :: resolve 189ms :: artifacts dl 4ms
  :: modules in use:
  com.databricks#spark-csv_2.10;1.3.0 from central in [default]
  com.univocity#univocity-parsers;1.5.1 from central in [default]
  org.apache.commons#commons-csv;1.1 from central in [default]
  ---------------------------------------------------------------------
  |                    |           modules          ||   artifacts   |
  |        conf        | number| search|dwnlded|evicted|| number|dwnlded|
  ---------------------------------------------------------------------
  |      default       |   3   |   0   |   0   |   0   ||   3   |   0   |
  ---------------------------------------------------------------------
:: retrieving :: org.apache.spark#spark-submit-parent
  confs: [default]
  0 artifacts copied, 3 already retrieved (0kB/7ms)


 Welcome to


    ____              __
   / __/__  ___ _____/ /__
  _\ \/ _ \/ _ `/ __/  '_/
 /___/ .__/\_,_/_/ /_/\_\   version 1.6.1
    /_/


 Spark context is available as sc, SQL context is available as sqlContext
> sparkDf <- read.df(sqlContext, "./flights", "com.databricks.spark.csv",
header="true", inferSchema = "false")
> sfoFlights <- select(filter(sparkDf, sparkDf$Dest == "SFO"),
"DayOfWeek", "Origin", "UniqueCarrier", "ArrDelayMinutes")
> aggs <- agg(group_by(sfoFlights, "DayOfWeek", "Origin",
"UniqueCarrier"), count(sparkDf$ArrDelayMinutes),
avg(sparkDf$ArrDelayMinutes))
```

```
> head(arrange(aggs, c('avg(ArrDelayMinutes)'), decreasing = TRUE), 10)
```

	DayOfWeek	Origin	UniqueCarrier	count(ArrDelayMinutes)	avg(ArrDelayMinutes)
1	7	SLC	AS	4	203.25
2	6	TUS	OO	4	168.25
3	3	RNO	UA	8	79.50
4	5	IAH	F9	5	77.60
5	4	TUS	OO	5	71.80
6	4	ABQ	OO	5	67.60
7	2	ABQ	OO	4	66.25
8	1	IAH	F9	4	61.25
9	4	DAL	WN	5	59.20
10	3	SUN	OO	5	59.00

Note that we loaded the additional com.databricks:spark-csv_2.10:1.3.0 package by supplying the --package flag on the command line; we can easily go distributed by using a Spark instance over a cluster of nodes or even analyze a larger dataset:

```
$ for i in $(seq 1 6); do wget http://www.transtats.bts.gov/Download/
On_Time_On_Time_Performance_2015_$i.zip; unzip -d flights On_Time_On_
Time_Performance_2015_$i.zip; hadoop fs -put -f flights/On_Time_On_Time_
Performance_2015_$i.csv flights; done


$ hadoop fs -ls flights
Found 7 items
-rw-r--r--   3 alex eng  211633432 2016-02-16 03:28 flights/On_Time_On_
Time_Performance_2015_1.csv
-rw-r--r--   3 alex eng  192791767 2016-02-16 03:28 flights/On_Time_On_
Time_Performance_2015_2.csv
-rw-r--r--   3 alex eng  227016932 2016-02-16 03:28 flights/On_Time_On_
Time_Performance_2015_3.csv
```

```
-rw-r--r--   3 alex eng  218600030 2016-02-16 03:28 flights/On_Time_On_
Time_Performance_2015_4.csv

-rw-r--r--   3 alex eng  224003544 2016-02-16 03:29 flights/On_Time_On_
Time_Performance_2015_5.csv

-rw-r--r--   3 alex eng  227418780 2016-02-16 03:29 flights/On_Time_On_
Time_Performance_2015_6.csv

-rw-r--r--   3 alex eng  235037955 2016-02-15 21:56 flights/On_Time_On_
Time_Performance_2015_7.csv
```

This will download and put the on-time performance data in the flight's directory (remember, as we discussed in *Chapter 1, Exploratory Data Analysis,* we would like to treat directories as big data datasets). We can now run the same analysis over the whole period of 2015 (for the available data):

```
> sparkDf <- read.df(sqlContext, "./flights", "com.databricks.spark.csv",
header="true")
> sfoFlights <- select(filter(sparkDf, sparkDf$Dest == "SFO"),
"DayOfWeek", "Origin", "UniqueCarrier", "ArrDelayMinutes")
> aggs <- cache(agg(group_by(sfoFlights, "DayOfWeek",
"Origin", "UniqueCarrier"), count(sparkDf$ArrDelayMinutes),
avg(sparkDf$ArrDelayMinutes)))
> head(arrange(aggs, c('avg(ArrDelayMinutes)'), decreasing = TRUE), 10)
    DayOfWeek Origin UniqueCarrier count(ArrDelayMinutes)
avg(ArrDelayMinutes)
```

	DayOfWeek	Origin	UniqueCarrier	count(ArrDelayMinutes)	avg(ArrDelayMinutes)
1	6	MSP	UA	1	122.00000
2	3	RNO	UA	8	79.50000
3	1	MSP	UA	13	68.53846
4	7	SAT	UA	1	65.00000
5	7	STL	UA	9	64.55556
6	1	ORD	F9	13	55.92308
7	1	MSO	OO	4	50.00000
8	2	MSO	OO	4	48.50000
9	5	CEC	OO	28	45.86957
10	3	STL	UA	13	43.46154

Note that we used a `cache()` call to pin the dataset to the memory as we will use it again later. This time it's Minneapolis/United on Saturday! However, you probably already know why: there is only one record for this combination of `DayOfWeek`, `Origin`, and `UniqueCarrier`; it's most likely an outlier. The average over about 30 flights for the previous outlier was reduced to 30 minutes:

```
> head(arrange(filter(filter(aggs, aggs$Origin == "SLC"),
aggs$UniqueCarrier == "AS"), c('avg(ArrDelayMinutes)'), decreasing =
TRUE), 100)
   DayOfWeek Origin UniqueCarrier count(ArrDelayMinutes)
avg(ArrDelayMinutes)
1          7   SLC            AS                       30
32.600000
2          2   SLC            AS                       30
10.200000
3          4   SLC            AS                       31
9.774194
4          1   SLC            AS                       30
9.433333
5          3   SLC            AS                       30
5.866667
6          5   SLC            AS                       31
5.516129
7          6   SLC            AS                       30
2.133333
```

Sunday still remains a problem in terms of delays. The limit to the amount of data we can analyze now is only the number of cores on the laptop and nodes in the cluster. Let's look at more complex machine learning models now.

Linear models

Linear methods play an important role in statistical modeling. As the name suggests, linear model assumes that the dependent variable is a weighted combination of independent variables. In R, the `lm` function performs a linear regression and reports the coefficients, as follows:

```
R> attach(iris)
R> lm(Sepal.Length ~ Sepal.Width)


Call:
```

```
lm(formula = Sepal.Length ~ Sepal.Width)


Coefficients:
(Intercept)   Sepal.Width
     6.5262       -0.2234
```

The summary function provides even more information:

```
R> model <- lm(Sepal.Length ~ Sepal.Width + Petal.Length + Petal.Width)
R> summary(model)


Call:
lm(formula = Sepal.Length ~ Sepal.Width + Petal.Length + Petal.Width)


Residuals:
     Min       1Q    Median       3Q      Max
-0.82816 -0.21989   0.01875  0.19709  0.84570


Coefficients:
              Estimate Std. Error t value Pr(>|t|)
(Intercept)    1.85600    0.25078   7.401 9.85e-12 ***
Sepal.Width    0.65084    0.06665   9.765  < 2e-16 ***
Petal.Length   0.70913    0.05672  12.502  < 2e-16 ***
Petal.Width   -0.55648    0.12755  -4.363 2.41e-05 ***
---
Signif. codes:  0 '***' 0.001 '**' 0.01 '*' 0.05 '.' 0.1 ' ' 1


Residual standard error: 0.3145 on 146 degrees of freedom
Multiple R-squared:  0.8586,  Adjusted R-squared:  0.8557
F-statistic: 295.5 on 3 and 146 DF,  p-value: < 2.2e-16
```

While we considered generalized linear models in *Chapter 3, Working with Spark and MLlib,* and we will also consider the glm implementation in R and SparkR shortly, linear models provide more information in general and are an excellent tool for working with noisy data and selecting the relevant attribute for further analysis.

Data analysis life cycle

While most of the statistical books focus on the analysis and best use of available data, the results of statistical analysis in general should also affect the search for the new sources of information. In the complete data life cycle, discussed at the end of *Chapter 3*, *Working with Spark and MLlib*, a data scientist should always transform the latest variable importance results into the theories of how to collect data. For example, if the ink usage analysis for home printers points to an increase in ink usage for photos, one could potentially collect more information about the format of the pictures, sources of digital images, and paper the user prefers to use. This approach turned out to be very productive in a real business situation even though not fully automated.

Specifically, here is a short description of the output that linear models provide:

- **Residuals**: These are statistics for the difference between the actual and predicted values. A lot of techniques exist to detect the problems with the models on patterns of the residual distribution, but this is out of scope of this book. A detailed residual table can be obtained with the `resid(model)` function.

- **Coefficients**: These are the actual linear combination coefficients; the t-value represents the ratio of the value of the coefficient to the estimate of the standard error: higher values mean a higher likelihood that this coefficient has a non-trivial effect on the dependent variable. The coefficients can also be obtained with `coef(model)` functions.

- **Residual standard error**: This reports the standard mean square error, the metric that is the target of optimization in a straightforward linear regression.

- **Multiple R-squared**: This is the fraction of the dependent variable variance that is explained by the model. The adjusted value accounts for the number of parameters in your model and is considered to be a better metric to avoid overfitting if the number of observations does not justify the complexity of the models, which happens even for big data problems.

- **F-statistic**: The measure of model quality. In plain terms, it measures how all the parameters in the model explain the dependent variable. The p-value provides the probability that the model explains the dependent variable just due to random chance. The values under 0.05 (or 5%) are, in general, considered satisfactory. While in general, a high value probably means that the model is probably not statistically valid and "nothing else matters, the low F-statistic does not always mean that the model will work well in practice, so it cannot be directly applied as a model acceptance criterion.

Once the linear models are applied, usually more complex `glm` or recursive models, such as decision trees and the `rpart` function, are applied to find interesting variable interactions. Linear models are good for establishing baseline on the other models that can improve.

Finally, ANOVA is a standard technique to study the variance if the independent variables are discrete:

```
R> aov <- aov(Sepal.Length ~ Species)
R> summary(aov)
            Df  Sum Sq  Mean Sq  F value  Pr(>F)
Species      2   63.21   31.606    119.3  <2e-16 ***
Residuals  147   38.96    0.265
---
Signif. codes:  0 '***' 0.001 '**' 0.01 '*' 0.05 '.' 0.1 ' ' 1
```

The measure of the model quality is F-statistics. While one can always run R algorithms with RDD using the pipe mechanism with `Rscript`, I will partially cover this functionality with respect to **Java Specification Request (JSR)** 223 Python integration later. In this section, I would like to explore specifically a generalized linear regression `glm` function that is implemented both in R and SparkR natively.

Generalized linear model

Once again, you can run either R `glm` or SparkR `glm`. The list of possible link and optimization functions for R implementation is provided in the following table:

The following list shows possible options for R `glm` implementation:

Family	Variance	Link
gaussian	gaussian	identity
binomial	binomial	logit, probit or cloglog
poisson	poisson	log, identity or sqrt
Gamma	Gamma	inverse, identity or log
inverse.gaussian	inverse.gaussian	$1/mu^2$
quasi	user-defined	user-defined

I will use a binary target, `ArrDel15`, which indicates whether the plane was more than 15 minutes late for the arrival. The independent variables will be `DepDel15`, `DayOfWeek`, `Month`, `UniqueCarrier`, `Origin`, and `Dest`:

```
R> flights <- read.table(unz("On_Time_On_Time_Performance_2015_7.zip",
"On_Time_On_Time_Performance_2015_7.csv"), nrows=1000000, header=T,
quote="\"", sep=",")

R> flights$DoW_ <- factor(flights$DayOfWeek,levels=c(1,2,3,4,5,6,7), labe
ls=c("Mon","Tue","Wed","Thu","Fri","Sat","Sun"))

R> attach(flights)

R> system.time(model <- glm(ArrDel15 ~ UniqueCarrier + DoW_ + Origin +
Dest, flights, family="binomial"))
```

While you wait for the results, open another shell and run `glm` in the `SparkR` mode on the full seven months of data:

```
sparkR> cache(sparkDf <- read.df(sqlContext, "./flights", "com.
databricks.spark.csv", header="true", inferSchema="true"))
```

```
DataFrame[Year:int, Quarter:int, Month:int, DayofMonth:int,
DayOfWeek:int, FlightDate:string, UniqueCarrier:string, AirlineID:int,
Carrier:string, TailNum:string, FlightNum:int, OriginAirportID:int,
OriginAirportSeqID:int, OriginCityMarketID:int, Origin:string,
OriginCityName:string, OriginState:string, OriginStateFips:int,
OriginStateName:string, OriginWac:int, DestAirportID:int,
DestAirportSeqID:int, DestCityMarketID:int, Dest:string,
DestCityName:string, DestState:string, DestStateFips:int,
DestStateName:string, DestWac:int, CRSDepTime:int, DepTime:int,
DepDelay:double, DepDelayMinutes:double, DepDel15:double,
DepartureDelayGroups:int, DepTimeBlk:string, TaxiOut:double,
WheelsOff:int, WheelsOn:int, TaxiIn:double, CRSArrTime:int,
ArrTime:int, ArrDelay:double, ArrDelayMinutes:double, ArrDel15:double,
ArrivalDelayGroups:int, ArrTimeBlk:string, Cancelled:double,
CancellationCode:string, Diverted:double, CRSElapsedTime:double,
ActualElapsedTime:double, AirTime:double, Flights:double,
Distance:double, DistanceGroup:int, CarrierDelay:double,
WeatherDelay:double, NASDelay:double, SecurityDelay:double,
LateAircraftDelay:double, FirstDepTime:int, TotalAddGTime:double,
LongestAddGTime:double, DivAirportLandings:int, DivReachedDest:double,
DivActualElapsedTime:double, DivArrDelay:double, DivDistance:double,
Div1Airport:string, Div1AirportID:int, Div1AirportSeqID:int,
Div1WheelsOn:int, Div1TotalGTime:double, Div1LongestGTime:double,
Div1WheelsOff:int, Div1TailNum:string, Div2Airport:string,
Div2AirportID:int, Div2AirportSeqID:int, Div2WheelsOn:int,
Div2TotalGTime:double, Div2LongestGTime:double, Div2WheelsOff:string,
Div2TailNum:string, Div3Airport:string, Div3AirportID:string,
Div3AirportSeqID:string, Div3WheelsOn:string, Div3TotalGTime:string,
Div3LongestGTime:string, Div3WheelsOff:string, Div3TailNum:string,
Div4Airport:string, Div4AirportID:string, Div4AirportSeqID:string,
```

```
Div4WheelsOn:string, Div4TotalGTime:string, Div4LongestGTime:string,
Div4WheelsOff:string, Div4TailNum:string, Div5Airport:string,
Div5AirportID:string, Div5AirportSeqID:string, Div5WheelsOn:string,
Div5TotalGTime:string, Div5LongestGTime:string, Div5WheelsOff:string,
Div5TailNum:string, :string]
sparkR> noNulls <- cache(dropna(selectExpr(filter(sparkDf,
sparkDf$Cancelled == 0), "ArrDel15", "UniqueCarrier", "format_
string('%d', DayOfWeek) as DayOfWeek", "Origin", "Dest"), "any"))

sparkR> sparkModel = glm(ArrDel15 ~ UniqueCarrier + DayOfWeek + Origin +
Dest, noNulls, family="binomial")
```

Here we try to build a model explaining delays as an effect of carrier, day of week, and origin on destination airports, which is captured by the formular construct `ArrDel15 ~ UniqueCarrier + DayOfWeek + Origin + Dest`.

Nulls, big data, and Scala

Note that in the SparkR case of `glm`, I had to explicitly filter out the non-cancelled flights and removed the NA — or nulls in the C/Java lingo. While R does this for you by default, NAs in big data are very common as the datasets are typically sparse and shouldn't be treated lightly. The fact that we have to deal with nulls explicitly in MLlib warns us about some additional information in the dataset and is definitely a welcome feature. The presence of an NA can carry information about the way the data was collected. Ideally, each NA should be accompanied by a small `get_na_info` method as to why this particular value was not available or collected, which leads us to the `Either` type in Scala.

Even though nulls are inherited from Java and a part of Scala, the `Option` and `Either` types are new and more robust mechanism to deal with special cases where nulls were traditionally used. Specifically, `Either` can provide a value or exception message as to why it was not computed; while `Option` can either provide a value or be `None`, which can be readily captured by the Scala pattern-matching framework.

One thing you will notice is that SparkR will run multiple threads, and even on a single node, it will consume CPU time from multiple cores and returns much faster even with a larger size of data. In my experiment on a 32-core machine, it was able to finish in under a minute (as opposed to 35 minutes for R `glm`). To get the results, as in the R model case, we need to run the `summary()` method:

```
> summary(sparkModel)
$coefficients
                     Estimate
(Intercept)       -1.518542340
```

```
UniqueCarrier_WN   0.382722232
UniqueCarrier_DL  -0.047997652
UniqueCarrier_OO   0.367031995
UniqueCarrier_AA   0.046737727
UniqueCarrier_EV   0.344539788
UniqueCarrier_UA   0.299290120
UniqueCarrier_US   0.069837542
UniqueCarrier_MQ   0.467597761
UniqueCarrier_B6   0.326240578
UniqueCarrier_AS  -0.210762769
UniqueCarrier_NK   0.841185903
UniqueCarrier_F9   0.788720078
UniqueCarrier_HA  -0.094638586
DayOfWeek_5        0.232234937
DayOfWeek_4        0.274016179
DayOfWeek_3        0.147645473
DayOfWeek_1        0.347349366
DayOfWeek_2        0.190157420
DayOfWeek_7        0.199774806
Origin_ATL        -0.180512251
...
```

The worst performer is NK (Spirit Airlines). Internally, SparkR uses limited-memory BFGS, which is a limited-memory quasi-Newton optimization method that is similar to the results obtained with R `glm` on the July data:

```
R> summary(model)

Call:
glm(formula = ArrDel15 ~ UniqueCarrier + DoW + Origin + Dest,
    family = "binomial", data = dow)

Deviance Residuals:
    Min       1Q    Median        3Q       Max
-1.4205   -0.7274   -0.6132   -0.4510    2.9414

Coefficients:
```

```
                   Estimate Std. Error z value Pr(>|z|)
(Intercept)       -1.817e+00  2.402e-01  -7.563 3.95e-14 ***
UniqueCarrierAS   -3.296e-01  3.413e-02  -9.658  < 2e-16 ***
UniqueCarrierB6    3.932e-01  2.358e-02  16.676  < 2e-16 ***
UniqueCarrierDL   -6.602e-02  1.850e-02  -3.568 0.000359 ***
UniqueCarrierEV    3.174e-01  2.155e-02  14.728  < 2e-16 ***
UniqueCarrierF9    6.754e-01  2.979e-02  22.668  < 2e-16 ***
UniqueCarrierHA    7.883e-02  7.058e-02   1.117 0.264066
UniqueCarrierMQ    2.175e-01  2.393e-02   9.090  < 2e-16 ***
UniqueCarrierNK    7.928e-01  2.702e-02  29.343  < 2e-16 ***
UniqueCarrierOO    4.001e-01  2.019e-02  19.817  < 2e-16 ***
UniqueCarrierUA    3.982e-01  1.827e-02  21.795  < 2e-16 ***
UniqueCarrierVX    9.723e-02  3.690e-02   2.635 0.008423 **
UniqueCarrierWN    6.358e-01  1.700e-02  37.406  < 2e-16 ***
dowTue             1.365e-01  1.313e-02  10.395  < 2e-16 ***
dowWed             1.724e-01  1.242e-02  13.877  < 2e-16 ***
dowThu             4.593e-02  1.256e-02   3.656 0.000256 ***
dowFri            -2.338e-01  1.311e-02 -17.837  < 2e-16 ***
dowSat            -2.413e-01  1.458e-02 -16.556  < 2e-16 ***
dowSun            -3.028e-01  1.408e-02 -21.511  < 2e-16 ***
OriginABI         -3.355e-01  2.554e-01  -1.314 0.188965
...
```

Other parameters of SparkR `glm` implementation are provided in the following table:

The following table shows a list of parameters for SparkR `glm` implementation:

Parameter	Possible Values	Comments
formula	A symbolic description like in R	Currently only a subset of formula operators are supported: '~', '.', ':', '+', and '-'
family	gaussian or binomial	Needs to be in quotes: gaussian -> linear regression, binomial -> logistic regression
data	DataFrame	Needs to be SparkR DataFrame, not data.frame
lambda	positive	Regularization coefficient
alpha	positive	Elastic-net mixing parameter (refer to glmnet's documentation for details)
standardize	TRUE or FALSE	User-defined

Parameter	Possible Values	Comments
`solver`	l-bfgs, normal or auto	auto will choose the algorithm automatically, l-bfgs means limited-memory BFGS, normal means using normal equation as an analytical solution to the linear regression problem

Reading JSON files in SparkR

Schema on Read is one of the convenient features of big data. The DataFrame class has the ability to figure out the schema of a text file containing a JSON record per line:

```
[akozlov@Alexanders-MacBook-Pro spark-1.6.1-bin-hadoop2.6]$ cat examples/
src/main/resources/people.json
{"name":"Michael"}
{"name":"Andy", "age":30}
{"name":"Justin", "age":19}


[akozlov@Alexanders-MacBook-Pro spark-1.6.1-bin-hadoop2.6]$ bin/sparkR

...


> people = read.json(sqlContext, "examples/src/main/resources/people.
json")
> dtypes(people)
[[1]]
[1] "age"     "bigint"

[[2]]
[1] "name"    "string"

> schema(people)
StructType
|-name = "age", type = "LongType", nullable = TRUE
|-name = "name", type = "StringType", nullable = TRUE
> showDF(people)
+----+-------+
| age|   name|
+----+-------+
```

```
|null|Michael|
|  30|   Andy|
|  19| Justin|
+----+-------+
```

Writing Parquet files in SparkR

As we mentioned in the previous chapter, the Parquet format is an efficient storage format, particularly for low cardinality columns. Parquet files can be read/written directly from R:

```
> write.parquet(sparkDf, "parquet")
```

You can see that the new Parquet file is 66 times smaller that the original zip file downloaded from the DoT:

```
[akozlov@Alexanders-MacBook-Pro spark-1.6.1-bin-hadoop2.6]$ ls -l On_
Time_On_Time_Performance_2015_7.zip parquet/ flights/

-rw-r--r--  1 akozlov  staff  26204213 Sep  9 12:21 /Users/akozlov/spark/
On_Time_On_Time_Performance_2015_7.zip


flights/:
total 459088
-rw-r--r--  1 akozlov  staff  235037955 Sep  9 12:20 On_Time_On_Time_
Performance_2015_7.csv
-rw-r--r--  1 akozlov  staff     12054 Sep  9 12:20 readme.html


parquet/:
total 848
-rw-r--r--  1 akozlov  staff         0 Jan 24 22:50 _SUCCESS
-rw-r--r--  1 akozlov  staff     10000 Jan 24 22:50 _common_metadata
-rw-r--r--  1 akozlov  staff     23498 Jan 24 22:50 _metadata
-rw-r--r--  1 akozlov  staff    394418 Jan 24 22:50 part-r-00000-9e2d0004-
c71f-4bf5-aafe-90822f9d7223.gz.parquet
```

Invoking Scala from R

Let's assume that one has an exceptional implementation of a numeric method in Scala that we want to call from R. One way of doing this would be to use the R system() function that invokes /bin/sh on Unix-like systems. However, the rscala package is a more efficient way that starts a Scala interpreter and maintains communication over TCP/IP network connection.

Here, the Scala interpreter maintains the state (memoization) between the calls. Similarly, one can define functions, as follows:

```
R> scala <- scalaInterpreter()
R> scala %~% 'def pri(i: Stream[Int]): Stream[Int] = i.head #:: pri(i.
tail filter  { x => { println("Evaluating " + x + "%" + i.head); x %
i.head != 0 } } )'
ScalaInterpreterReference... engine: javax.script.ScriptEngine
R> scala %~% 'val primes = pri(Stream.from(2))'
ScalaInterpreterReference... primes: Stream[Int]
R> scala %~% 'primes take 5 foreach println'
2
Evaluating 3%2
3
Evaluating 4%2
Evaluating 5%2
Evaluating 5%3
5
Evaluating 6%2
Evaluating 7%2
Evaluating 7%3
Evaluating 7%5
7
Evaluating 8%2
Evaluating 9%2
Evaluating 9%3
Evaluating 10%2
Evaluating 11%2
Evaluating 11%3
Evaluating 11%5
Evaluating 11%7
```

```
11
R> scala %~% 'primes take 5 foreach println'
2
3
5
7
11
R> scala %~% 'primes take 7 foreach println'
2
3
5
7
11
Evaluating 12%2
Evaluating 13%2
Evaluating 13%3
Evaluating 13%5
Evaluating 13%7
Evaluating 13%11
13
Evaluating 14%2
Evaluating 15%2
Evaluating 15%3
Evaluating 16%2
Evaluating 17%2
Evaluating 17%3
Evaluating 17%5
Evaluating 17%7
Evaluating 17%11
Evaluating 17%13
17
R>
```

R from Scala can be invoked using the ! or !! Scala operators and `Rscript` command:

```
[akozlov@Alexanders-MacBook-Pro ~]$ cat << EOF > rdate.R
> #!/usr/local/bin/Rscript
>
> write(date(), stdout())
> EOF
[akozlov@Alexanders-MacBook-Pro ~]$ chmod a+x rdate.R
[akozlov@Alexanders-MacBook-Pro ~]$ scala
Welcome to Scala version 2.11.7 (Java HotSpot(TM) 64-Bit Server VM, Java
1.8.0_40).
Type in expressions to have them evaluated.
Type :help for more information.

scala> import sys.process._
import sys.process._

scala> val date = Process(Seq("./rdate.R")).!!
date: String =
"Wed Feb 24 02:20:09 2016
"
```

Using Rserve

A more efficient way is to use the similar TCP/IP binary transport protocol to communicate with R with `Rsclient/Rserve` (http://www.rforge.net/Rserve). To start `Rserve` on a node that has R installed, perform the following action:

```
[akozlov@Alexanders-MacBook-Pro ~]$ wget http://www.rforge.net/Rserve/
snapshot/Rserve_1.8-5.tar.gz

[akozlov@Alexanders-MacBook-Pro ~]$ R CMD INSTALL Rserve_1.8-5.tar.gz
...
[akozlov@Alexanders-MacBook-Pro ~]$ R CMD INSTALL Rserve_1.8-5.tar.gz

[akozlov@Alexanders-MacBook-Pro ~]$ $ R -q CMD Rserve

R version 3.2.3 (2015-12-10) -- "Wooden Christmas-Tree"
```

```
Copyright (C) 2015 The R Foundation for Statistical Computing
Platform: x86_64-apple-darwin13.4.0 (64-bit)


R is free software and comes with ABSOLUTELY NO WARRANTY.
You are welcome to redistribute it under certain conditions.
Type 'license()' or 'licence()' for distribution details.


  Natural language support but running in an English locale


R is a collaborative project with many contributors.
Type 'contributors()' for more information and
'citation()' on how to cite R or R packages in publications.


Type 'demo()' for some demos, 'help()' for on-line help, or
'help.start()' for an HTML browser interface to help.
Type 'q()' to quit R.


Rserv started in daemon mode.
```

By default, `Rserv` opens a connection on `localhost:6311`. The advantage of the binary network protocol is that it is platform-independent and multiple clients can communicate with the server. The clients can connect to `Rserve`.

Note that, while passing the results as a binary object has its advantages, you have to be careful with the type mappings between R and Scala. `Rserve` supports other clients, including Python, but I will also cover JSR 223-compliant scripting at the end of this chapter.

Integrating with Python

Python has slowly established ground as a de-facto tool for data science. It has a command-line interface and decent visualization via matplotlib and ggplot, which is based on R's ggplot2. Recently, Wes McKinney, the creator of Pandas, the time series data-analysis package, has joined Cloudera to pave way for Python in big data.

Setting up Python

Python is usually part of the default installation. Spark requires version 2.7.0+.

If you don't have Python on Mac OS, I recommend installing the Homebrew package manager from `http://brew.sh`:

```
[akozlov@Alexanders-MacBook-Pro spark(master)]$ ruby -e "$(curl -fsSL
https://raw.githubusercontent.com/Homebrew/install/master/install)"
==> This script will install:
/usr/local/bin/brew
/usr/local/Library/...
/usr/local/share/man/man1/brew.1

...

[akozlov@Alexanders-MacBook-Pro spark(master)]$ brew install python

...
```

Otherwise, on a Unix-like system, Python can be compiled from the source distribution:

```
$ export PYTHON_VERSION=2.7.11
$ wget -O - https://www.python.org/ftp/python/$PYTHON_VERSION/Python-
$PYTHON_VERSION.tgz | tar xzvf -
$ cd $HOME/Python-$PYTHON_VERSION
$ ./configure--prefix=/usr/local --enable-unicode=ucs4--enable-shared
LDFLAGS="-Wl,-rpath /usr/local/lib"
$ make; sudo make altinstall
$ sudo ln -sf /usr/local/bin/python2.7 /usr/local/bin/python
```

It is good practice to place it in a directory different from the default Python installation. It is normal to have multiple versions of Python on a single system, which usually does not lead to problems as Python separates the installation directories. For the purpose of this chapter, as for many machine learning takes, I'll also need a few packages. The packages and specific versions may differ across installations:

```
$ wget https://bootstrap.pypa.io/ez_setup.py
$ sudo /usr/local/bin/python ez_setup.py
$ sudo /usr/local/bin/easy_install-2.7 pip
$ sudo /usr/local/bin/pip install --upgrade avro nose numpy scipy pandas
statsmodels scikit-learn iso8601 python-dateutil python-snappy
```

If everything compiles—SciPy uses a Fortran compiler and libraries for linear algebra—we are ready to use Python 2.7.11!

 Note that if one wants to use Python with the `pipe` command in a distributed environment, Python needs to be installed on every node in the network.

PySpark

As `bin/sparkR` launches R with preloaded Spark context, `bin/pyspark` launches Python shell with preloaded Spark context and Spark driver running. The `PYSPARK_PYTHON` environment variable can be used to point to a specific Python version:

```
[akozlov@Alexanders-MacBook-Pro spark-1.6.1-bin-hadoop2.6]$ export
PYSPARK_PYTHON=/usr/local/bin/python
[akozlov@Alexanders-MacBook-Pro spark-1.6.1-bin-hadoop2.6]$ bin/pyspark
Python 2.7.11 (default, Jan 23 2016, 20:14:24)
[GCC 4.2.1 Compatible Apple LLVM 7.0.2 (clang-700.1.81)] on darwin
Type "help", "copyright", "credits" or "license" for more information.
Welcome to
      ____              __
     / __/__  ___ _____/ /__
    _\ \/ _ \/ _ `/ __/  '_/
   /__ / .__/\_,_/_/ /_/\_\   version 1.6.1
      /_/

Using Python version 2.7.11 (default, Jan 23 2016 20:14:24)
SparkContext available as sc, HiveContext available as sqlContext.
>>>
```

PySpark directly supports most of MLlib functionality on Spark RDDs (http://spark.apache.org/docs/latest/api/python), but it is known to lag a few releases behind the Scala API (http://spark.apache.org/docs/latest/api/python). As of the 1.6.0+ release, it also supports DataFrames (http://spark.apache.org/docs/latest/sql-programming-guide.html):

```
>>> sfoFlights = sqlContext.sql("SELECT Dest, UniqueCarrier,
ArrDelayMinutes FROM parquet.parquet")
>>> sfoFlights.groupBy(["Dest", "UniqueCarrier"]).agg(func.
avg("ArrDelayMinutes"), func.count("ArrDelayMinutes")).
sort("avg(ArrDelayMinutes)", ascending=False).head(5)
```

```
[Row(Dest=u'HNL', UniqueCarrier=u'HA', avg(ArrDelayMinut
es)=53.70967741935484, count(ArrDelayMinutes)=31), Row(Dest=u'IAH',
UniqueCarrier=u'F9', avg(ArrDelayMinutes)=43.064516129032256,
count(ArrDelayMinutes)=31), Row(Dest=u'LAX', UniqueCarrier=u'DL', av
g(ArrDelayMinutes)=39.68691588785047, count(ArrDelayMinutes)=214),
Row(Dest=u'LAX', UniqueCarrier=u'WN', avg(ArrDelayMinut
es)=29.704453441295545, count(ArrDelayMinutes)=247), Row(Dest=u'MSO',
UniqueCarrier=u'OO', avg(ArrDelayMinutes)=29.551724137931036,
count(ArrDelayMinutes)=29)]
```

Calling Python from Java/Scala

As this is really a book about Scala, we should also mention that one can call Python code and its interpreter directly from Scala (or Java). There are a few options available that will be discussed in this chapter.

Using sys.process._

Scala, as well as Java, can call OS processes via spawning a separate thread, which we already used for interactive analysis in *Chapter 1, Exploratory Data Analysis*: the .! method will start the process and return the exit code, while .!! will return the string that contains the output:

```
scala> import sys.process._
import sys.process._


scala> val retCode = Process(Seq("/usr/local/bin/python", "-c", "import
socket; print(socket.gethostname())")).!
Alexanders-MacBook-Pro.local
retCode: Int = 0


scala> val lines = Process(Seq("/usr/local/bin/python", "-c", """from
datetime import datetime, timedelta; print("Yesterday was {}".
format(datetime.now()-timedelta(days=1)))""")).!!
lines: String =
"Yesterday was 2016-02-12 16:24:53.161853
"
```

Let's try a more complex SVD computation (similar to the one we used in SVD++ recommendation engine, but this time, it invokes BLAS C-libraries at the backend). I created a Python executable that takes a string representing a matrix and the required rank as an input and outputs an SVD approximation with the provided rank:

```python
#!/usr/bin/env python

import sys
import os
import re

import numpy as np
from scipy import linalg
from scipy.linalg import svd

np.set_printoptions(linewidth=10000)

def process_line(input):
    inp = input.rstrip("\r\n")
    if len(inp) > 1:
        try:
            (mat, rank) = inp.split("|")
            a = np.matrix(mat)
            r = int(rank)
        except:
            a = np.matrix(inp)
            r = 1
        U, s, Vh = linalg.svd(a, full_matrices=False)
        for i in xrange(r, s.size):
            s[i] = 0
        S = linalg.diagsvd(s, s.size, s.size)
        print(str(np.dot(U, np.dot(S, Vh))).replace(os.linesep, ";"))

if __name__ == '__main__':
    map(process_line, sys.stdin)
```

Let's call it svd.py and put in in the current directory. Given a matrix and rank as an input, it produces an approximation of a given rank:

```
$ echo -e "1,2,3;2,1,2;3,2,1;7,8,9|3" | ./svd.py
[[ 1.   2.   3.]; [ 2.   1.   2.]; [ 3.   2.   1.]; [ 7.   8.   9.]]
```

To call it from Scala, let's define the following #<<< method in our DSL:

```scala
scala> implicit class RunCommand(command: String) {
     |    def #<<< (input: String)(implicit buffer: StringBuilder) =  {
     |       val process = Process(command)
     |       val io = new ProcessIO (
     |          in  => { in.write(input getBytes "UTF-8"); in.close},
     |          out => { buffer append scala.io.Source.fromInputStream(out).
getLines.mkString("\n"); buffer.append("\n"); out.close() },
     |          err => { scala.io.Source.fromInputStream(err).getLines().
foreach(System.err.println) })
     |       (process run io).exitValue
     |    }
     | }
defined class RunCommand
```

Now, we can use the #<<< operator to call Python's SVD method:

```scala
scala> implicit val buffer = new StringBuilder()
buffer: StringBuilder =

scala> if ("./svd.py" #<<< "1,2,3;2,1,2;3,2,1;7,8,9|1" == 0)
Some(buffer.toString) else None
res77: Option[String] = Some([[ 1.84716691  2.02576751  2.29557674];
[ 1.48971176  1.63375041  1.85134741]; [ 1.71759947  1.88367234
2.13455611]; [ 7.19431647  7.88992728  8.94077601]])
```

Note that as we requested the resulting matrix rank to be one, all rows and columns are linearly dependent. We can even pass several lines of input at a time, as follows:

```scala
scala> if ("./svd.py" #<<< """
     | 1,2,3;2,1,2;3,2,1;7,8,9|0
     | 1,2,3;2,1,2;3,2,1;7,8,9|1
     | 1,2,3;2,1,2;3,2,1;7,8,9|2
     | 1,2,3;2,1,2;3,2,1;7,8,9|3""" == 0) Some(buffer.toString) else None
res80: Option[String] =
Some([[ 0.  0.  0.]; [ 0.  0.  0.]; [ 0.  0.  0.]; [ 0.  0.  0.]]
[[ 1.84716691  2.02576751  2.29557674]; [ 1.48971176  1.63375041
1.85134741]; [ 1.71759947  1.88367234  2.13455611]; [ 7.19431647
7.88992728  8.94077601]]
```

```
[[ 0.9905897    2.02161614   2.98849663]; [ 1.72361156   1.63488399
1.66213642]; [ 3.04783513   1.89011928   1.05847477]; [ 7.04822694
7.88921926   9.05895373]]
```

```
[[ 1.   2.   3.]; [ 2.   1.   2.]; [ 3.   2.   1.]; [ 7.   8.   9.]])
```

Spark pipe

SVD decomposition is usually a pretty heavy operation, so the relative overhead of calling Python in this case is small. We can avoid this overhead if we keep the process running and supply several lines at a time, like we did in the last example. Both Hadoop MR and Spark implement this approach. For example, in Spark, the whole computation will take only one line, as shown in the following:

```
scala> sc.parallelize(List("1,2,3;2,1,2;3,2,1;7,8,9|0",
"1,2,3;2,1,2;3,2,1;7,8,9|1", "1,2,3;2,1,2;3,2,1;7,8,9|2",
"1,2,3;2,1,2;3,2,1;7,8,9|3"),4).pipe("./svd.py").collect.foreach(println)
```

```
[[ 0.   0.   0.]; [ 0.   0.   0.]; [ 0.   0.   0.]; [ 0.   0.   0.]]
```

```
[[ 1.84716691   2.02576751   2.29557674]; [ 1.48971176   1.63375041
1.85134741]; [ 1.71759947   1.88367234   2.13455611]; [ 7.19431647
7.88992728   8.94077601]]
```

```
[[ 0.9905897    2.02161614   2.98849663]; [ 1.72361156   1.63488399
1.66213642]; [ 3.04783513   1.89011928   1.05847477]; [ 7.04822694
7.88921926   9.05895373]]
```

```
[[ 1.   2.   3.]; [ 2.   1.   2.]; [ 3.   2.   1.]; [ 7.   8.   9.]]
```

The whole pipeline is ready to be distributed across a cluster of multicore workstations! I think you will be in love with Scala/Spark already.

Note that debugging the pipelined executions might be tricky as the data is passed from one process to another using OS pipes.

Jython and JSR 223

For completeness, we need to mention Jython, a Java implementation of Python (as opposed to a more familiar C implementation, also called CPython). Jython avoids the problem of passing input/output via OS pipelines by allowing the users to compile Python source code to Java byte codes, and running the resulting bytecodes on any Java virtual machine. As Scala also runs in Java virtual machine, it can use the Jython classes directly, although the reverse is not true in general; Scala classes sometimes are not compatible to be used by Java/Jython.

JSR 223

In this particular case, the request is for "Scripting for the JavaTM Platform" and was originally filed on Nov 15th 2004 (`https://www.jcp.org/en/jsr/detail?id=223`). At the beginning, it was targeted towards the ability of the Java servlet to work with multiple scripting languages. The specification requires the scripting language maintainers to provide a Java JAR with corresponding implementations. Portability issues hindered practical implementations, particularly when platforms require complex interaction with OS, such as dynamic linking in C or Fortran. Currently, only a handful languages are supported, with R and Python being supported, but in incomplete form.

Since Java 6, JSR 223: Scripting for Java added the `javax.script` package that allows multiple scripting languages to be called through the same API as long as the language provides a script engine. To add the Jython scripting language, download the latest Jython JAR from the Jython site at `http://www.jython.org/downloads.html`:

```
$ wget -O jython-standalone-2.7.0.jar http://search.maven.org/
remotecontent?filepath=org/python/jython-standalone/2.7.0/jython-
standalone-2.7.0.jar
```

```
[akozlov@Alexanders-MacBook-Pro Scala]$ scala -cp jython-standalone-
2.7.0.jar
Welcome to Scala version 2.11.7 (Java HotSpot(TM) 64-Bit Server VM, Java
1.8.0_40).
Type in expressions to have them evaluated.
Type :help for more information.


scala> import javax.script.ScriptEngine;
...
scala> import javax.script.ScriptEngineManager;
...
scala> import javax.script.ScriptException;
...
scala> val manager = new ScriptEngineManager();
manager: javax.script.ScriptEngineManager = javax.script.
ScriptEngineManager@3a03464


scala> val engines = manager.getEngineFactories();
```

```
engines: java.util.List[javax.script.ScriptEngineFactory] = [org.python.
jsr223.PyScriptEngineFactory@4909b8da, jdk.nashorn.api.scripting.
NashornScriptEngineFactory@68837a77, scala.tools.nsc.interpreter.
IMain$Factory@1324409e]
```

Now, I can use the Jython/Python scripting engine:

```
scala> val engine = new ScriptEngineManager().getEngineByName("jython");

engine: javax.script.ScriptEngine = org.python.jsr223.
PyScriptEngine@6094de13


scala> engine.eval("from datetime import datetime, timedelta; yesterday =
str(datetime.now()-timedelta(days=1))")
res15: Object = null


scala> engine.get("yesterday")
res16: Object = 2016-02-12 23:26:38.012000
```

It is worth giving a disclaimer here that not all Python modules are available in Jython. Modules that require a C/Fortran dynamic linkage for the library that doesn't exist in Java are not likely to work in Jython. Specifically, NumPy and SciPy are not supported in Jython as they rely on C/Fortran. If you discover some other missing modules, you can try copying the .py file from a Python distribution to a sys.path Jython directory—if this works, consider yourself lucky.

Jython has the advantage of accessing Python-rich modules without the necessity of starting the Python runtime on each call, which might result in a significant performance saving:

```
scala> val startTime = System.nanoTime
startTime: Long = 54384084381087


scala> for (i <- 1 to 100) {
     |     engine.eval("from datetime import datetime, timedelta; yesterday
= str(datetime.now()-timedelta(days=1))")
     |     val yesterday = engine.get("yesterday")
     | }


scala> val elapsed = 1e-9 * (System.nanoTime - startTime)
elapsed: Double = 0.270837934


scala> val startTime = System.nanoTime
```

```
startTime: Long = 54391560460133


scala> for (i <- 1 to 100) {
     |     val yesterday = Process(Seq("/usr/local/bin/python", "-c",
"""from datetime import datetime, timedelta; print(datetime.now()-
timedelta(days=1))""")).!!
     | }


scala> val elapsed = 1e-9 * (System.nanoTime - startTime)
elapsed: Double = 2.221937263
```

Jython JSR 223 call is 10 times faster!

Summary

R and Python are like bread and butter for a data scientist. Modern frameworks tend to be interoperable and borrow from each other's strength. In this chapter, I went over the plumbing of interoperability with R and Python. Both of them have packages (R) and modules (Python) that became very popular and extend the current Scala/Spark functionality. Many consider R and Python existing libraries to be crucial for their implementations.

This chapter demonstrated a few ways to integrate these packages and provide the tradeoffs of using these integrations so that we can proceed on to the next chapter, looking at the NLP, where functional programming has been traditionally used from the start.

9
NLP in Scala

This chapter describes a few common techniques of **Natural Language Processing** (**NLP**), specifically, the ones that can benefit from Scala. There are some NLP packages in the open source out there. The most famous of them is probably NLTK (`http://www.nltk.org`), which is written in Python, and ostensibly even a larger number of proprietary software solutions emphasizing different aspects of NLP. It is worth mentioning Wolf (`https://github.com/wolfe-pack`), FACTORIE (`http://factorie.cs.umass.edu`), and ScalaNLP (`http://www.scalanlp.org`), and skymind (`http://www.skymind.io`), which is partly proprietary. However, few open source projects in this area remain active for a long period of time for one or another reason. Most projects are being eclipsed by Spark and MLlib capabilities, particularly, in the scalability aspect.

Instead of giving a detailed description of each of the NLP projects, which also might include speech-to-text, text-to-speech, and language translators, I will provide a few basic techniques focused on leveraging Spark MLlib in this chapter. The chapter comes very naturally as the last analytics chapter in this book. Scala is a very natural-language looking computer language and this chapter will leverage the techniques I developed earlier.

NLP arguably is the core of AI. Originally, the AI was created to mimic the humans, and natural language parsing and understanding is an indispensable part of it. Big data techniques has started to penetrate NLP, even though traditionally, NLP is very computationally intensive and is regarded as a small data problem. NLP often requires extensive deep learning techniques, and the volume of data of all written texts appears to be not so large compared to the logs volumes generated by all the machines today and analyzed by the big data machinery.

Even though the Library of Congress counts millions of documents, most of them can be digitized in PBs of actual digital data, a volume that any social websites is able to collect, store, and analyze within a few seconds. Complete works of most prolific authors can be stored within a few MBs of files (refer to *Table 09-1*). Nonetheless, the social network and ADTECH companies parse text from millions of users and in hundreds of contexts every day.

The complete works of	When lived	Size
Plato	428/427 (or 424/423) - 348/347 BC	2.1 MB
William Shakespeare	26 April 1564 (baptized) - 23 April 1616	3.8 MB
Fyodor Dostoevsky	11 November 1821 - 9 February 1881	5.9 MB
Leo Tolstoy	9 September 1828 - 20 November 1910	6.9 MB
Mark Twain	November 30, 1835 - April 21, 1910	13 MB

Table 09-1. Complete Works collections of some famous writers (most can be acquired on Amazon.com today for a few dollars, later authors, although readily digitized, are more expensive)

The natural language is a dynamic concept that changes over time, technology, and generations. We saw the appearance of emoticons, three-letter abbreviations, and so on. Foreign languages tend to borrow from each other; describing this dynamic ecosystem is a challenge on itself.

As in the previous chapters, I will focus on how to use Scala as a tool to orchestrate the language analysis rather than rewriting the tools in Scala. As the topic is so large, I will not claim to cover all aspects of NLP here.

In this chapter, we will cover the following topics:

- Discussing NLP with the example of text processing pipeline and stages
- Learning techniques for simple text analysis in terms of bags
- Learning about **Term Frequency Inverse Document Frequency** (TF-IDF) technique that goes beyond simple bag analysis and de facto the standard in **Information Retrieval (IR)**
- Learning about document clustering with the example of the **Latent Dirichlet Allocation (LDA)** approach
- Performing semantic analysis using word2vec n-gram-based algorithms

Text analysis pipeline

Before we proceed to detailed algorithms, let's look at a generic text-processing pipeline depicted in *Figure 9-1*. In text analysis, the input is usually presented as a stream of characters (depending on the specific language).

Lexical analysis has to do with breaking this stream into a sequence of words (or lexemes in linguistic analysis). Often it is also called tokenization (and the words called the tokens). **ANother Tool for Language Recognition (ANTLR)** (`http://www.antlr.org/`) and Flex (`http://flex.sourceforge.net`) are probably the most famous in the open source community. One of the classical examples of ambiguity is lexical ambiguity. For example, in the phrase *I saw a bat. bat* can mean either an animal or a baseball bat. We usually need context to figure this out, which we will discuss next:

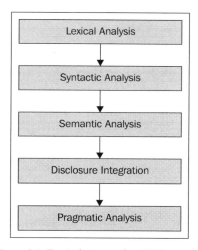

Figure 9-1. Typical stages of an NLP process.

Syntactic analysis, or parsing, traditionally deals with matching the structure of the text with grammar rules. This is relatively more important for computer languages that do not allow any ambiguity. In natural languages, this process is usually called chunking and tagging. In many cases, the meaning of the word in human language can be subject to context, intonation, or even body language or facial expression. The value of such analysis, as opposed to the big data approach, where the volume of data trumps complexity is still a contentious topic—one example of the latter is the word2vec approach, which will be described later.

Semantic analysis is the process of extracting language-independent meaning from the syntactic structures. As much as possible, it also involves removing features specific to particular cultural and linguistic contexts, to the extent that such a project is possible. The sources of ambiguity at this stage are: phrase attachment, conjunction, noun group structure, semantic ambiguity, anaphoric non-literal speech, and so on. Again, word2vec partially deals with these issues.

Disclosure integration partially deals with the issue of the context: the meaning of a sentence or an idiom can depend on the sentences or paragraphs before that. Syntactic analysis and cultural background play an important role here.

Finally, pragmatic analysis is yet another layer of complexity trying to reinterpret what is said in terms of what the intention was. How does this change the state of the world? Is it actionable?

Simple text analysis

The straightforward representation of the document is a bag of words. Scala, and Spark, provides an excellent paradigm to perform analysis on the word distributions. First, we read the whole collection of texts, and then count the unique words:

```
$ bin/spark-shell
Welcome to


      ____              __
     / __/__  ___ _____/ /__
    _\ \/ _ \/ _ `/ __/  '_/
   /___/ .__/\_,_/_/ /_/\_\   version 1.6.1
      /_/


Using Scala version 2.10.5 (Java HotSpot(TM) 64-Bit Server VM, Java
1.8.0_40)
Type in expressions to have them evaluated.
Type :help for more information.
Spark context available as sc.
SQL context available as sqlContext.


scala> val leotolstoy = sc.textFile("leotolstoy").cache
```

```
leotolstoy: org.apache.spark.rdd.RDD[String] = leotolstoy
MapPartitionsRDD[1] at textFile at <console>:27


scala> leotolstoy.flatMap(_.split("\\W+")).count
res1: Long = 1318234


scala> val shakespeare = sc.textFile("shakespeare").cache
shakespeare: org.apache.spark.rdd.RDD[String] = shakespeare
MapPartitionsRDD[7] at textFile at <console>:27


scala> shakespeare.flatMap(_.split("\\W+")).count
res2: Long = 1051958
```

This gives us just an estimate of the number of distinct words in the repertoire of quite different authors. The simplest way to find intersection between the two corpuses is to find the common vocabulary (which will be quite different as *Leo Tolstoy* wrote in Russian and French, while *Shakespeare* was an English-writing author):

```
scala> :silent


scala> val shakespeareBag = shakespeare.flatMap(_.split("\\W+")).map(_.
toLowerCase).distinct


scala> val leotolstoyBag = leotolstoy.flatMap(_.split("\\W+")).map(_.
toLowerCase).distinct
leotolstoyBag: org.apache.spark.rdd.RDD[String] = MapPartitionsRDD[27] at
map at <console>:29


scala> println("The bags intersection is " + leotolstoyBag.
intersection(shakespeareBag).count)
The bags intersection is 11552
```

A few thousands word indices are manageable with the current implementations. For any new story, we can determine whether it is more likely to be written by Leo Tolstoy or *William Shakespeare*. Let's take a look at *The King James Version of the Bible*, which also can be downloaded from Project Gutenberg (https://www.gutenberg.org/files/10/10-h/10-h.htm):

```
$ (mkdir bible; cd bible; wget http://www.gutenberg.org/cache/epub/10/pg10.txt)
```

```
scala> val bible = sc.textFile("bible").cache
```

```
scala> val bibleBag = bible.flatMap(_.split("\\W+")).map(_.toLowerCase).distinct
```

```
scala>:silent
```

```
scala> bibleBag.intersection(shakespeareBag).count
res5: Long = 7250
```

```
scala> bibleBag.intersection(leotolstoyBag).count
res24: Long = 6611
```

This seems reasonable as the religious language was popular during the Shakespearean time. On the other hand, plays by *Anton Chekhov* have a larger intersection with the *Leo Tolstoy* vocabulary:

```
$ (mkdir chekhov; cd chekhov;
 wget http://www.gutenberg.org/cache/epub/7986/pg7986.txt
 wget http://www.gutenberg.org/cache/epub/1756/pg1756.txt
 wget http://www.gutenberg.org/cache/epub/1754/1754.txt
 wget http://www.gutenberg.org/cache/epub/13415/pg13415.txt)
```

```
scala> val chekhov = sc.textFile("chekhov").cache
chekhov: org.apache.spark.rdd.RDD[String] = chekhov MapPartitionsRDD[61]
at textFile at <console>:27
```

```
scala> val chekhovBag = chekhov.flatMap(_.split("\\W+")).map(_.toLowerCase).distinct
```

```
chekhovBag: org.apache.spark.rdd.RDD[String] = MapPartitionsRDD[66] at
distinct at <console>:29
```

```
scala> chekhovBag.intersection(leotolstoyBag).count
res8: Long = 8263
```

```
scala> chekhovBag.intersection(shakespeareBag).count
res9: Long = 6457
```

This is a very simple approach that works, but there are a number of commonly known improvements we can make. First, a common technique is to stem the words. In many languages, words have a common part, often called root, and a changeable prefix or suffix, which may depend on the context, gender, time, and so on. Stemming is the process of improving the distinct count and intersection by approximating this flexible word form to the root, base, or a stem form in general. The stem form does not need to be identical to the morphological root of the word, it is usually sufficient that related words map to the same stem, even if this stem is not in itself a valid grammatical root. Secondly, we probably should account for the frequency of the words—while we will describe more elaborate methods in the next section, for the purpose of this exercise, we'll exclude the words with very high count, that usually are present in any document such as articles and possessive pronouns, which are usually called stop words, and the words with very low count. Specifically, I'll use the optimized **Porter Stemmer** implementation that I described in more detail at the end of the chapter.

 The `http://tartarus.org/martin/PorterStemmer/` site contains some of the Porter Stemmer implementations in Scala and other languages, including a highly optimized ANSI C, which may be more efficient, but here I will provide another optimized Scala version that can be used immediately with Spark.

The Stemmer example will stem the words and count the relative intersections between them, removing the stop words:

```
def main(args: Array[String]) {

    val stemmer = new Stemmer

    val conf = new SparkConf().
      setAppName("Stemmer").
```

```
        setMaster(args(0))

    val sc = new SparkContext(conf)

    val stopwords = scala.collection.immutable.TreeSet(
      "", "i", "a", "an", "and", "are", "as", "at", "be", "but",
        "by", "for", "from", "had", "has", "he", "her", "him", "his",
        "in", "is", "it", "its", "my", "not", "of", "on", "she",
        "that", "the", "to", "was", "were", "will", "with", "you"
    ) map { stemmer.stem(_) }

    val bags = for (name <- args.slice(1, args.length)) yield {
      val rdd = sc.textFile(name).map(_.toLowerCase)
      if (name == "nytimes" || name == "nips" || name == "enron")
        rdd.filter(!_.startsWith("zzz_")).flatMap(_.split("_"))
          .map(stemmer.stem(_))
          .distinct.filter(!stopwords.contains(_)).cache
      else {
        val withCounts = rdd.flatMap(_.split("\\W+"))
          .map(stemmer.stem(_)).filter(!stopwords.contains(_))
          .map((_, 1)).reduceByKey(_+_)
        val minCount = scala.math.max(1L, 0.0001 *
          withCounts.count.toLong)
        withCounts.filter(_._2 > minCount).map(_._1).cache
      }
    }

    val cntRoots = (0 until { args.length - 1 }).map(i =>
      Math.sqrt(bags(i).count.toDouble))

    for(l <- 0 until { args.length - 1 }; r <- l until
      { args.length - 1 }) {
      val cnt = bags(l).intersection(bags(r)).count
      println("The intersect " + args(l+1) + " x " + args(r+1) + "
        is: " + cnt + " (" +
        (cnt.toDouble / cntRoots(l) / cntRoots(r)) + ")")
    }

    sc.stop
    }
}
```

When one runs the main class example from the command line, it outputs the stemmed bag sizes and intersection for datasets specified as parameters (these are directories in the home filesystem with documents):

```
$ sbt "run-main org.akozlov.examples.Stemmer local[2] shakespeare
leotolstoy chekhov nytimes nips enron bible"
```

[info] Loading project definition from /Users/akozlov/Src/Book/ml-in-scala/chapter09/project

[info] Set current project to NLP in Scala (in build file:/Users/akozlov/Src/Book/ml-in-scala/chapter09/)

[info] Running org.akozlov.examples.Stemmer local[2] shakespeare leotolstoy chekhov nytimes nips enron bible

The intersect shakespeare x shakespeare is: 10533 (1.0)

The intersect shakespeare x leotolstoy is: 5834 (0.5293670391596142)

The intersect shakespeare x chekhov is: 3295 (0.4715281914492153)

The intersect shakespeare x nytimes is: 7207 (0.4163369701270161)

The intersect shakespeare x nips is: 2726 (0.27457329089479504)

The intersect shakespeare x enron is: 5217 (0.34431535832271265)

The intersect shakespeare x bible is: 3826 (0.45171392986714726)

The intersect leotolstoy x leotolstoy is: 11531 (0.9999999999999999)

The intersect leotolstoy x chekhov is: 4099 (0.5606253333241973)

The intersect leotolstoy x nytimes is: 8657 (0.47796976891152176)

The intersect leotolstoy x nips is: 3231 (0.3110369262979765)

The intersect leotolstoy x enron is: 6076 (0.38326210407266764)

The intersect leotolstoy x bible is: 3455 (0.3898604013063757)

The intersect chekhov x chekhov is: 4636 (1.0)

The intersect chekhov x nytimes is: 3843 (0.33463022711780555)

The intersect chekhov x nips is: 1889 (0.28679311682962116)

The intersect chekhov x enron is: 3213 (0.31963226496874225)

The intersect chekhov x bible is: 2282 (0.40610513998395287)

The intersect nytimes x nytimes is: 28449 (1.0)

The intersect nytimes x nips is: 4954 (0.30362042173997206)

The intersect nytimes x enron is: 11273 (0.45270741164576034)

The intersect nytimes x bible is: 3655 (0.2625720159205085)

The intersect nips x nips is: 9358 (1.0000000000000002)

The intersect nips x enron is: 4888 (0.3422561629856124)

The intersect nips x bible is: 1615 (0.20229053645165143)

```
The intersect enron x enron is: 21796 (1.0)

The intersect enron x bible is: 2895 (0.23760453654690084)

The intersect bible x bible is: 6811 (1.0)

[success] Total time: 12 s, completed May 17, 2016 11:00:38 PM
```

This, in this case, just confirms the hypothesis that Bible's vocabulary is closer to *William Shakespeare* than to Leo Tolstoy and other sources. Interestingly, modern vocabularies of *NY Times* articles and Enron's e-mails from the previous chapters are much closer to *Leo Tolstoy's*, which is probably more an indication of the translation quality.

Another thing to notice is that the pretty complex analysis took about *40* lines of Scala code (not counting the libraries, specifically the Porter Stemmer, which is about ~ *100* lines) and about 12 seconds. The power of Scala is that it can leverage other libraries very efficiently to write concise code.

Serialization

We already talked about serialization in *Chapter 6, Working with Unstructured Data*. As Spark's tasks are executed in different threads and potentially JVMs, Spark does a lot of serialization/deserialization when passing the objects. Potentially, I could use `map { val stemmer = new Stemmer; stemmer.stem(_) }` instead of `map { stemmer.stem(_) }`, but the latter reuses the object for multiple iterations and seems to be linguistically more appealing. One suggested performance optimization is to use *Kryo serializer*, which is less flexible than the Java serializer, but more performant. However, for integrative purpose, it is much easier to just make every object in the pipeline serializable and use default Java serialization.

As another example, let's compute the distribution of word frequencies, as follows:

```
scala> val bags = for (name <- List("shakespeare", "leotolstoy",
"chekhov", "nytimes", "enron", "bible")) yield {
     |       sc textFile(name) flatMap { _.split("\\W+") } map {
_.toLowerCase } map { stemmer.stem(_) } filter { ! stopwords.contains(_)
} cache()
     | }
bags: List[org.apache.spark.rdd.RDD[String]] = List(MapPartitionsRDD[93]
at filter at <console>:36, MapPartitionsRDD[98] at filter at
<console>:36, MapPartitionsRDD[103] at filter at <console>:36,
MapPartitionsRDD[108] at filter at <console>:36, MapPartitionsRDD[113] at
filter at <console>:36, MapPartitionsRDD[118] at filter at <console>:36)
```

```scala
scala> bags reduceLeft { (a, b) => a.union(b) } map { (_, 1) }
reduceByKey { _+_ } collect() sortBy(- _._2) map { x => scala.math.
log(x._2) }
```

```
res18: Array[Double] = Array(10.27759958298627, 10.1152465449837,
10.058652004037477, 10.046635061754612, 9.999615579630348,
9.855399641729074, 9.834405391348684, 9.801233318497372,
9.792667717430884, 9.76347807952779, 9.742496866444002,
9.655474810542554, 9.630365631415676, 9.623244409181346,
9.593355351246755, 9.517604459155686, 9.515837804297965,
9.47231994707559, 9.45930760329985, 9.441531454869693, 9.435561763085358,
9.426257878198653, 9.378985497953893, 9.355997944398545,
9.34862295977619, 9.300820725104558, 9.25569607369698, 9.25320827220336,
9.229162126216771, 9.20391980417326, 9.19917830726999, 9.167224080902555,
9.153875834995056, 9.137877200242468, 9.129889247578555,
9.090430075303626, 9.090091799380007, 9.083075020930307,
9.077722847361343, 9.070273383079064, 9.0542711863262...
```

. . .

The distribution of relative frequencies on the log-log scale is presented in the following diagram. With the exception of the first few tokens, the dependency of frequency on rank is almost linear:

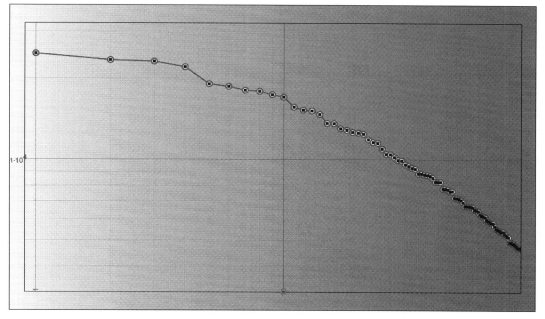

Figure 9-2. A typical distribution of word relative frequencies on log-log scale (Zipf's Law)

MLlib algorithms in Spark

Let's halt at MLlib that complements other NLP libraries written in Scala. MLlib is primarily important because of scalability, and thus supports a few of the data preparation and text processing algorithms, particularly in the area of feature construction (http://spark.apache.org/docs/latest/ml-features.html).

TF-IDF

Although the preceding analysis can already give a powerful insight, the piece of information that is missing from the analysis is term frequency information. The term frequencies are relatively more important in information retrieval, where the collection of documents need to be searched and ranked in relation to a few terms. The top documents are usually returned to the user.

TF-IDF is a standard technique where term frequencies are offset by the frequencies of the terms in the corpus. Spark has an implementation of the TF-IDF. Spark uses a hash function to identify the terms. This approach avoids the need to compute a global term-to-index map, but can be subject to potential hash collisions, the probability of which is determined by the number of buckets of the hash table. The default feature dimension is $2^{20}=1,048,576$.

In the Spark implementation, each document is a line in the dataset. We can convert it into to an RDD of iterables and compute the hashing by the following code:

```
scala> import org.apache.spark.mllib.feature.HashingTF
import org.apache.spark.mllib.feature.HashingTF


scala> import org.apache.spark.mllib.linalg.Vector
import org.apache.spark.mllib.linalg.Vector


scala> val hashingTF = new HashingTF
hashingTF: org.apache.spark.mllib.feature.HashingTF = org.apache.spark.
mllib.feature.HashingTF@61b975f7


scala> val documents: RDD[Seq[String]] = sc.textFile("shakepeare").map(_.
split("\\W+").toSeq)
documents: org.apache.spark.rdd.RDD[Seq[String]] = MapPartitionsRDD[263]
at map at <console>:34


scala> val tf = hashingTF transform documents
tf: org.apache.spark.rdd.RDD[org.apache.spark.mllib.linalg.Vector] =
MapPartitionsRDD[264] at map at HashingTF.scala:76
```

When computing `hashingTF`, we only need a single pass over the data, applying IDF needs two passes: first to compute the IDF vector and second to scale the term frequencies by IDF:

```scala
scala> tf.cache
res26: tf.type = MapPartitionsRDD[268] at map at HashingTF.scala:76


scala> import org.apache.spark.mllib.feature.IDF
import org.apache.spark.mllib.feature.IDF


scala> val idf = new IDF(minDocFreq = 2) fit tf
idf: org.apache.spark.mllib.feature.IDFModel = org.apache.spark.mllib.feature.IDFModel@514bda2d


scala> val tfidf = idf transform tf
tfidf: org.apache.spark.rdd.RDD[org.apache.spark.mllib.linalg.Vector] = MapPartitionsRDD[272] at mapPartitions at IDF.scala:178


scala> tfidf take(10) foreach println
(1048576,[3159,3543,84049,582393,787662,838279,928610,961626,1021219,1021
273],[3.9626355004005083,4.556357737874695,8.380602528651274,8.1577369746
83708,11.513471982269106,9.316247404932888,10.666174121881904,11.51347198
2269106,8.07948477778396,11.002646358503116])

(1048576,[267794,1021219],[8.783442874448122,8.07948477778396])

(1048576,[0],[0.5688129477150906])

(1048576,[3123,3370,3521,3543,96727,101577,114801,116103,497275,504006,50
8606,843002,962509,980206],[4.207164322003765,2.9674322162952897,4.125144
122691999,2.2781788689373474,2.132236195047438,3.2951341639027754,1.92045
75904855747,6.318664992090735,11.002646358503116,3.1043838099579815,5.451
238364272918,11.002646358503116,8.43769700104158,10.30949917794317])

(1048576,[0,3371,3521,3555,27409,89087,104545,107877,552624,735790,910062
,943655,962421],[0.5688129477150906,3.442878442319589,4.125144122691999,4
.462482535201062,5.023254392629403,5.160262034409286,5.646060083831103,4.
712188947797486,11.002646358503116,7.006282204641219,6.216822672821767,11
.513471982269106,8.898512204232908])

(1048576,[3371,3543,82108,114801,149895,279256,582393,597025,838279,91518
1],[3.442878442319589,2.2781788689373474,6.017670811187438,3.840915180971
1495,7.893585399642122,6.625632265652778,8.157736974683708,10.41485969360
0997,9.316247404932888,11.513471982269106])

(1048576,[3123,3555,413342,504006,690950,702035,980206],[4.20716432200376
5,4.462482535201062,3.4399651117812313,3.1043838099579815,11.513471982269
106,11.002646358503116,10.30949917794317])
```

```
(1048576,[0],[0.5688129477150906])

(1048576,[97,1344,3370,100898,105489,508606,582393,736902,838279,1026302]
,[2.533299776544098,23.026943964538212,2.9674322162952897,0.0,11.22578990
9817326,5.451238364272918,8.157736974683708,10.30949917794317,9.316247404
932888,11.513471982269106])

(1048576,[0,1344,3365,114801,327690,357319,413342,692611,867249,965170],[
4.550503581720725,23.026943964538212,2.7455719545259836,1.920457590485574
7,8.268278849083533,9.521041817578901,3.4399651117812313,0.0,6.6614417183
49489,0.0])
```

Here we see each document represented by a set of terms and their scores.

LDA

LDA in Spark MLlib is a clustering mechanism, where the feature vectors represent the counts of words in a document. The model maximizes the probability of observing the word counts, given the assumption that each document is a mixture of topics and the words in the documents are generated based on **Dirichlet distribution** (a generalization of beta distribution on multinomial case) for each of the topic independently. The goal is to derive the (latent) distribution of the topics and the parameters of the words generation statistical model.

The MLlib implementation is based on 2009 LDA paper (http://www.jmlr.org/papers/volume10/newman09a/newman09a.pdf) and uses GraphX to implement a distributed **Expectation Maximization** (**EM**) algorithm for assigning topics to the documents.

Let's take the Enron e-mail corpus discussed in *Chapter 7, Working with Graph Algorithms*, where we tried to figure out communications graph. For e-mail clustering, we need to extract the body of the e-mail and place is as a single line in the training file:

```
$ mkdir enron
$ cat /dev/null > enron/all.txt
$ for f in $(find maildir -name \*\. -print); do cat $f | sed
'1,/^$/d;/^$/d' | tr "\n\r" "  " >> enron/all.txt; echo "" >> enron/all.
txt; done
$
```

Now, let's use Scala/Spark to construct a corpus dataset containing the document ID, followed by a dense array of word counts in the bag:

```
$ spark-shell --driver-memory 8g --executor-memory 8g --packages com.
github.fommil.netlib:all:1.1.2
Ivy Default Cache set to: /home/alex/.ivy2/cache
```

The jars for the packages stored in: /home/alex/.ivy2/jars

:: loading settings :: url = jar:file:/opt/cloudera/parcels/CDH-
5.5.2-1.cdh5.5.2.p0.4/jars/spark-assembly-1.5.0-cdh5.5.2-hadoop2.6.0-
cdh5.5.2.jar!/org/apache/ivy/core/settings/ivysettings.xml

com.github.fommil.netlib#all added as a dependency

:: resolving dependencies :: org.apache.spark#spark-submit-parent;1.0

  confs: [default]

    found com.github.fommil.netlib#all;1.1.2 in central

    found net.sourceforge.f2j#arpack_combined_all;0.1 in central

    found com.github.fommil.netlib#core;1.1.2 in central

    found com.github.fommil.netlib#netlib-native_ref-osx-x86_64;1.1 in
central

    found com.github.fommil.netlib#native_ref-java;1.1 in central

    found com.github.fommil#jniloader;1.1 in central

    found com.github.fommil.netlib#netlib-native_ref-linux-x86_64;1.1 in
central

    found com.github.fommil.netlib#netlib-native_ref-linux-i686;1.1 in
central

    found com.github.fommil.netlib#netlib-native_ref-win-x86_64;1.1 in
central

    found com.github.fommil.netlib#netlib-native_ref-win-i686;1.1 in
central

    found com.github.fommil.netlib#netlib-native_ref-linux-armhf;1.1 in
central

    found com.github.fommil.netlib#netlib-native_system-osx-x86_64;1.1 in
central

    found com.github.fommil.netlib#native_system-java;1.1 in central

    found com.github.fommil.netlib#netlib-native_system-linux-x86_64;1.1 in
central

    found com.github.fommil.netlib#netlib-native_system-linux-i686;1.1 in
central

    found com.github.fommil.netlib#netlib-native_system-linux-armhf;1.1 in
central

    found com.github.fommil.netlib#netlib-native_system-win-x86_64;1.1 in
central

    found com.github.fommil.netlib#netlib-native_system-win-i686;1.1 in
central

downloading https://repo1.maven.org/maven2/net/sourceforge/f2j/arpack_
combined_all/0.1/arpack_combined_all-0.1-javadoc.jar ...

```
[SUCCESSFUL ] net.sourceforge.f2j#arpack_combined_all;0.1!arpack_
combined_all.jar (513ms)
```

downloading https://repo1.maven.org/maven2/com/github/fommil/netlib/
core/1.1.2/core-1.1.2.jar ...

```
[SUCCESSFUL ] com.github.fommil.netlib#core;1.1.2!core.jar (18ms)
```

downloading https://repo1.maven.org/maven2/com/github/fommil/netlib/
netlib-native_ref-osx-x86_64/1.1/netlib-native_ref-osx-x86_64-1.1-
natives.jar ...

```
[SUCCESSFUL ] com.github.fommil.netlib#netlib-native_ref-osx-
x86_64;1.1!netlib-native_ref-osx-x86_64.jar (167ms)
```

downloading https://repo1.maven.org/maven2/com/github/fommil/netlib/
netlib-native_ref-linux-x86_64/1.1/netlib-native_ref-linux-x86_64-1.1-
natives.jar ...

```
[SUCCESSFUL ] com.github.fommil.netlib#netlib-native_ref-linux-
x86_64;1.1!netlib-native_ref-linux-x86_64.jar (159ms)
```

downloading https://repo1.maven.org/maven2/com/github/fommil/netlib/
netlib-native_ref-linux-i686/1.1/netlib-native_ref-linux-i686-1.1-
natives.jar ...

```
[SUCCESSFUL ] com.github.fommil.netlib#netlib-native_ref-linux-
i686;1.1!netlib-native_ref-linux-i686.jar (131ms)
```

downloading https://repo1.maven.org/maven2/com/github/fommil/netlib/
netlib-native_ref-win-x86_64/1.1/netlib-native_ref-win-x86_64-1.1-
natives.jar ...

```
[SUCCESSFUL ] com.github.fommil.netlib#netlib-native_ref-win-
x86_64;1.1!netlib-native_ref-win-x86_64.jar (210ms)
```

downloading https://repo1.maven.org/maven2/com/github/fommil/netlib/
netlib-native_ref-win-i686/1.1/netlib-native_ref-win-i686-1.1-natives.jar
...

```
[SUCCESSFUL ] com.github.fommil.netlib#netlib-native_ref-win-
i686;1.1!netlib-native_ref-win-i686.jar (167ms)
```

downloading https://repo1.maven.org/maven2/com/github/fommil/netlib/
netlib-native_ref-linux-armhf/1.1/netlib-native_ref-linux-armhf-1.1-
natives.jar ...

```
[SUCCESSFUL ] com.github.fommil.netlib#netlib-native_ref-linux-
armhf;1.1!netlib-native_ref-linux-armhf.jar (110ms)
```

downloading https://repo1.maven.org/maven2/com/github/fommil/netlib/
netlib-native_system-osx-x86_64/1.1/netlib-native_system-osx-x86_64-1.1-
natives.jar ...

```
[SUCCESSFUL ] com.github.fommil.netlib#netlib-native_system-osx-
x86_64;1.1!netlib-native_system-osx-x86_64.jar (54ms)
```

downloading https://repo1.maven.org/maven2/com/github/fommil/netlib/
netlib-native_system-linux-x86_64/1.1/netlib-native_system-linux-x86_64-
1.1-natives.jar ...

```
   [SUCCESSFUL ] com.github.fommil.netlib#netlib-native_system-linux-
x86_64;1.1!netlib-native_system-linux-x86_64.jar (47ms)

downloading https://repo1.maven.org/maven2/com/github/fommil/netlib/
netlib-native_system-linux-i686/1.1/netlib-native_system-linux-i686-1.1-
natives.jar ...

   [SUCCESSFUL ] com.github.fommil.netlib#netlib-native_system-linux-
i686;1.1!netlib-native_system-linux-i686.jar (44ms)

downloading https://repo1.maven.org/maven2/com/github/fommil/netlib/
netlib-native_system-linux-armhf/1.1/netlib-native_system-linux-armhf-
1.1-natives.jar ...

[SUCCESSFUL ] com.github.fommil.netlib#netlib-native_system-linux-
armhf;1.1!netlib-native_system-linux-armhf.jar (35ms)

downloading https://repo1.maven.org/maven2/com/github/fommil/netlib/
netlib-native_system-win-x86_64/1.1/netlib-native_system-win-x86_64-1.1-
natives.jar ...

   [SUCCESSFUL ] com.github.fommil.netlib#netlib-native_system-win-
x86_64;1.1!netlib-native_system-win-x86_64.jar (62ms)

downloading https://repo1.maven.org/maven2/com/github/fommil/netlib/
netlib-native_system-win-i686/1.1/netlib-native_system-win-i686-1.1-
natives.jar ...

   [SUCCESSFUL ] com.github.fommil.netlib#netlib-native_system-win-
i686;1.1!netlib-native_system-win-i686.jar (55ms)

downloading https://repo1.maven.org/maven2/com/github/fommil/netlib/
native_ref-java/1.1/native_ref-java-1.1.jar ...

   [SUCCESSFUL ] com.github.fommil.netlib#native_ref-java;1.1!native_ref-
java.jar (24ms)

downloading https://repo1.maven.org/maven2/com/github/fommil/
jniloader/1.1/jniloader-1.1.jar ...

   [SUCCESSFUL ] com.github.fommil#jniloader;1.1!jniloader.jar (3ms)

downloading https://repo1.maven.org/maven2/com/github/fommil/netlib/
native_system-java/1.1/native_system-java-1.1.jar ...

   [SUCCESSFUL ] com.github.fommil.netlib#native_system-java;1.1!native_
system-java.jar (7ms)

:: resolution report :: resolve 3366ms :: artifacts dl 1821ms
   :: modules in use:
   com.github.fommil#jniloader;1.1 from central in [default]
   com.github.fommil.netlib#all;1.1.2 from central in [default]
   com.github.fommil.netlib#core;1.1.2 from central in [default]
   com.github.fommil.netlib#native_ref-java;1.1 from central in [default]
   com.github.fommil.netlib#native_system-java;1.1 from central in
[default]
```

```
  com.github.fommil.netlib#netlib-native_ref-linux-armhf;1.1 from central
in [default]
  com.github.fommil.netlib#netlib-native_ref-linux-i686;1.1 from central
in [default]
  com.github.fommil.netlib#netlib-native_ref-linux-x86_64;1.1 from
central in [default]
  com.github.fommil.netlib#netlib-native_ref-osx-x86_64;1.1 from central
in [default]
  com.github.fommil.netlib#netlib-native_ref-win-i686;1.1 from central in
[default]
  com.github.fommil.netlib#netlib-native_ref-win-x86_64;1.1 from central
in [default]
  com.github.fommil.netlib#netlib-native_system-linux-armhf;1.1 from
central in [default]
  com.github.fommil.netlib#netlib-native_system-linux-i686;1.1 from
central in [default]
  com.github.fommil.netlib#netlib-native_system-linux-x86_64;1.1 from
central in [default]
  com.github.fommil.netlib#netlib-native_system-osx-x86_64;1.1 from
central in [default]
  com.github.fommil.netlib#netlib-native_system-win-i686;1.1 from central
in [default]
  com.github.fommil.netlib#netlib-native_system-win-x86_64;1.1 from
central in [default]
  net.sourceforge.f2j#arpack_combined_all;0.1 from central in [default]
  :: evicted modules:
  com.github.fommil.netlib#core;1.1 by [com.github.fommil.
netlib#core;1.1.2] in [default]
  ---------------------------------------------------------------
  |                    |          modules          ||   artifacts    |
  |        conf        | number| search|dwnlded|evicted|| number|dwnlded|
  ---------------------------------------------------------------
  |      default       |  19   |  18   |  18   |   1   ||   17  |   17  |
  ---------------------------------------------------------------
...
scala> val enron = sc textFile("enron")
enron: org.apache.spark.rdd.RDD[String] = MapPartitionsRDD[1] at textFile
at <console>:21


scala> enron.flatMap(_.split("\\W+")).map(_.toLowerCase).distinct.count
```

```
res0: Long = 529199

scala> val stopwords = scala.collection.immutable.TreeSet ("", "i", "a",
"an", "and", "are", "as", "at", "be", "but", "by", "for", "from", "had",
"has", "he", "her", "him", "his", "in", "is", "it", "its", "not", "of",
"on", "she", "that", "the", "to", "was", "were", "will", "with", "you")

stopwords: scala.collection.immutable.TreeSet[String] = TreeSet(, a, an,
and, are, as, at, be, but, by, for, from, had, has, he, her, him, his, i,
in, is, it, its, not, of, on, she, that, the, to, was, were, will, with,
you)

scala>


scala> val terms = enron.flatMap(x => if (x.length < 8192) x.toLowerCase.
split("\\W+") else Nil).filterNot(stopwords).map(_,1).reduceByKey(_+_).
collect.sortBy(- _._2).slice(0, 1000).map(_._1)

terms: Array[String] = Array(enron, ect, com, this, hou, we, s, have,
subject, or, 2001, if, your, pm, am, please, cc, 2000, e, any, me, 00,
message, 1, corp, would, can, 10, our, all, sent, 2, mail, 11, re,
thanks, original, know, 12, 713, http, may, t, do, 3, time, 01, ees, m,
new, my, they, no, up, information, energy, us, gas, so, get, 5, about,
there, need, what, call, out, 4, let, power, should, na, which, one, 02,
also, been, www, other, 30, email, more, john, like, these, 03, mark,
04, attached, d, enron_development, their, see, 05, j, forwarded, market,
some, agreement, 09, day, questions, meeting, 08, when, houston, doc,
contact, company, 6, just, jeff, only, who, 8, fax, how, deal, could, 20,
business, use, them, date, price, 06, week, here, net, 15, 9, 07, group,
california,...

scala> def getBagCounts(bag: Seq[String]) = { for(term <- terms) yield {
bag.count(_==term) } }

getBagCounts: (bag: Seq[String])Array[Int]


scala> import org.apache.spark.mllib.linalg.Vectors

import org.apache.spark.mllib.linalg.Vectors


scala> val corpus = enron.map(x => { if (x.length < 8192) Some(x.
toLowerCase.split("\\W+").toSeq) else None } ).map(x => { Vectors.
dense(getBagCounts(x.getOrElse(Nil)).map(_.toDouble).toArray)
}).zipWithIndex.map(_.swap).cache

corpus: org.apache.spark.rdd.RDD[(Long, org.apache.spark.mllib.linalg.
Vector)] = MapPartitionsRDD[14] at map at <console>:30


scala> import org.apache.spark.mllib.clustering.{LDA,
DistributedLDAModel}
```

```
import org.apache.spark.mllib.clustering.{LDA, DistributedLDAModel}

scala> import org.apache.spark.mllib.linalg.Vectors
import org.apache.spark.mllib.linalg.Vectors

scala> val ldaModel = new LDA().setK(10).run(corpus)
...
scala> ldaModel.topicsMatrix.transpose
res2: org.apache.spark.mllib.linalg.Matrix =
207683.78495933366   79745.88417942637   92118.63972404732   ... (1000
total)
35853.48027575886    4725.178508682296   111214.8860582083   ...
135755.75666585402   54736.471356209106  93289.65563593085   ...
39445.796099155996   6272.534431534215   34764.02707696523   ...
329786.21570967307   602782.9591026317   42212.22143362559   ...
62235.09960154089    12191.826543794878  59343.24100019015   ...
210049.59592560542   160538.9650732507   40034.69756641789   ...
53818.14660186875    6351.853448001488   125354.26708575874  ...
44133.150537842856   4342.697652158682   154382.95646078113  ...
90072.97362336674    21132.629704311104  93683.40795807641   ...
```

We can also list the words and their relative importance for the topic in the descending order:

```
scala> ldaModel.describeTopics foreach { x : (Array[Int], Array[Double])
=> { print(x._1.slice(0,10).map(terms(_)).mkString(":")); print("-> ");
print(x._2.slice(0,10).map(_.toFloat).mkString(":")); println } }
com:this:ect:or:if:s:hou:2001:00:we-> 0.054606363:0.024220783:0.02096761:
0.013669214:0.0132700335:0.012969772:0.012623918:0.011363528:0.010114557:
0.009587474

s:this:hou:your:2001:or:please:am:com:new-> 0.029883621:0.027119286:0.013
396418:0.012856948:0.01218803:0.01124849:0.010425644:0.009812181:0.008742
722:0.0070441025

com:this:s:ect:hou:or:2001:if:your:am-> 0.035424445:0.024343235:0.0151826
28:0.014283071:0.013619815:0.012251413:0.012221165:0.011411696:0.01028402
4:0.009559739

would:pm:cc:3:thanks:e:my:all:there:11-> 0.047611523:0.034175437:0.022914
853:0.019933242:0.017208714:0.015393614:0.015366959:0.01393391:0.01257752
5:0.011743208
```

```
ect:com:we:can:they:03:if:also:00:this-> 0.13815293:0.0755843:0.065043546
:0.015290086:0.0121941045:0.011561104:0.011326733:0.010967959:0.010653805
:0.009674695

com:this:s:hou:or:2001:pm:your:if:cc-> 0.016605735:0.015834121:0.01289918
:0.012708308:0.0125788655:0.011726159:0.011477625:0.010578845:0.010555539
:0.009609056

com:ect:we:if:they:hou:s:00:2001:or-> 0.05537054:0.04231919:0.023271963:0
.012856676:0.012689817:0.012186356:0.011350313:0.010887237:0.010778923:0.
010662295

this:s:hou:com:your:2001:or:please:am:if-> 0.030830953:0.016557815:0.0142
36835:0.013236604:0.013107091:0.0126846135:0.012257128:0.010862533:0.0102
7849:0.008893094

this:s:or:pm:com:your:please:new:hou:2001-> 0.03981197:0.013273305:0.0128
72894:0.011672661:0.011380969:0.010689667:0.009650983:0.009605533:0.00953
5899:0.009165275

this:com:hou:s:or:2001:if:your:am:please-> 0.024562683:0.02361607:0.01377
0585:0.013601272:0.01269994:0.012360005:0.011348433:0.010228578:0.0096196
28:0.009347991
```

To find out the top documents per topic or top topics per document, we need to convert this model to `DistributedLDA` or `LocalLDAModel`, which extend `LDAModel`:

```scala
scala> ldaModel.save(sc, "ldamodel")


scala> val sameModel = DistributedLDAModel.load(sc, "ldamode21")


scala> sameModel.topDocumentsPerTopic(10) foreach { x : (Array[Long],
Array[Double]) => { print(x._1.mkString(":")); print("-> "); print(x._2.
map(_.toFloat).mkString(":")); println } }
```

```
59784:50745:52479:60441:58399:49202:64836:52490:67936:67938-> 0.97146696:
0.9713364:0.9661418:0.9661132:0.95249915:0.9519995:0.94945914:0.94944507:
0.8977366:0.8791358

233009:233844:233007:235307:233842:235306:235302:235293:233020:233857->
0.9962034:0.9962034:0.9962034:0.9962034:0.9962034:0.99620336:0.9954057:0.
9954057:0.9954057:0.9954057

14909:115602:14776:39025:115522:288507:4499:38955:15754:200876-> 0.839639
07:0.83415157:0.8319566:0.8303818:0.8291597:0.8281472:0.82739806:0.827251
7:0.82579833:0.8243338

237004:71818:124587:278308:278764:278950:233672:234490:126637:123664-> 0.
99929106:0.9968135:0.9964454:0.99644524:0.996445:0.99644494:0.99644476:0.
9964447:0.99644464:0.99644417
```

```
156466:82237:82252:82242:341376:82501:341367:340197:82212:82243-> 0.99716
955:0.94635135:0.9431836:0.94241136:0.9421047:0.9410431:0.94075173:0.9406
304:0.9402021:0.94014835

335708:336413:334075:419613:417327:418484:334157:335795:337573:334160->
0.987011:0.98687994:0.9865438:0.96953565:0.96953565:0.96953565:0.9588571:
0.95852506:0.95832515:0.9581657

243971:244119:228538:226696:224833:207609:144009:209548:143066:195299->
0.7546907:0.7546907:0.59146744:0.59095955:0.59090924:0.45532238:0.4506441
7:0.44945204:0.4487876:0.44833568

242260:214359:126325:234126:123362:233304:235006:124195:107996:334829->
0.89615464:0.8961442:0.8106028:0.8106027:0.8106023:0.8106023:0.8106021:0.
8106019:0.76834095:0.7570231

209751:195546:201477:191758:211002:202325:197542:193691:199705:329052->
0.913124:0.9130985:0.9130918:0.9130672:0.5525752:0.5524637:0.5524494:0.55
2405:0.55240136:0.5026157

153326:407544:407682:408098:157881:351230:343651:127848:98884:129351-> 0.
97206575:0.97206575:0.97206575:0.97206575:0.97206575:0.9689198:0.968068:0
.9659192:0.9657442:0.96553063
```

Segmentation, annotation, and chunking

When the text is presented in digital form, it is relatively easy to find words as we can split the stream on non-word characters. This becomes more complex in spoken language analysis. In this case, segmenters try to optimize a metric, for example, to minimize the number of distinct words in the lexicon and the length or complexity of the phrase (*Natural Language Processing with Python* by *Steven Bird et al, O'Reilly Media Inc*, 2009).

Annotation usually refers to parts-of-speech tagging. In English, these are nouns, pronouns, verbs, adjectives, adverbs, articles, prepositions, conjunctions, and interjections. For example, in the phrase *we saw the yellow dog*, *we* is a pronoun, *saw* is a verb, *the* is an article, *yellow* is an adjective, and *dog* is a noun.

In some languages, the chunking and annotation depends on context. For example, in Chinese, 爱江山人 literally translates to *love country person* and can mean either *country-loving person* or *love country-person*. In Russian, *казнить нельзя помиловать*, literally translating to *execute not pardon*, can mean *execute, don't pardon*, or *don't execute, pardon*. While in written language, this can be disambiguated using commas, in a spoken language this is usually it is very hard to recognize the difference, even though sometimes the intonation can help to segment the phrase properly.

For techniques based on word frequencies in the bags, some extremely common words, which are of little value in helping select documents, are explicitly excluded from the vocabulary. These words are called stop words. There is no good general strategy for determining a stop list, but in many cases, this is to exclude very frequent words that appear in almost every document and do not help to differentiate between them for classification or information retrieval purposes.

POS tagging

POS tagging probabilistically annotates each word with it's grammatical function—noun, verb, adjective, and so on. Usually, POS tagging serves as an input to syntactic and semantic analysis. Let's demonstrate POS tagging on the FACTORIE toolkit example, a software library written in Scala (http://factorie.cs.umass.edu). To start, you need to download the binary image or source files from https://github.com/factorie/factorie.git and build it:

```
$ git clone https://github.com/factorie/factorie.git
...
$ cd factorie
$ git checkout factorie_2.11-1.2
...
$ mvn package -Pnlp-jar-with-dependencies
```

After the build, which also includes model training, the following command will start a network server on port 3228:

```
$ $ bin/fac nlp --wsj-forward-pos --conll-chain-ner
java -Xmx6g -ea -Djava.awt.headless=true -Dfile.encoding=UTF-8 -server
-classpath ./src/main/resources:./target/classes:./target/factorie_2.11-
1.2-nlp-jar-with-dependencies.jar
found model
18232
Listening on port 3228
...
```

Now, all traffic to port 3228 will be interpreted (as text), and the output will be tokenized and annotated:

```
$ telnet localhost 3228
Trying ::1...
Connected to localhost.
Escape character is '^]'.
```

But I warn you, if you don't tell me that this means war, if you still
try to defend the infamies and horrors perpetrated by that Antichrist--I
really believe he is Antichrist--I will have nothing more to do with you
and you are no longer my friend, no longer my 'faithful slave,' as you
call yourself! But how do you do? I see I have frightened you--sit down
and tell me all the news.

```
1    1    But    CC    O
2    2    I      PRP   O
3    3    warn   VBP   O
4    4    you    PRP   O
5    5    ,            O
6    6    if     IN    O
7    7    you    PRP   O
8    8    do     VBP   O
9    9    n't    RB    O
10   10   tell   VB    O
11   11   me     PRP   O
12   12   that   IN    O
13   13   this   DT    O
14   14   means  VBZ   O
15   15   war    NN    O
16   16   ,      ,     O
17   17   if     IN    O
18   18   you    PRP   O
19   19   still  RB    O
20   20   try    VBP   O
21   21   to     TO    O
22   22   defend VB    O
23   23   the    DT    O
24   24   infamies   NNS   O
25   25   and    CC    O
26   26   horrors    NNS   O
27   27   perpetrated    VBN   O
28   28   by     IN    O
29   29   that   DT    O
30   30   Antichrist    NNP   O
```

```
31  31  --       :   O
32  1   I    PRP   O
33  2   really    RB   O
34  3   believe    VBP   O
35  4   he    PRP   O
36  5   is    VBZ   O
37  6   Antichrist     NNP   U-MISC
38  7   --       :   O
39  1   I    PRP   O
40  2   will     MD   O
41  3   have    VB   O
42  4   nothing    NN   O
43  5   more    JJR   O
44  6   to    TO   O
45  7   do    VB   O
46  8   with    IN   O
47  9   you    PRP   O
48  10  and    CC   O
49  11  you    PRP   O
50  12  are    VBP   O
51  13  no    RB   O
52  14  longer    RBR   O
53  15  my    PRP$   O
54  16  friend    NN   O
55  17  ,    ,   O
56  18  no    RB   O
57  19  longer    RB   O
58  20  my   PRP$   O
59  21  '    POS   O
60  22  faithful    NN   O
61  23  slave    NN   O
62  24  ,    ,   O
63  25  '    ''   O
64  26  as    IN   O
65  27  you    PRP   O
66  28  call    VBP   O
```

```
67   29   yourself     PRP   O
68   30   !        .    O
69   1    But      CC   O
70   2    how      WRB  O
71   3    do       VBP  O
72   4    you      PRP  O
73   5    do       VB   O
74   6    ?        .    O
75   1    I        PRP  O
76   2    see      VBP  O
77   3    I        PRP  O
78   4    have     VBP  O
79   5    frightened   VBN   O
80   6    you      PRP  O
81   7    --       :    O
82   8    sit      VB   O
83   9    down     RB   O
84   10   and      CC   O
85   11   tell     VB   O
86   12   me       PRP  O
87   13   all      DT   O
88   14   the      DT   O
89   15   news     NN   O
90   16   .        .    O
```

This POS is a single-path left-right tagger that can process the text as a stream. Internally, the algorithm uses probabilistic techniques to find the most probable assignment. Let's also look at other techniques that do not use grammatical analysis and yet proved to be very useful for language understanding and interpretation.

Using word2vec to find word relationships

Word2vec has been developed by Tomas Mikolov at Google, around 2012. The original idea behind word2vec was to demonstrate that one might improve efficiency by trading the model's complexity for efficiency. Instead of representing a document as bags of words, word2vec takes each word context into account by trying to analyze n-grams or skip-grams (a set of surrounding tokens with potential the token in question skipped). The words and word contexts themselves are represented by an array of floats/doubles u_t. The objective function is to maximize log likelihood:

$$\frac{1}{T} \sum_{t=1}^{T} \sum_{j=-k}^{k} \log p\left(w_{t+j} \mid w_t\right)$$

Where:

$$p\left(w_j \mid w_i\right) = \frac{\exp\left(u_j^T u_i\right)}{\sum_k \exp\left(u_k^T u_i\right)}$$

By choosing the optimal u_t and to get a comprehensive word representation (also called **map optimization**). Similar words are found based on cosine similarity metric (dot product) of u_t. Spark implementation uses hierarchical softmax, which reduces the complexity of computing the conditional probability to $O\left(\log(V)\right)$, or log of the vocabulary size V, as opposed to $O(V)$, or proportional to V. The training is still linear in the dataset size, but is amenable to big data parallelization techniques.

Word2vec is traditionally used to predict the most likely word given context or find similar words with a similar meaning (synonyms). The following code trains in word2vec model on *Leo Tolstoy's Wars and Peace,* and finds synonyms for the word *circle*. I had to convert the Gutenberg's representation of *War and Peace* to a single-line format by running the `cat 2600.txt | tr "\n\r" " " > warandpeace.txt` command:

```scala
scala> val word2vec = new Word2Vec
word2vec: org.apache.spark.mllib.feature.Word2Vec = org.apache.spark.
mllib.feature.Word2Vec@58bb4dd


scala> val model = word2vec.fit(sc.textFile("warandpeace").map(_.
split("\\W+").toSeq)
model: org.apache.spark.mllib.feature.Word2VecModel = org.apache.spark.
mllib.feature.Word2VecModel@6f61b9d7


scala> val synonyms = model.findSynonyms("life", 10)
synonyms: Array[(String, Double)] = Array((freedom,1.704344822168997),
(universal,1.682276637692245), (conception,1.6776193389148586),
(relation,1.6760497906519414), (humanity,1.67601036253831),
(consists,1.6637604144872544), (recognition,1.6526169382380496),
(subjection,1.6496559771230317), (activity,1.646671198014248),
(astronomy,1.6444424059160712))


scala> synonyms foreach println
(freedom,1.704344822168997)
(universal,1.682276637692245)
(conception,1.6776193389148586)
(relation,1.6760497906519414)
(humanity,1.67601036253831)
(consists,1.6637604144872544)
(recognition,1.6526169382380496)
(subjection,1.6496559771230317)
(activity,1.646671198014248)
(astronomy,1.6444424059160712)
```

While in general, it is hard to some with an objective function, and freedom is not listed as a synonym to life in the English Thesaurus, the results do make sense.

Each word in the word2vec model is represented as an array of doubles. Another interesting application is to find associations *a to b is the same as c to ?* by performing subtraction *vector(a) - vector(b) + vector(c)*:

```scala
scala> val a = model.getVectors.filter(_._1 == "monarchs").map(_._2).head
a: Array[Float] = Array(-0.0044642715, -0.0013227836, -0.011506443,
0.03691717, 0.020431392, 0.013427449, -0.0036369907, -0.013460356,
-3.8938568E-4, 0.02432113, 0.014533845, 0.004130258, 0.00671316,
-0.009344602, 0.006229065, -0.005442078, -0.0045390734, -0.0038824948,
-6.5973646E-4, 0.021729799, -0.011289608, -0.0030690092, -0.011423801,
0.009100784, 0.011765533, 0.0069619063, 0.017540144, 0.011198071,
0.026103685, -0.017285397, 0.0045515243, -0.0044477824, -0.0074411617,
-0.023975836, 0.011371289, -0.022625357, -2.6478301E-5, -0.010510282,
0.010622139, -0.009597833, 0.014937023, -0.01298345, 0.0016747514,
0.01172987, -0.001512275, 0.022340108, -0.009758578, -0.014942565,
0.0040697413, 0.0015349758, 0.010246878, 0.0021413323, 0.008739062,
0.007845526, 0.006857361, 0.01160148, 0.008595...

scala> val b = model.getVectors.filter(_._1 == "princess").map(_._2).head
b: Array[Float] = Array(0.13265875, -0.04882792, -0.08409957,
-0.04067986, 0.009084379, 0.121674284, -0.11963971, 0.06699862,
-0.20277102, 0.26296946, -0.058114383, 0.076021515, 0.06751665,
-0.17419271, -0.089830205, 0.2463593, 0.062816426, -0.10538805,
0.062085453, -0.2483566, 0.03468293, 0.20642486, 0.3129267, -0.12418643,
-0.12557726, 0.06725172, -0.03703333, -0.10810595, 0.06692443,
-0.046484336, 0.2433963, -0.12762263, -0.18473054, -0.084376186,
0.0037174677, -0.0040220995, -0.3419341, -0.25928706, -0.054454487,
0.09521076, -0.041567303, -0.13727514, -0.04826158, 0.13326299,
0.16228828, 0.08495835, -0.18073058, -0.018380836, -0.15691829,
0.056539804, 0.13673553, -0.027935665, 0.081865616, 0.07029694,
-0.041142456, 0.041359138, -0.2304657, -0.17088272, -0.14424285,
-0.0030700471, -0...

scala> val c = model.getVectors.filter(_._1 == "individual").map(_._2).head
c: Array[Float] = Array(-0.0013353615, -0.01820516, 0.007949033,
0.05430816, -0.029520465, -0.030641818, -6.607431E-4, 0.026548808,
0.04784935, -0.006470232, 0.041406438, 0.06599842, 0.0074243015,
0.041538745, 0.0030222891, -0.003932073, -0.03154199, -0.028486902,
0.022139633, 0.05738223, -0.03890591, -0.06761177, 0.0055152955,
-0.02480924, -0.053222697, -0.028698998, -0.005315235, 0.0582403,
-0.0024816995, 0.031634405, -0.027884213, 6.0290704E-4, 1.9750209E-
4, -0.05563172, 0.023785716, -0.037577976, 0.04134448, 0.0026664822,
-0.019832063, -0.0011898747, 0.03160933, 0.031184288, 0.0025268437,
-0.02718441, -0.07729341, -0.009460656, 0.005344515, -0.05110715,
0.018468754, 0.008984449, -0.0053139487, 0.0053904117, -0.01322933,
-0.015247412, 0.009819351, 0.038043085, 0.044905875, 0.00402788...
```

```
scala> model.findSynonyms(new DenseVector((for(i <- 0 until 100) yield
(a(i) - b(i) + c(i)).toDouble).toArray), 10) foreach println
(achievement,0.9432423663884002)
(uncertainty,0.9187759184842362)
(leader,0.9163721499105207)
(individual,0.9048367510621271)
(instead,0.8992079672038455)
(cannon,0.8947818781378154)
(arguments,0.8883634101905679)
(aims,0.8725107984356915)
(ants,0.8593842583047755)
(War,0.8530727227924755)
```

This can be used to find relationships in the language.

A Porter Stemmer implementation of the code

Porter Stemmer was first developed around the 1980s and there are many implementations. The detailed steps and original reference are provided at http://tartarus.org/martin/PorterStemmer/def.txt. It consists of roughly 6-9 steps of suffix/endings replacements, some of which are conditional on prefix or stem. I will provide a Scala-optimized version with the book code repository. For example, step 1 covers the majority of stemming cases and consists of 12 substitutions: the last 8 of which are conditional on the number of syllables and the presence of vowels in the stem:

```
def step1(s: String) = {
  b = s
  // step 1a
  processSubList(List(("sses", "ss"), ("ies","i"),
    ("ss","ss"), ("s", "")), _>=0)
  // step 1b
  if (!(replacer("eed", "ee", _>0)))
  {
    if ((vowelInStem("ed") && replacer("ed", "", _>=0)) ||
      (vowelInStem("ing") && replacer("ing", "", _>=0)))
    {
      if (!processSubList(List(("at", "ate"), ("bl","ble"),
      ("iz","ize")), _>=0 ) )
      {
        // if this isn't done, then it gets more confusing.
```

```
        if (doublec() && b.last != 'l' && b.last != 's' &&
          b.last != 'z') { b = b.substring(0, b.length - 1) }
        else
          if (calcM(b.length) == 1 && cvc("")) { b = b + "e" }
      }
    }
  }
  // step 1c
  (vowelInStem("y") && replacer("y", "i", _>=0))
  this
}
```

The complete code is available at `https://github.com/alexvk/ml-in-scala/blob/master/chapter09/src/main/scala/Stemmer.scala`.

Summary

In this chapter, I described basic NLP concepts and demonstrated a few basic techniques. I hoped to demonstrate that pretty complex NLP concepts could be expressed and tested in a few lines of Scala code. This is definitely just the tip of the iceberg as a lot of NLP techniques are being developed now, including the ones based on in-CPU parallelization as part of GPUs. (refer to, for example, **Puck** at `https://github.com/dlwh/puck`). I also gave a flavor of major Spark MLlib NLP implementations.

In the next chapter, which will be the final chapter of this book, I'll cover systems and model monitoring.

10
Advanced Model Monitoring

Even though this is the last chapter of the book, it can hardly be an afterthought even though monitoring in general often is in practical situations, quite unfortunately. Monitoring is a vital deployment component for any long execution cycle component and thus is part of the finished product. Monitoring can significantly enhance product experience and define future success as it improves problem diagnostic and is essential to determine the improvement path.

One of the primary rules of successful software engineering is to create systems as if they were targeted for personal use when possible, which fully applies to monitoring, diagnostic, and debugging—quite hapless name for fixing existing issues in software products. Diagnostic and debugging of complex systems, particularly distributed systems, is hard, as the events often can be arbitrary interleaved and program executions subject to race conditions. While there is a lot of research going in the area of distributed system devops and maintainability, this chapter will scratch the service and provide guiding principle to design a maintainable complex distributed system.

To start with, a pure functional approach, which Scala claims to follow, spends a lot of time avoiding side effects. While this idea is useful in a number of aspects, it is hard to imagine a useful program that has no effect on the outside world, the whole idea of a data-driven application is to have a positive effect on the way the business is conducted, a well-defined side effect.

Monitoring clearly falls in the side effect category. Execution needs to leave a trace that the user can later parse in order to understand where the design or implementation went awry. The trace of the execution can be left by either writing something on a console or into a file, usually called a log, or returning an object that contains the trace of the program execution, and the intermediate results. The latter approach, which is actually more in line with functional programming and monadic philosophy, is actually more appropriate for the distributed programming but often overlooked. This would have been an interesting topic for research, but unfortunately the space is limited and I have to discuss the practical aspects of monitoring in contemporary systems that is almost always done by logging. Having the monadic approach of carrying an object with the execution trace on each call can certainly increase the overhead of the interprocess or inter-machine communication, but saves a lot of time in stitching different pieces of information together.

Let's list the naive approaches to debugging that everyone who needed to find a bug in the code tried:

- Analyzing program output, particularly logs produced by simple print statements or built-in logback, java.util.logging, log4j, or the slf4j façade
- Attaching a (remote) debugger
- Monitoring CPU, disk I/O, memory (to resolve higher level resource-utilization issues)

More or less, all these approaches fail if we have a multithreaded or distributed system — and Scala is inherently multithreaded as Spark is inherently distributed. Collecting logs over a set of nodes is not scalable (even though a few successful commercial systems exist that do this). Attaching a remote debugger is not always possible due to security and network restrictions. Remote debugging can also induce substantial overhead and interfere with the program execution, particularly for ones that use synchronization. Setting the debug level to the DEBUG or TRACE level helps sometimes, but leaves you at the mercy of the developer who may or may not have thought of a particular corner case you are dealing with right at the moment. The approach we take in this book is to open a servlet with enough information to glean into program execution and application methods real-time, as much as it is possible with the current state of Scala and Scalatra.

Enough about the overall issues of debugging the program execution. Monitoring is somewhat different, as it is concerned with only high-level issue identification. Intersection with issue investigation or resolution happens, but usually is outside of monitoring. In this chapter, we will cover the following topics:

- Understanding major areas for monitoring and monitoring goals
- Learning OS tools for Scala/Java monitoring to support issue identification and debugging
- Learning about MBeans and MXBeans
- Understanding model performance drift
- Understanding A/B testing

System monitoring

While there are other types of monitoring dealing specifically with ML-targeted tasks, such as monitoring the performance of the models, let me start with basic system monitoring. Traditionally, system monitoring is a subject of operating system maintenance, but it is becoming a vital component of any complex application, specifically running over a set of distributed workstations. The primary components of the OS are CPU, disk, memory, network, and energy on battery-powered machines. The traditional OS-like tools for monitoring system performance are provided in the following table. We limit them to Linux tools as this is the platform for most Scala applications, even though other OS vendors provide OS monitoring tools such as **Activity Monitor**. As Scala runs in Java JVM, I also added Java-specific monitoring tools that are specific to JVMs:

Area	Programs	Comments
CPU	`htop, top, sar-u`	`top` has been the most often used performance diagnostic tool, as CPU and memory have been the most constraint resources. With the advent of distributed programming, network and disk tend to be the most constraint.
Disk	`iostat, sar -d, lsof`	The number of open files, provided by `lsof`, is often a constraining resource as many big data applications and daemons tend to keep multiple files open.
Memory	`top, free, vmstat, sar -r`	Memory is used by OS in multiple ways, for example to maintain disk I/O buffers so that having extra buffered and cached memory helps performance.

Area	Programs	Comments
Network	`ifconfig, netstat, tcpdump, nettop, iftop, nmap`	Network is how the distributed systems talk and is an important OS component. From the application point of view, watch for errors, collisions, and dropped packets as an indicator of problems.
Energy	`powerstat`	While power consumption is traditionally not a part of OS monitoring, it is nevertheless a shared resource, which recently became one of the major costs for maintaining a working system.
Java	`jconsole, jinfo, jcmd, jmc`	All these tools allow you to examine configuration and run-time properties of an application. **Java Mission Control (JMC)** is shipped with JDK starting with version 7u40.

Table 10.1. Common Linux OS monitoring tools

In many cases, the tools are redundant. For example, the CPU and memory information can be obtained with `top`, `sar`, and `jmc` commands.

There are a few tools for collecting this information over a set of distributed nodes. Ganglia is a BSD-licensed scalable distributed monitoring system (`http://ganglia.info`). It is based on a hierarchical design and is very careful about data structure and algorithm designs. It is known to scale to 10,000s of nodes. It consists of a gmetad daemon that is collects information from multiple hosts and presents it in a web interface, and gmond daemons running on each individual host. The communication happens on the 8649 port by default, which spells Unix. By default, gmond sends information about CPU, memory, and network, but multiple plugins exist for other metrics (or can be created). Gmetad can aggregate the information and pass it up the hierarchy chain to another gmetad daemon. Finally, the data is presented in a Ganglia web interface.

Graphite is another monitoring tool that stores numeric time-series data and renders graphs of this data on demand. The web app provides a /render endpoint to generate graphs and retrieve raw data via a RESTful API. Graphite has a pluggable backend (although it has it's own default implementation). Most of the modern metrics implementations, including scala-metrics used in this chapter, support sending data to Graphite.

Process monitoring

The tools described in the previous section are not application-specific. For a long-running process, it often necessary to provide information about the internal state to either a monitoring a graphing solution such as Ganglia or Graphite, or just display it in a servlet. Most of these solutions are read-only, but in some cases, the commands give the control to the users to modify the state, such as log levels, or to trigger garbage collection.

Monitoring, in general is supposed to do the following:

- Provide high-level information about program execution and application-specific metrics
- Potentially, perform health-checks for critical components
- Might incorporate alerting and thresholding on some critical metrics

I have also seen monitoring to include update operations to either update the logging parameters or test components, such as trigger model scoring with predefined parameters. The latter can be considered as a part of parameterized health check.

Let's see how it works on the example of a simple Hello World web application that accepts REST-like requests and assigns a unique ID for different users written in the Scalatra framework (http://scalatra.org), a lightweight web-application development framework in Scala. The application is supposed to respond to CRUD HTTP requests to create a unique numeric ID for a user. To implement the service in Scalatra, we need just to provide a Scalate template. The full documentation can be found at http://scalatra.org/2.4/guides/views/scalate.html, the source code is provided with the book and can be found in chapter10 subdirectory:

```
class SimpleServlet extends Servlet {
  val logger = LoggerFactory.getLogger(getClass)
  var hwCounter: Long = 0L
  val hwLookup: scala.collection.mutable.Map[String,Long] =
    scala.collection.mutable.Map()
  val defaultName = "Stranger"
  def response(name: String, id: Long) = { "Hello %s! Your id
    should be %d.".format(if (name.length > 0) name else
    defaultName, id) }
  get("/hw/:name") {
    val name = params("name")
    val startTime = System.nanoTime
    val retVal = response(name, synchronized { hwLookup.get(name)
      match { case Some(id) => id; case _ => hwLookup += name -> {
      hwCounter += 1; hwCounter } ; hwCounter } } )
```

```
        logger.info("It took [" + name + "] " + (System.nanoTime -
          startTime) + " " + TimeUnit.NANOSECONDS)
        retVal
    }
  }
```

First, the code gets the `name` parameter from the request (REST-like parameter parsing is also supported). Then, it checks the internal HashMap for existing entries, and if the entry does not exist, it creates a new index using a synchronized call to increment `hwCounter` (in a real-world application, this information should be persistent in a database such as HBase, but I'll skip this layer in this section for the purpose of simplicity). To run the application, one needs to download the code, start `sbt`, and type `~;jetty:stop;jetty:start` to enable continuous run/compilation as in *Chapter 7, Working with Graph Algorithms*. The modifications to the file will be immediately picked up by the build tool and the jetty server will restart:

```
[akozlov@Alexanders-MacBook-Pro chapter10]$ sbt

[info] Loading project definition from /Users/akozlov/Src/Book/ml-in-
scala/chapter10/project

[info] Compiling 1 Scala source to /Users/akozlov/Src/Book/ml-in-scala/
chapter10/project/target/scala-2.10/sbt-0.13/classes...

[info] Set current project to Advanced Model Monitoring (in build file:/
Users/akozlov/Src/Book/ml-in-scala/chapter10/)

> ~;jetty:stop;jetty:start

[success] Total time: 0 s, completed May 15, 2016 12:08:31 PM

[info] Compiling Templates in Template Directory: /Users/akozlov/Src/
Book/ml-in-scala/chapter10/src/main/webapp/WEB-INF/templates

SLF4J: Failed to load class "org.slf4j.impl.StaticLoggerBinder".

SLF4J: Defaulting to no-operation (NOP) logger implementation

SLF4J: See http://www.slf4j.org/codes.html#StaticLoggerBinder for further
details.

[info] starting server ...

[success] Total time: 1 s, completed May 15, 2016 12:08:32 PM

1. Waiting for source changes... (press enter to interrupt)

2016-05-15 12:08:32.578:INFO::main: Logging initialized @119ms

2016-05-15 12:08:32.586:INFO:oejr.Runner:main: Runner

2016-05-15 12:08:32.666:INFO:oejs.Server:main: jetty-9.2.1.v20140609

2016-05-15 12:08:34.650:WARN:oeja.AnnotationConfiguration:main:
ServletContainerInitializers: detected. Class hierarchy: empty

2016-15-05 12:08:34.921: [main] INFO  o.scalatra.servlet.ScalatraListener
- The cycle class name from the config: ScalatraBootstrap
```

```
2016-15-05 12:08:34.973: [main] INFO  o.scalatra.servlet.ScalatraListener
- Initializing life cycle class: ScalatraBootstrap

2016-15-05 12:08:35.213: [main] INFO  o.f.s.servlet.ServletTemplateEngine
- Scalate template engine using working directory: /var/folders/p1/y7ygx_
4507q34vhd60q115p80000gn/T/scalate-6339535024071976693-workdir

2016-05-15 12:08:35.216:INFO:oejsh.ContextHandler:main: Started o.e.j
.w.WebAppContext@1ef7fe8e{/,file:/Users/akozlov/Src/Book/ml-in-scala/
chapter10/target/webapp/,AVAILABLE}{file:/Users/akozlov/Src/Book/ml-in-
scala/chapter10/target/webapp/}

2016-05-15 12:08:35.216:WARN:oejsh.RequestLogHandler:main: !RequestLog

2016-05-15 12:08:35.237:INFO:oejs.ServerConnector:main: Started ServerCon
nector@68df9280{HTTP/1.1}{0.0.0.0:8080}

2016-05-15 12:08:35.237:INFO:oejs.Server:main: Started @2795ms2016-15-05
12:03:52.385: [main] INFO  o.f.s.servlet.ServletTemplateEngine - Scalate
template engine using working directory: /var/folders/p1/y7ygx_4507q34vhd
60q115p80000gn/T/scalate-3504767079718792844-workdir

2016-05-15 12:03:52.387:INFO:oejsh.ContextHandler:main: Started o.e.j
.w.WebAppContext@1ef7fe8e{/,file:/Users/akozlov/Src/Book/ml-in-scala/
chapter10/target/webapp/,AVAILABLE}{file:/Users/akozlov/Src/Book/ml-in-
scala/chapter10/target/webapp/}

2016-05-15 12:03:52.388:WARN:oejsh.RequestLogHandler:main: !RequestLog

2016-05-15 12:03:52.408:INFO:oejs.ServerConnector:main: Started ServerCon
nector@68df9280{HTTP/1.1}{0.0.0.0:8080}

2016-05-15 12:03:52.408:INFO:oejs.Server:main: Started @2796mss
```

When the servlet is started on port 8080, issue a browser request:

 I pre-created the project for this book, but if you want to create a Scalatra project from scratch, there is a `gitter` command in `chapter10/bin/create_project.sh`. Gitter will create a `project/build.scala` file with a Scala object, extending build that will set project parameters and enable the Jetty plugin for the SBT.

`http://localhost:8080/hw/Joe`.

The output should look similar to the following screenshot:

Figure 10-1: The servlet web page.

If you call the servlet with a different name, it will assign a distinct ID, which will be persistent across the lifetime of the application.

As we also enabled console logging, you will also see something similar to the following command on the console:

```
2016-15-05 13:10:06.240: [qtp1747585824-26] INFO  o.a.examples.
ServletWithMetrics - It took [Joe] 133225 NANOSECONDS
```

While retrieving and analyzing logs, which can be redirected to a file, is an option and there are multiple systems to collect, search, and analyze logs from a set of distributed servers, it is often also important to have a simple way to introspect the running code. One way to accomplish this is to create a separate template with metrics, however, Scalatra provides metrics and health support to enable basic implementations for counts, histograms, rates, and so on.

I will use the Scalatra metrics support. The `ScalatraBootstrap` class has to implement the `MetricsBootstrap` trait. The `org.scalatra.metrics.MetricsSupport` and `org.scalatra.metrics.HealthChecksSupport` traits provide templating similar to the Scalate templates, as shown in the following code.

The following is the content of the `ScalatraTemplate.scala` file:

```scala
import org.akozlov.examples._

import javax.servlet.ServletContext
import org.scalatra.LifeCycle
import org.scalatra.metrics.MetricsSupportExtensions._
import org.scalatra.metrics._

class ScalatraBootstrap extends LifeCycle with MetricsBootstrap {
  override def init(context: ServletContext) = {
    context.mount(new ServletWithMetrics, "/")
    context.mountMetricsAdminServlet("/admin")
    context.mountHealthCheckServlet("/health")
    context.installInstrumentedFilter("/*")
  }
}
```

The following is the content of the `ServletWithMetrics.scala` file:

```scala
package org.akozlov.examples

import org.scalatra._
import scalate.ScalateSupport
```

```scala
import org.scalatra.ScalatraServlet
import org.scalatra.metrics.{MetricsSupport, HealthChecksSupport}
import java.util.concurrent.atomic.AtomicLong
import java.util.concurrent.TimeUnit
import org.slf4j.{Logger, LoggerFactory}

class ServletWithMetrics extends Servlet with MetricsSupport with
  HealthChecksSupport {
  val logger = LoggerFactory.getLogger(getClass)
  val defaultName = "Stranger"
  var hwCounter: Long = 0L
  val hwLookup: scala.collection.mutable.Map[String,Long] =
    scala.collection.mutable.Map()  val hist =
    histogram("histogram")
  val cnt =  counter("counter")
  val m = meter("meter")
  healthCheck("response", unhealthyMessage = "Ouch!") {
    response("Alex", 2) contains "Alex" }
  def response(name: String, id: Long) = { "Hello %s! Your id
    should be %d.".format(if (name.length > 0) name else
    defaultName, id) }

  get("/hw/:name") {
    cnt += 1
    val name = params("name")
    hist += name.length
    val startTime = System.nanoTime
    val retVal = response(name, synchronized { hwLookup.get(name)
      match { case Some(id) => id; case _ => hwLookup += name -> {
      hwCounter += 1; hwCounter } ; hwCounter } } )s
    val elapsedTime = System.nanoTime - startTime
    logger.info("It took [" + name + "] " + elapsedTime + " " +
      TimeUnit.NANOSECONDS)
    m.mark(1)
    retVal
  }
```

If you run the server again, the `http://localhost:8080/admin` page will show a set of links for operational information, as shown in the following screenshot:

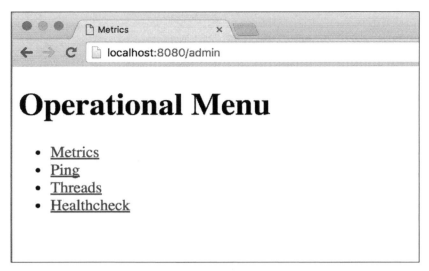

Figure 10-2: The admin servlet web page

The **Metrics** link will lead to the metrics servlet depicted in *Figure 10-3*. The `org.akozlov.exampes.ServletWithMetrics.counter` will have a global count of requests, and `org.akozlov.exampes.ServletWithMetrics.histogram` will show the distribution of accumulated values, in this case, the name lengths. More importantly, it will compute `50`, `75`, `95`, `98`, `99`, and `99.9` percentiles. The meter counter will show rates for the last `1`, `5`, and `15` minutes:

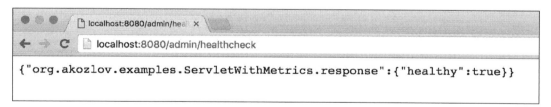

```
{
  "version" : "3.0.0",
  "gauges" : { },
  "counters" : {
    "com.codahale.metrics.servlet.InstrumentedFilter.activeRequests" : {
      "count" : 1
    },
    "org.akozlov.examples.ServletWithMetrics.counter" : {
      "count" : 3
    }
  },
  "histograms" : {
    "org.akozlov.examples.ServletWithMetrics.histogram" : {
      "count" : 3,
      "max" : 6,
      "mean" : 4.417153998557605,
      "min" : 3,
      "p50" : 4.0,
      "p75" : 6.0,
      "p95" : 6.0,
      "p98" : 6.0,
      "p99" : 6.0,
      "p999" : 6.0,
      "stddev" : 1.25749956766925
    }
  },
  "meters" : {
    "com.codahale.metrics.servlet.InstrumentedFilter.responseCodes.badRequest" : {
      "count" : 0,
      "m15_rate" : 0.0,
      "m1_rate" : 0.0,
      "m5_rate" : 0.0,
      "mean_rate" : 0.0,
```

Figure 10-3: The metrics servlet web page

Finally, one can write health checks. In this case, I will just check whether the result of the response function contains the string that it has been passed as a parameter. Refer to the following *Figure 10.4*:

```
localhost:8080/admin/healthcheck

{"org.akozlov.examples.ServletWithMetrics.response":{"healthy":true}}
```

Figure 10-4: The health check servlet web page.

The metrics can be configured to report to Ganglia or Graphite data collection servers or periodically dump information into a log file.

Endpoints do not have to be read-only. One of the pre-configured components is the timer, which measures the time to complete a task — which can be used for measuring scoring performance. Let's put the code in the `ServletWithMetrics` class:

```
get("/time") {
  val sleepTime = scala.util.Random.nextInt(1000)
  val startTime = System.nanoTime
  timer("timer") {
    Thread.sleep(sleepTime)
    Thread.sleep(sleepTime)
    Thread.sleep(sleepTime)
  }
  logger.info("It took [" + sleepTime + "] " + (System.nanoTime
    - startTime) + " " + TimeUnit.NANOSECONDS)
  m.mark(1)
}
```

Accessing `http://localhost:8080/time` will trigger code execution, which will be timed with a timer in metrics.

Analogously, the put operation, which can be created with the `put()` template, can be used to either adjust the run-time parameters or execute the code in-situ — which, depending on the code, might need to be secured in production environments.

JSR 110

JSR 110 is another **Java Specification Request (JSR)**, commonly known as **Java Management Extensions (JMX)**. JSR 110 specifies a number of APIs and protocols in order to be able to monitor the JVM executions remotely. A common way to access JMX Services is via the `jconsole` command that will connect to one of the local processes by default. To connect to a remote host, you need to provide the `-Dcom.sun.management.jmxremote.port=portNum` property on the Java command line. It is also advisable to enable security (SSL or password-based authentication). In practice, other monitoring tools use JMX for monitoring, as well as managing the JVM, as JMX allows callbacks to manage the system state.

You can provide your own metrics that are exposed via JMX. While Scala runs in JVM, the implementation of JMX (via MBeans) is very Java-specific, and it is not clear how well the mechanism will play with Scala. JMX Beans can certainly be exposed as a servlet in Scala though.

The JMX MBeans can usually be examined in JConsole, but we can also expose it as `/jmx servlet`, the code provided in the book repository (`https://github.com/alexvk/ml-in-scala`).

Model monitoring

We have covered basic system and application metrics. Lately, a new direction evolved for using monitoring components to monitor statistical model performance. The statistical model performance covers the following:

- How the model performance evolved over time
- When is the time to retire the model
- Model health check

Performance over time

ML models deteriorate with time, or 'age': While this process is not still well understood, the model performance tends to change with time, if even due to concept drift, where the definition of the attributes change, or the changes in the underlying dependencies. Unfortunately, model performance rarely improves, at least in my practice. Thus, it is imperative to keep track of models. One way to do this is by monitoring the metrics that the model is intended to optimize, as in many cases, we do not have a ready-labeled set of data.

In many cases, the model performance deterioration is not related directly to the quality of the statistical modeling, even though simpler models such as linear and logistic regression tend to be more stable than more complex models such as decision trees. Schema evolution or unnoticed renaming of attributes may cause the model to not perform well.

Part of model monitoring should be running the health check, where a model periodically scores either a few records or a known scored set of data.

Criteria for model retiring

A very common case in practical deployments is that data scientists come with better sets of models every few weeks. However, if this does not happen, one needs come up with a set of criteria to retire a model. As real-world traffic rarely comes with the scored data, for example, the data that is already scored, the usual way to measure model performance is via a proxy, which is the metric that the model is supposed to improve.

A/B testing

A/B testing is a specific case of controlled experiment in e-commerce setting. A/B testing is usually applied to versions of a web page where we direct completely independent subset of users to each of the versions. The dependent variable to test is usually the response rate. Unless any specific information is available about users, and in many cases, it is not unless a cookie is placed in the computer, the split is random. Often the split is based on unique userID, but this is known not to work too well across multiple devices. A/B testing is subject to the same assumptions the controlled experiments are subject to: the tests should be completely independent and the distribution of the dependent variable should be `i.i.d.`. Even though it is hard to imagine that all people are truly `i.i.d.`, the A/B test has been shown to work for practical problems.

In modeling, we split the traffic to be scored into two or multiple channels to be scored by two or multiple models. Further, we need to measure the cumulative performance metric for each of the channels together with estimated variance. Usually, one of the models is treated as a baseline and is associated with the null hypothesis, and for the rest of the models, we run a t-test, comparing the ratio of the difference to the standard deviation.

Summary

This chapter described system, application, and model monitoring goals together with the existing monitoring solutions for Scala, and specifically Scalatra. Many metrics overlap with standard OS or Java monitoring, but we also discussed how to create application-specific metrics and health checks. We talked about a new emerging field of model monitoring in an ML application, where statistical models are subject to deterioration, health, and performance monitoring. I also touched on monitoring distributed systems, a topic that really deserves much more space, which unfortunately, I did not have.

This is the end of the book, but in no way is it the end of the journey. I am sure, new frameworks and applications are being written as we speak. Scala has been a pretty awesome and succinct development tool in my practice, with which I've been able to achieve results in hours instead of days, which is the case with more traditional tools, but it is yet to win the popular support, which I am pretty sure it. We just need to emphasize its advantages in the modern world of interactive analysis, complex data, and distributed processing.

Index

Made in the USA
Monee, IL
01 June 2021